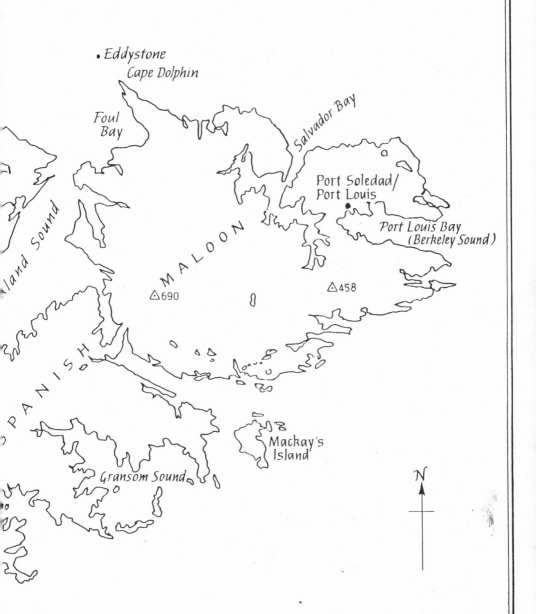

FALKLAND ISLANDS

Using names applicable in 1813-1815

△458 High points (feet)

THE WRECK OF THE ISABELLA

By the same author:

Submarines of the World, Salamander (1991).

Modern Submarine Warfare, Salamander (1987).

Illustrated Directory of Modern Weapons Systems, Salamander (1985).

Modern Land Warfare, Salamander (1987). (With Chris Foss).

Combat Arms: Submarines, Salamander (1989).

Modern Naval Combat, Salmander (1986) (with Chris Foss).

The World's Navies, Salamander (1991).

Battlefield, Brian Trodd (1991).

A Short History of the Office of the Master-General of the Ordnance, Ministry of Defence (1973).

and many more.

THE WRECK
OF THE
ISABELLA

by
DAVID MILLER

NAVAL INSTITUTE PRESS
ANNAPOLIS, MARYLAND

© David Miller, 1995
First published in Great Britain in 1995
by Leo Cooper, Pen & Sword Books Limited

Published and distributed in the United States of America and Canada
by the Naval Institute Press,
118 Maryland Avenue,
Annapolis, Maryland 21402–5035

Library of Congress Catalog Card Number 95–67721
ISBN 1–55750–768–6

This edition is authorized for sale only in
the United States, its territories and possessions,
and Canada

Printed in Great Britain

THIS BOOK IS DEDICATED TO
BERTHA S DODGE,
TEACHER, TRAVELLER, FRIEND AND AUTHOR,
WHO REDISCOVERED CHARLES BARNARD, AND TO
WHOM I AM GREATLY INDEBTED

CONTENTS

TABLES

PREFACE

While in the Falkland Islands in 1985 I visited New Island, one of the most westerly in the group, where my host, Tony Chater, pointed to a large stone hut. 'That', he told me, 'was raised on the foundations of the hut built by the American Crusoe'. My interest aroused, I eventually managed to obtain a copy of the journal of that 'crusoe,' who turned out to be Captain Charles Barnard, his book having been originally published in 1828, but later rediscovered and republished with considerable additional notes by Mrs Bertha Dodge in 1979.

That book whetted my interest in the subject and I started a lengthy correspondence with Mrs Dodge, culminating in a most happy visit to meet her in 1992. In our discussions she told me that she felt that there was probably even more to the tale than she had been able to discover and we agreed that I would take on the search for new material. This book is the result.

This is a most exciting story, as full of high adventure, colourful characters and curious twists as any novel. The events to be related took place between 1813 and 1815 in what was then a very obscure part of the world and caused little excitement at the time in the two countries involved. Great Britain had been at war with France for many years so the affair of the wreck of the merchant brig, *Isabella*, aroused only minor interest, while in the United States attention was focused on events much closer to home, as the War of 1812 ran its course. A few scattered newspaper reports on the fate of the sealing-brig *Nanina* appeared and there was some indignation over the behaviour of the British with various versions of the story appearing in American mariners' journals up to the 1870s, but the full story, including the surprising denouement, has never been told.

Everything in this book has been researched from contemporary sources; a note on these sources, and an explanation of how they have been used and interpreted is at Appendix D. Suffice it to say that the story is related in straight narrative form and readers can refer to footnotes for further explanation and to endnotes for detailed attribution of sources, as they feel necessary. Where direct verbal or written quotes from contemporary sources are used in every case they use the exact words, spelling, grammar and punctuation of the original.

The story concerns three ships and inevitably many nautical terms are involved. These are all explained in the glossary at Appendix A. Wherever possible, contemporary nineteenth century names and terminology are used to describe events aboard the ships, the names of places in the Falkland Islands and of the islands' wildlife. There is, however, a solitary exception to this, the word 'rook', which is explained in the text.

There are many novels about the navies in the Napoleonic Wars, but in all but a few of those books the heroes' ships tend to be in good repair, to sail wherever and whenever required, to be well-manned and to be under the command of brave and determined officers. This book gives the reality of life in distant waters, where many of the ships were in shocking disrepair, the crews short-handed and sickly, and in some cases, at least, the officers were exhausted by many years of warfare. Also, although the sailing man-of-war was the most complicated and advanced piece of machinery known to man at that time, it was still constrained to a great degree by the weather particularly, of course, the wind. Thus, as will be seen, captains often simply could not sail when ordered and waiting for a good wind might take up to a fortnight; sometimes, indeed, the captain could not follow a particular course at all, simply because he could not weather a headland.

ACKNOWLEDGEMENTS

A book such as this could only be written with the help of many people. Above all, I must thank Mrs Bertha Dodge, who rediscovered Charles Barnard and has given me great encouragement to carry out more research on the subject and to publish the findings. My book does not seek to replace hers and I commend all those who enjoy this book to read Barnard's own account of his adventures in her book, *Marooned*. I thank both her and Syracuse University Press for permission to base Part 4 of this book on Barnard's journal.

I also wish to thank the staffs of the Public Record Office at Kew and Chancery Lane in London, and of the National Archives in Washington, DC, for their unfailing help and courtesy. Among the many individuals who have helped me with their specialized knowledge are:

– *The American background*: Mrs Bertha Dodge, author of *Marooned*, of Vermont, USA.

– *Australian aspects of the story*: Ian Henderson of Yaroomba, Queensland.

– *Sailing ships of the era*: Peter Goodwin, Keeper of HMS *Victory*.

– *Navigation in and around the Falkland Islands*: Major E. Southby-Tailyour, Royal Marines (Retired).

– *The D'Aranda family*: The Genealogical Society; The Huguenot Society Library; Mrs Joy Saynor of Shoreham and Mrs M.L. Meaden of Sevenoaks, both in Kent; Essex County Record Office; Bob Carpenter of Chelmsford; Sue Twyman, Parish Administrator, Calne; Derek Kyte, Bremhill; City Records Office, Southampton.

– *The Durie family*: Director of Cultural Services, Isle of Wight; Dunfermline District Museum.

– *The Lundin family*: Mrs Violet Meldrum of Auchtermairnie Mill; Sir

John Gilmour, Bt, of Montravie; David Read and David Crichton of Kennoway; all in Fifeshire, Scotland.

– *Sir Henry Hayes*: M.W. Walker, Esq, Freemason's Hall, Dublin, Eire; A.H.B. Crosbie, Esq of Cobh, Eire; Michael Bogle, Curator, Vaucluse House, Sydney, Australia; National Museum of Ireland; National Gallery of Ireland.

INTRODUCTION

The breathless and exciting newspaper 'exclusive' is no modern phenomenon and the readers of *The Times* of London came across just such a despatch on Saturday, 29 January, 1814:

'The circumstances of his Majesty's sloop *Nancy*, of 18 guns, having proceeded from Buenos Ayres to the Falkland islands in quest of some shipwrecked mariners and passengers, we believe, has already been mentioned, and of their having been saved in consequence; but the following extracts of a letter from an officer on board that ship has never yet met the public eye:-

'We yesterday arrived in this roadstead (Buenos Ayres) after encountering a series of the most tempestuous weather I have yet experienced; we from unceasing perseverance have executed the important service sent upon. The Anicers islands, upon which we discovered the wrecked people, are dangerous in the extreme, and surrounded by numerous and extensive reefs; upon one of which we had a most miraculous escape; had the vessel gone to pieces, not a soul would have been saved from the steepness of the shore and heavy surf.'

'We were a month upon our passage, and three-and-twenty days in returning, and had constant gales during our stay in the islands. The weather was so piercing cold, with snow and hail, that the crew could not keep the deck or perform the least duty, and we were all but a complete wreck when we returned. It was with great difficulty we patched her up to bring us here. She is now past going to sea, and our limbs and sinews are so dreadfully contracted, that I fear some of them will be in a similar situation. I am just going to take a boatload to the hospital. We found on the islands the unhappy people we went in search of (48 in number), except two American seamen; but from our long passage there, and the prospect of another one back, we should not have been able, for want of provisions, to bring them all away, had we not most fortunately captured an American, on board of which we put

33, and took ourselves 15. The American arrived safely at Rio Janeiro, as soon as we did at Buenos Ayres. Sir H HAYES, Bart, Captain DUCIE, of the 73rd regiment, his wife, and two children, were amongst those we brought off; also the Master of the vessel they were wrecked in.'

The letter we have seen from his Majesty's ship *Nancy* speaks in the highest terms of the unwearied exertions of her Commander, Lieutenant D'ARANDA: he will, with the rest of his officers and crew, have, for the remainder of their lives, the pleasing recollection, that by these exertions they have saved the lives of nearly 50 of their fellow creatures.'[1]

The *Times*' story certainly made exciting reading, and would have raised vivid pictures in readers' imaginations of intrepid British sailors battling their way through stormy seas to rescue shipwrecked mariners on a gale-swept, uninhabited island in the remote southern Ocean. Like so many newspaper stories, much of what it said was close to the truth, but unfortunately it also contained errors of fact and left unreported some deeds which would have cast a quite different light on events.

The correspondent neither explained what an American vessel was doing in the 'Anicer islands' (or Falkland islands, as they were more commonly called), nor why she was captured. He skipped quickly over the question of the two missing Americans and totally failed to mention that three British seamen had also been cruelly abandoned in the islands. His readers may also have wondered why a British naval officer should have had such a Spanish-sounding name as D'Aranda and how a 'Sir H Hayes, Bart' came to be on board.

Finally, the last paragraph proved to be totally inaccurate, since, for the remainder of his long life, Lieutenant William D'Aranda, RN, was to look back on this episode not with pleasure at having rescued so many people, but with bitterness. All that it brought him, he told anyone who would listen, was trouble, sickness, disappointment and financial ruin.

Many stories about war concern themselves with admirals, generals, or political leaders, but in this case, all such high-ranking and experienced people were far away, and unable to influence events. The story is, instead, about some young and very ordinary people – a captain and a lieutenant from the army, the commander of a Royal Navy brig and the masters of two merchant vessels, together with assorted sailors, passengers, Marines, their womenfolk and three children, who accompanied them. All of these found themselves in truly unusual circumstances, where they had to look to themselves and to each other for salvation in the remote, wild, deserted and little-known Falkland Islands. Most behaved well, but at least two were

2

downright wicked; some were strong and many were weak; and some of the leaders led from the front, while others, despite their rank, kept well to the rear. But, in all except a very few cases, they did their best and here, after nearly two centuries, is their story.

PART 1

The Last Voyage of the *Isabella*

CHAPTER 1

On 4 December, 1812, the merchant brig *Isabella* lay, ready to sail, in Port Jackson harbour in the British convict colony of New South Wales.* One of the passengers took the trouble to note that the temperature was over 90° Fahrenheit, but the people on the deck were well used to such heat, and a happy, laughing group of passengers surrounded His Excellency The Governor, Lieutenant-Colonel Lachlan Macquarie, accompanied by Major Maclean and several other officers of his staff, who had come to wish them 'God's Speed' on their long voyage 'home'.

As usual, the passengers included a number of military men, some of them accompanied by their wives and families, who were leaving the garrison to return to the home country on furlough or on posting to a new appointment. There was also a small number of former convicts – both men and women – who had not only completed their sentences or obtained pardons, but who had also, by fair means or foul, accumulated sufficient money to pay for the long voyage.

Standing by the tiller was the vessel's master, a glum-looking man with no known friends and a habit of taciturnity bordering on rudeness. He was not noticeably eager to depart, even though his ship had already been delayed for eleven days to await the Governor's despatches, which were held up pending the completion of an important Court Martial. Despite his appearance the master was ever-careful where money was concerned and had ensured that he had a certificate to this effect, which would enable the owners to submit an account for demurrage on his arrival in London.

The farewells complete, the Governor and his suite went over the side to their boat and the passengers waved goodbye as they were rowed back to the shore. Within minutes the crew had made sail and soon the *Isabella* was heading out towards the ocean and the long voyage, which, all being well, would take her half-way around the world to that great centre of the British Empire, known simply as 'home'.

* Now the State of New South Wales in the Commonwealth of Australia.

7

The ship to which this group were entrusting their lives was the *Isabella*, a moderately-sized, but stoutly built brig of 193 tons burthen, designed to carry both passengers and cargo. She was armed with ten cannon, although the chances of her resisting any serious attack were slim. Indeed, she had already been captured once, as she had been built in Venice as *La Perla* and sailed under the French flag for some years before being captured by the British privateer *St Josef* on 14 January, 1806, off the port of Algiers. After lengthy proceedings in the Prize Court at Malta she had sailed to England, where she was eventually sold to her present owners, Messrs Keir, Buxton & Co of London on 11 December, 1811.[2]

Isabella sailed for New South Wales in March 1812 by way of Madeira where her drunken mate had to be discharged and a new man taken on from a British vessel which happened to be in port. She then had a rough passage to Rio de Janeiro, where after repairing the storm damage she sailed on again. She arrived at Port Jackson (present-day Sydney) on 8 September, 1812, where she discharged her cargo of wines, spirits, building materials, soap, candles, cloth and other goods for sale. The latter even included three boxes of ladies' hats, suggesting that the penal colony was already achieving a degree of sophistication.[3]

For her return passage *Isabella* carried 34 passengers and a mixed cargo which included 18,983 salted fur and hair sealskins, 91 caskets of sperm and black oil, 17 tons of pearl shells, 72 sealskins and 24 oxhides. In addition, deep in her hold lay five pipes of madeira wine, the balance of a shipment which the owners had taken aboard on the outward voyage and which would be well matured on arrival in England.*

The government was paying for the passage of the military personnel and their families, but the private passengers naturally paid their own expenses. In the case of Joseph Holt this cost him thirty pounds each for himself, his wife, his son and three servants, which gained him a ten feet by eight feet space in the steerage in which to construct a cabin for himself and Mrs Holt, a space immediately outside for their son's cot to hang, and room elsewhere for the three servants to sling their hammocks. On top of this, Holt had to provide all his own provisions and sufficient water-casks to hold 120 gallons for each person. The family provisions included a load of biscuits, salted beef and pork, a cask of raisins, forty pounds of tea, one 160 pounds of sugar, as well as twelve dozen bottles of wine and no less than twenty gallons of rum.[4]

The crew of the *Isabella* was twenty strong. The Master was George Higton, who had been appointed just before leaving London, and the mate was George Davis, who had been taken on at Madeira. Of the remaining

---

* A 'pipe' was a wooden wine cask with a capacity of 105 British gallons (478 litres).

eighteen men, two were American, one German, one Spanish, and the others British, among whom the only personality of note was Samuel Ansell, an extremely quarrelsome young sailor, who suffered from periodic 'black rages'. These did not seem to his comrades necessarily to be caused by drink, however, as was usually the case with sailors, and during these he lost all control, which on several occasions led him to cause serious injury to his comrades.

Isabella ploughed steadily on her way, taking a great sweep to the south-east to avoid the southern tip of New Zealand. Fortunately for the passengers during the first five days the weather was fine, but on the sixth there was a sudden gale, which forced Higton to heave-to for twenty hours, although this brief excitement was followed by another long period of fine weather with a steady breeze.

The passengers had noticed that the Master drank much liquor, but they had no special reason to doubt his competence until the fifteenth night when, at one o'clock in the morning, there were sudden shouts of alarm and the passengers rushed onto the maindeck to see what was going on. One of the first to arrive was an experienced mariner, Captain Richard Brookes, who was returning to England as a passenger and he quickly saw that the ship was in great peril, as she was being blown to leeward towards a huge rocky promontory. In the absence of any firm orders from Higton or Davis, Brookes assumed command, ordering the sailors to hoist more sail and giving a string of clear orders to the helmsman. He carefully nursed the vessel off the lee-shore and was soon able to reassure the anxious passengers that the danger had passed, although he remained by the helmsman's side until they were well clear of the cape.

To the surprise of the onlookers, Captain Higton had come on deck just after Captain Brookes and then done nothing to prevent one of his passengers taking charge, standing quietly, if anxiously, to one side. But as Brookes relinquished control he turned to Higton and told him that he and his crew were very much to blame for not keeping a better lookout. They must have known, Brookes said, that they were near to Campbell's Island and it was sheer carelessness to have allowed the ship to get so close and with that Brookes turned on his heel and went below. Up to that point he had been very careful not to criticize the Master, for whom it must have been embarrassing to have a more experienced mariner aboard, but the danger had been very real and Higton had done nothing to take command of the deck himself, which augured badly for the future.

CHAPTER 2

The passengers were as disparate a group as might be imagined and, in order to understand what happened later, it is necessary to get to know them a little better. What might be termed the 'respectable' group comprised two Army officers, a master mariner, fourteen Royal Marines, four wives and two children. Also aboard, however, were some less respectable people: six male and four female former convicts, together with, as it turned out, a stowaway.

Robert Durie and his family were returning home to Scotland on twelve months' leave on 'private affairs.' Durie stood out for two reasons: his uniform and his wife. He was a captain in His Majesty's 73rd Regiment of Foot[5] and the senior military officer on board, which gave him great status among the passengers, all of whom had been living in a penal colony run by the Army. Durie had also been appointed by the Governor to command the draft of fourteen Royal Marines who were taking passage on the *Isabella*.

Durie was born at Craigluscar, just outside Dunfermline in Scotland in 1777 and purchased a commission into the 73rd Regiment of Foot in 1804, at the unusually advanced age of 27. He was serving as a lieutenant with the First Battalion of that regiment in Scotland when it was ordered to New South Wales to overthrow the illegal régime that had displaced Governor Bligh in 1808. The battalion made a leisurely journey south, embarking at Leith in Scotland on 13 January, 1809, eventually reaching the Isle of Wight off England's south coast in early March.

There the 32-year old bachelor met Joanna-Ann Ross, the widow of a Lieutenant-Colonel Ross, who had died some three years previously in Inverness. The couple were married by special licence in the parish church at Freshwater on 22 April, their witnesses being two of Durie's brother officers in the 73rd Regiment, also en route to New South Wales: Lieutenants David Rose and Charles McIntosh.[6] The speed of events suggests that this was a whirlwind romance and the family's subsequent history makes it more likely that the personable Joanna-Ann swept the younger man off his feet, rather than the other way around!

TABLE I

ABOARD THE BRITISH MERCHANT BRIG "ISABELLA":
SAILED FROM PORT JACKSON, NEW SOUTH WALES 4 December, 1812
WRECKED ON THE FALKLAND ISLANDS 8 February, 1813

THE CREW
Master: George Higton. Mate: George Davis.
Foremast Hands: Joseph Albrook; Samuel Ansell; Jose Antonio
(Portuguese); John Babtist; Hans Brockner; John Brown;
Joseph Ellis; Daniel Elrict; Ford ("an American"); James
Hubbart; John Gordon; Charles Lewis; James Louder; Angus
McCoy; James Moss; James Read; William Robarts; John
Servester.

PASSENGERS
THE DURIE PARTY Captain Robert Durie, His Majesty's 73rd
Regiment of Foot (senior military officer aboard and in
command of the Royal Marines); Mrs Joanna-Ann Durie; Miss
Agnes Durie (aged 1½).

ROYAL MARINES
Sergeant William Bean; Private Robert Andrews; Private John
Bellingham; Drummer John Brind; Private William Catford;
Private Thomas Green; Drummer William Hughes; Private
William Johnson; Private James Rea; Private Richard Rowell;
Corporal Richard Sargent; Private James Spooner; Private
Richard Walton; Private Joseph Woolley.

WIVES OF ROYAL MARINES
Mrs Elizabeth Bean; Mrs Hughes.

THE HOLT PARTY "General" Joseph Holt (former convict,
pardoned in 1812); Mrs Hester Holt; Joseph Harrison Holt,
(aged 13); John Burns, Philip Harney, Edward Kilbride
(pardoned convicts, employed as servants by "General" Holt).

THE HAYES PARTY Sir Henry Browne Hayes: Samuel Breakwell
(both pardoned convicts).

OTHER MALE PASSENGERS Captain Richard Brookes (merchant
captain returning to England); Lieutenant Richard Lundin,
73rd Regiment.

STOW AWAY William Mattinson.

OTHER FEMALE PASSENGERS Mrs Mary Bindell; Mrs Connolly; Mrs
Elizabeth Davis; Mrs Mary Anne Spencer (all ex-convicts and
former prostitutes).

TOTALS
Crew   20
Passengers   20
Royal Marines   14

GRAND TOTAL   54

The new Mrs Durie had two children by Lieutenant-Colonel Ross, but she obviously made very rapid arrangements for them to be looked after by relatives, as they were not with her when she set off with her new husband when they sailed for New South Wales on 8 May. The battalion, comprising some 600 men, accompanied by no less than one hundred wives and sixty children, was accommodated aboard the man-of-war HMS *Hindoostan*, which was accompanied by the naval storeship, *Dromedary*.[7] These two vessels arrived in Sydney on 4 January, 1810, after a voyage of no less than eight and a half months, which was very slow, even by the standards of the day.

Once in New South Wales Durie was appointed commandant of the troops at Paramatta, some fourteen miles inland from Port Jackson. After a few months the Governor appointed him to be the resident magistrate for the area, for which he was paid an additional five shillings a day from the Police Fund, which was, no doubt, a very welcome addition to the family income.[8]

While they were at Paramatta the Duries' first child, Agnes, was born, being baptised at George's River on 30 June[9]. Then, on his promotion to captain in 1811 he decided to take twelve months' home leave and said farewell to their comrades in the 73rd, who were to remain in New South Wales until January, 1814, and boarded the *Isabella* just before she sailed. Agnes was just eighteen months old and Mrs Durie was in the seventh month of another pregnancy, but apparently untroubled by the fact that she must inevitably give birth while on the high seas.

Durie was an ineffective man, very disinclined to influence events and usually electing, despite his rank, to follow, rather than to lead. He was later described as 'chicken-hearted', which, as events were to prove, was a well-deserved criticism.[10] Mrs Durie, on the other hand, was a woman with a very powerful personality, whose considerable charm overlay a steely character. She was tough, even by the standards of the time, having reputedly followed the late Colonel Ross on many of his postings and she had just completed two years in Australia with Durie at a time when the vast majority of women in the colony were convicts. When their adventures were over, one of the other passengers observed that, taking Captain and Mrs Durie together, she was by far the better soldier, while an American she was to meet later went even further and recorded that she had '*the sympathizing heart that distinguishes the tygress*'.

By far the most impressive of the passengers was the Irishman, Joseph Holt, a powerful-looking man, five feet ten inches tall and stockily built. He wore his black hair long and had a beard under his chin, but shaved the rest of his face, a curious fashion, for which he was to reveal the reason later. He had heavy, bushy eye-brows, and his eyes were dark and penetrating, giving an impression of great suppressed energy. In his manner, however, he was simple and unaffected, and had a ready wit, being very inclined to make jokes, but, even so, he was quite capable of assuming a most commanding demeanour when the occasion demanded and was very stubborn, being prepared to argue his case vehemently when he felt himself to be in the right.

His story was well-known in outline, if not in detail, to all aboard the *Isabella*. Born in 1756, he was the son of a Protestant farmer in southern Ireland, and a descendant of one of the settler families introduced into the country at the end of the sixteenth century. Although not well educated, he became a farmer and businessman, as well as accumulating a number of official appointments. In his own words: 'I was deputy alnager [parish constable] under Sir John Blaquiere, which produced me from £80 to £100 a-year, [and] I had, by agencies, £60 more. I was also chief barony constable, tory-hunter, catcher of thieves, coiners, pickpockets, and murderers, which produced me £50 more. Had I been mean enough to take bribes, I might have made it £150. I was likewise overseer and projector of roads, leveller of hills and filler up of hollows, making crooked ways straight and rugged places smooth, which I may justly say produced me £50 more. So I was well-off. But with all these advantages, I was made a rebel.'[11]

When the great rebellion of 1798 broke out, which was, as usual, a predominantly Catholic uprising against the British, Holt was denounced as a rebel, quite unjustly, by a local landowner who had taken a dislike to him. Despite his Protestant background and his well-proven support of the government through his various appointments, a squad of soldiers was immediately sent to arrest him. Holt was absent on business and so the soldiers, assuming from their instructions that he must be a proven rebel, without further ado razed his farm to the ground, typical of the misunderstandings that have bedevilled Anglo-Irish relationships down the centuries. When he returned home Holt was furious that his loyalty to the Crown had been so cruelly rewarded, but being apprehensive that he would be arrested if he gave himself up, he felt that he had no alternative but to join the rebels.

Once in the hills, his natural ability and air of authority quickly earned him a position of prominence, and he was soon in command of some 13,000 men, despite being a Protestant in an essentially Catholic movement. He showed very considerable tactical and administrative skills, and was acknowledged on both sides to have behaved with honour, becoming known to all in Ireland as 'General Holt'.

The rebellion petered out after a few months and, as the British forces began to mop up the remnants, Holt recognized the inevitable and negotiated his surrender through an intermediary, giving himself up in November, 1798. He was treated with considerable respect and was neither tried nor humiliated, although the major provision of the agreement was that he should be exiled to the recently founded penal colony of New South Wales.

Holt's wife, Hester, insisted on accompanying him, together with their two sons, and he was able to pay for their passage on the same ship, the transport *Minerva*, which left Cork on 24 August, 1799. The 'passengers' eventually comprised 165 men and twenty-six women, of whom the vast majority were convicts, most of them criminals (or what passed for criminals in those hard times), but a few were former rebels. Holt regarded these other rebels with some puzzlement, since he did not suffer fools gladly and in his view they not only had little reason for joining the rebellion, but had then done little to further it, apart from getting themselves arrested. There were two priests, Father James Harold and the Reverend Henry Fulton, a Catholic and a Protestant respectively, and two former Army officers, Captains Alcock and St Leger, who were lucky not to have been shot for desertion. Finally there was Dr O'Connor who had earned a comfortable living administering fairly harmless potions to society ladies in Dublin, before he dabbled, so unsuccessfully, in politics.

Minerva arrived in Rio de Janeiro on 20 October, sailing again on 8 November. The voyage was the fastest on record up to that time, her best day's run being no less than 272 nautical miles. It was also a relatively happy voyage, the master, Captain Salkeld, being a humane man, who allowed the prisoners regular exercise and good rations and there was even some frivolity, usually (or so he claimed) provoked by Holt. On one occasion in Rio, Holt persuaded the Reverend Fulton to take his first taste of cayenne pepper and the cleric was soon in agony, having put a spoonful straight into his mouth. He ran around the deck shouting that he had been poisoned and was dying, whereupon Holt solicitously suggested that Father Harold should be summoned to administer the last rites. Such a truly appalling prospect for a good Protestant minister made Fulton's state ten times worse, and reduced the onlookers to helpless laughter.

Minerva entered Port Jackson on 11 January, 1800, sailing past Pinchgut Island where the first sign of habitation was the skeleton of a murderer swinging from a gibbet. Once ashore Holt soon found work as a farm bailiff, but his reputation as a rebel resulted in his being arrested several times on suspicion of complicity in the various convict mutinies. He was released on each occasion, until in 1804 he was found guilty (unjustly, he claimed) of participation in an Irish-led revolt and banished to Norfolk Island. He managed to return to Sydney, however, and continued to prosper, supported by his wife, Hester, who stuck with him throughout all his many adventures.

Holt eventually obtained his pardon in 1811 and then decided that, despite his prosperity, he needed to see his native Ireland again. His eldest son was well-established with his own farm which he declined to leave, but Holt sold his property, realizing well over two thousand pounds sterling. He left the colony in the *Isabella*, accompanied by his wife, their youngest son, and three menservants, all former convicts who had completed their sentences.[12]

If Holt was liked and respected, the same could not be said of the second prominent passenger, although he, too, was a Protestant Irishman. Sir Henry Browne Hayes was born in Cork in 1762, the son of a reputable and wealthy brewer, and was described by a contemporary as being 'straight-made, rather fresh-coloured, a little pock-marked and brown hair, with remarkable whiskers, about five foot seven inches high.'[13]

He appears to have behaved in an eccentric manner from an early age: on the one hand he became a captain in the militia and a sheriff of the county, while on the other, his father was so angry with his misbehaviour that he disowned him, having at first left him a considerable inheritance in his Will and then cancelled it in a codicil*. Hayes was knighted on 8 October, 1790, for the trifling achievement of conveying an invitation from the Mayor and Corporation of Cork to the Lord Lieutenant to dine with them, knighthoods being liberally disbursed in Ireland at that time to ensure loyalty.

When his wife died, Hayes' behaviour became even more erratic and he was involved in a notorious criminal case, which changed his life. In June, 1797 he decided that he wanted to marry a Quaker heiress, a Miss Pike, who spurned his advances. Undeterred, at one o'clock on the morning of 22 July Hayes had a message delivered to Miss Pike, falsely stating that her mother had been taken seriously ill. The anxious young woman dressed hurriedly, rushed to the waiting coach and was half-way to Cork when the coach was stopped and she was dragged into a waiting chaise, driven by Sir Henry. The abductor then drove her to his house where a bogus priest, dressed in borrowed vestments, performed a 'marriage ceremony'. The unfortunate Miss Pike managed to gain the attention of a passing gentleman, who rescued her before the erring knight had his evil way with her and Hayes was declared an outlaw.

Despite a price of £500 on his head, Hayes lived openly in Cork, but he eventually invited his barber to turn him in and claim the reward. After a sensational trial in April, 1801, Hayes, to his very considerable surprise and alarm, was sentenced to death, that being the mandatory punishment for abduction, although the judge did add a recommendation for mercy. Hayes was a Mason and his local lodge in Cork presented a 'Memorial in favour of our esteemed, but unfortunate Brother,' which may well have played some small part in the sentence being commuted by King George III to transportation.

---

* According to Irish custom the Will would have been read first, thus giving Hayes the impression that he had inherited his father's wealth, and only then would the codicil have been read, in which the bequest was cancelled and the wealth passed to others. Information supplied by A.H.P. Crosbie, Esq, of Cobh.

Hayes travelled out on board the *Atlas* and behaved so badly that he managed to offend almost everyone else on board. The Master, Captain Brookes, agreed to Hayes paying for a cabin instead of living in squalor with the other convicts, but even so, the two took a great dislike to each other. More importantly, Hayes managed to enrage one of the other passengers, who left the ship at Rio, reached Port Jackson first, and secured an appointment as a magistrate. As a result, as soon as Hayes arrived in the colony he was charged and sent to prison for six months. Thereafter, he was in almost constant trouble with the authorities and associated, from choice, with the worst characters in the colony. He was exiled several times, the first occasion being to Norfolk Island and the second to Van Diemen's Land, and was also twice sent to the Newcastle coal-mines.

Despite all this, he was never short of money and built a spacious home for himself, Vaucluse House, which still stands in an enviable position overlooking Sydney Harbour. The house was built on snake-infested land, so, to everyone's amusement, Hayes paid for 500 bags of turf to be imported from Ireland, which he used to surround the house in a form of earthen moat. He claimed that since St Patrick had banished snakes from Ireland no snake would cross the sacred turf and it goes without saying that from that day to this the house has been completely free of snakes! Hayes also founded freemasonry in Australia, holding the first meeting, despite a prohibition by the Governor, on 14 May, 1803, which resulted in one of his numerous trips into exile.

When Governor Bligh (of mutiny on the *Bounty* fame) arrived in 1806, Sir Harry, never one to follow fashion, was one of the few to befriend him and passed information to the deeply unpopular Governor. The garrison troops mutinied in 1808 and Bligh was so grateful for Hayes' help that he made out a pardon for him, but was unable to give it legal authority as the rebels had purloined the colony's great seal.

Major Johnstone, leader of the mutiny, sent Hayes to the coal-mines for eight months, but on his return to Sydney the Irishman immediately renewed his criticisms of the rebel government and would have been sent to the mines yet again had not the new, legitimate governor, Lieutenant Colonel Macquarie, arrived with the 73rd Foot and deposed the illegal regime. When he returned to England, Bligh, by now promoted to rear-admiral, wrote to the Secretary for the Colonies asking for a pardon for Hayes.[14] As a result, Governor Macquarie was instructed to issue the necessary certificate, which he did on 6 January, 1812.[15]

Despite his behaviour, there is no doubt that Hayes had a certain way with him, being known to all, from Governor to convict, as 'Sir Harry'. The more educated in the colony and on board the *Isabella* treated him with contempt tinged with amusement, while he was surprisingly popular with other convicts, partly because they were impressed that a real knight could become a convict too, and partly because he was permanently at war with authority, frequently saying the things that they themselves felt, but dared not express. Hayes was accompanied on board by Samuel Breakwell, a friend and business partner, and also an ex-convict.

In addition to Captain Durie, there was a second officer of the 73rd Foot on board; the 21 year-old Lieutenant Richard Lundin. Another Scot, he came from a long-established family which traced its ancestry to Robert Lundin, the younger son of King William the Lion, who ruled Scotland between 1165 and 1214. The family seat was at Auchtermairnie outside Kennoway in Fifeshire, only a short distance from the Duries' home at Craigluscar. Lundin purchased his commission as an ensign in the 73rd in June 1808 and then a further sum of money assured his subsequent promotion to lieutenant in 1810. He was on board the *Isabella* to return home to Scotland on leave and had also been given Governor Macquarie's despatches to deliver to the Colonial Office.

Captain Richard Brookes, who had saved them all off Campbell's Island, was a very experienced master mariner who was travelling back to England as a passenger in order to take his wife and children to Australia, and to collect a new ship. Like some of the others on board the *Isabella*, he too had a slightly murky past, his notoriety arising from the voyage of the *Atlas* in which Sir Harry Hayes had sailed, which was, without exception, the worst in the entire history of convict transports to Australia. The convicts joined *Atlas* in Ireland in December 1801 and many were in such poor shape on coming aboard that one actually died on being turned back by the ship's physician and two more before the ship weighed anchor. The only exception to this was Sir Harry Hayes, who, as might be expected, was in the very best of good health.

It was customary for masters to carry some goods in their ships to be sold either en route or at the destination, but Brookes, whose first command it was, took matters to excess. His merchandise was crammed into every space, with the companionways cluttered, half the hospital taken over and even part of the prison-deck used as storage space. As a result it was very difficult to move about the vessel, which was so deeply laden that air scuttles taking air to the prison-deck had to be kept closed, making the atmosphere inside even fouler than normal.

By the time *Atlas* reached Rio de Janeiro fifteen prisoners had died with many more seriously ill, and all the survivors were landed on an island in Rio Bay. This was not the magnanimous gesture it first appeared to be, however, as when the prisoners were reembarked, they discovered that Brookes had used the opportunity to move the stores and create extra space so that he could buy yet more goods! Brookes also managed to come to blows with the passenger, Surgeon Jamieson, who so disliked Hayes, a fight which Hayes claimed to have stopped.

Atlas was under orders to sail direct from Rio to New South Wales, but Brookes diverted into Cape Town on the spurious grounds that the convicts had mutinied, the troops were sick and the ship was running short of provisions. The real reason, however, was that a rumour had reached him that there was a glut of European goods in New South Wales and so Brookes believed that he would get a better price for his goods at Cape Town.

Atlas left the Cape in bad weather and the lot of the prisoners became even worse, with scurvy breaking out, food running low and water in short supply. By the time they reached Port Jackson, 220 days out of Cork, a total of sixty-five people had died, with another four expiring before they could be taken ashore. The condition of the prisoners was immediately seen to be so bad that the Governor set up a board of inquiry, which found that Brookes had been extremely negligent and that the large number of deaths was due to 'want of proper attention to cleanliness, the want of free circulation of air, and the lumbered state of the prison and hospital.'

Despite such a damning report, Brookes was never prosecuted for maltreatment of the prisoners, although the Governor exacted a somewhat mild form of retribution by preventing him from landing and selling some 2,166 gallons of spirits and 120 gallons of wine.[16] Despite this, Brookes continued to captain convict transports, but these all delivered their human cargo in good condition, so it appears that he had learnt his lesson. By 1812 Brookes was a very experienced master mariner and Holt, who certainly knew about the notorious voyage of the *Atlas*, did not allow this to blind him to Brookes' seamanship.

There was also a detachment of fourteen Royal Marines on board the *Isabella*. These men had been part of a forty-nine-strong group which had been sent out in 1803 with a 'transport' of 307 convicts to found a settlement at Port Philip.[17] On their arrival Lieutenant-Governor Collins disliked the site and after a lengthy delay was given authority to go instead to Van Diemen's Land (now Tasmania), and they arrived at the River Duncan settlement in February, 1804. Collins once again objected to the location and moved a short distance to a new site, which he named Hobart after the then Secretary-of-State for the Colonies.

The faithful Marines soldiered on from 1803 until 1811 when someone in London remembered them and Governor Macquarie was instructed to visit the men and sort things out. On his arrival Macquarie found that only forty-two Marines remained, seven, including both officers, having died. Following his instructions from London, the Governor offered the survivors a choice between leaving the Corps and becoming settlers in Hobart or returning to England. Twenty-eight decided to stay, but fourteen wanted to go home, of whom the senior was Sergeant William Bean.

The Governor took a personal interest in the well-being of these men and ensured that they were properly accommodated aboard the *Isabella*. He clearly felt sympathy for them, since, as he said in this despatches, they were 'well entitled to every reasonable indulgence from Government on account of their long and faithful service at the Derwent, where they have often experienced severe Privations without ever uttering a murmur or complaint.' In the absence of a Royal Marine officer, the Governor placed Captain Durie in command, although their day-to-day affairs were managed by Sergeant Bean.[18]

The Marines formed a separate group aboard the *Isabella* and organized their own mess for cooking and feeding, to which they reluctantly admitted Mattinson, of whom more shortly. A more welcome member was Sir Harry Hayes, the tawdry glamour of his title and the seemingly romantic nature of his past misdeeds being reinforced by a ready supply of money. The Marines were also loud in expressions of admiration of his ability to utter the most colourful curses and to play some of the more popular bar games of the time.

Isabella's passenger list included no less than nine females, of whom Mrs Durie, her daughter Agnes and Mrs Holt have already been mentioned. Two of the Royal Marines were also accompanied by their wives: Mrs Bean, the sergeant's wife, and Mrs Hughes, whose husband was the drummer.

The other four women were returning former convicts, who had completed their sentences and had all been able to find the cost of the passage, which was by no means cheap.[19] In the custom of the time, they were all referred to as 'Mrs,' although none was accompanied by a husband, if, indeed, one had existed in the first place. They were almost certainly prostitutes, who had earned the money for their return aboard the *Isabella* in the Port Jackson brothels.

Mary Bindell became the mistress of the unpopular Captain Higton, master of the *Isabella*, soon after leaving Port Jackson. Two others were more shadowy: Mrs Davis was considered by one of the roughest of the sailors, Ansell, to be his sweetheart, although this was probably not reciprocated, and both she and the third of the group, Mrs Connolly, were later to have their liquor supply stopped because of persistent drunkenness.

That left Mary-Ann Spencer, who, despite her background, seems to have been a cut above the others, as she became the lover of Lieutenant Lundin while crossing the Pacific. What is, perhaps, more surprising is that she was accepted as a friend by Mrs Durie and, for much of the adventures that were to come, the officer's wife and a fellow-officer's mistress became close companions.

19

The last of the passengers aboard the *Isabella* was a stowaway, a notorious and deeply detested character named William Mattinson, who had become known throughout the penal colony as an evil, drunken menace; no mean achievement in a community not exactly short of malefactors and he was not even a convict! Mattinson had arrived in New South Wales some six months previously, claiming to have been a sailing-master or a gunner (his story tended to change) in the Royal Navy, who had, so he told his cronies, been court-martialled in India for persistent drunkenness. He went on to claim that he had been discharged locally and abandoned, following which he had signed-on as a crewman aboard a merchant vessel from Bombay and jumped ship in Port Jackson.

Mattinson's career in the colony was spectacular. He rapidly ran up huge debts, spending all his money on gambling and liquor, and also took a delight in starting fights, with the more people involved and the more damage done, the greater his delight. As a result he made himself extremely unpopular with the authorities, the tradesmen, the publicans and the convicts alike. When the *Isabella* was preparing to sail Mattinson stowed himself aboard and had avoided detection by the crew, but was discovered at the last minute by a military officer whose task was to search every ship before it sailed, to ensure that no convicts were aboard. This officer took Mattinson ashore, as there was a law that nobody could leave the colony owing money (and Mattinson owed a great deal) where he proudly presented the prisoner to his creditors. The officer was, however, very taken aback when the creditors cursed him roundly and told him that he had done them a great disservice, unanimously declaring that they would annul all Mattinson's debts on the sole condition that he left New South Wales, never to return!

Higton told Mattinson that under no circumstances would he be allowed back on board the *Isabella*, but despite this the man somehow managed it, presumably with the connivance of at least one member of the crew. By the time he was discovered *Isabella* was well out to sea and, since it was too late for the ship to turn round to deposit him back on the shore, she sailed on with her unwelcome passenger.[20]

CHAPTER 3

Three weeks after leaving Port Jackson *Isabella* was approaching Cape Horn, and both crew and passengers were looking forward to Christmas when, on 24 December, a heavy gale struck, forcing Captain Higton to heave-to for fifty-six hours. Four sails were lost, and the maincourse and a foresail damaged, while the rough weather seriously hampered their long-planned Christmas festivities. As frequently happened in those latitudes, however, the violent winds were followed by a calm, which gave the crew a chance to sort out the rigging, before the winds picked up and they were on their way again.

They had a clear view of Cape Horn as the ship passed that dreaded landfall and later they passed Staten Island, which, the sailors solemnly told the credulous passengers, was inhabited by Patagonian cannibals, who particularly relished the flesh of Christians. Once in the Atlantic Higton headed north-eastwards, telling the passengers that he intended to call at the Falkland Islands to replenish his stock of water, which was running low. It seemed that some years previously he had met a whaling captain in the south seas who had told him of a Spanish settlement in the islands, so he headed there, despite, as Lundin acidly reported: 'our captain never reflected upon the difficulty of finding the port in question, of which he did not even know the name, nor had he a chart on a large enough scale to enable him to find any harbour.'

Their vessel was approaching these little-known islands when, with characteristic indecision, Higton finally admitted that his chart was not good enough for the purpose and changed his mind, saying that he would leave the islands well to starboard.[21] It soon transpired, however, that the wind was driving the *Isabella* towards the islands and Holt was standing on deck late in the afternoon of 7 February, 1813, when he heard Brookes advise Higton to order a tack, so that they would pass around the islands to the south. Holt later went below to his cabin and was resting there, talking to his wife, when the door opened and Higton staggered in, considerably the worse for drink, holding a bottle and behaving even more erratically than usual. 'Why do they ask me what harbour we are going to enter?' he shouted at the astonished Irishman. 'I refuse absolutely to let anyone know what harbour I am taking us to. If the ship sinks and everyone aboard perishes, who will have the responsibility – who? Only me, that's who!'

Holt wanted to calm the master on whom they all depended, but could not avoid giving one of his characteristically ironic replies: 'Well, Captain,' he said, 'if everyone drowns it doesn't really matter where the responsibility lies, since nobody will remain alive to prosecute.'

The subtlety of this was lost on Higton, who left the cabin and stomped off down the passageway. Hearing a door open and the sound of Mrs Bindell's voice, Holt realised that the master had gone to seek solace in his mistress's arms and began to wonder whether they would all survive the night.

At about two o'clock in the morning of 8 February Holt heard Higton go on deck and order a change of course and then return to his cabin. About an hour later the Irishman was woken yet again by the sound of running feet outside his cabin, followed by frantic shouting outside Mrs Bindell's door. Then a grumbling Higton clumped past, climbed to the deck and shouted an order to change course. Holt lay uneasily in his cot as the motion of the ship seemed to change and a dull, monotonous noise gradually became louder.

Suddenly there were loud shouts of alarm from the deck above and he heard one voice shout 'Rocks to larboard!' followed immediately by another 'Breakers to starboard!' Holt and his wife leapt out of bed and, calling their young son into the cabin, started to dress as rapidly as they could. Holt knew that he would have to exert himself if his family was to survive, but first he followed his invariable custom of ensuring that God was with them.

They had just sunk to their knees beside the bed to implore the Almighty's gracious interference when there was a tremendous crash and they were all thrown to the deck. They picked themselves up and Mrs Holt put their son between them and shouted dramatically to her husband above the noise, 'Let us all, linked in each other's arms, go to our watery graves together.'

Holt paused for a moment to comfort his wife and then decided that they must go up to the deck. Being, as always, a prudent man, he donned his greatcoat before leaving the security of the cabin, partly because it would keep him warm, but also because his money was hidden in the garment's pockets and lining. On deck all was confusion and noise as sailors, Marines and passengers ran hither and thither, while the wind roared, the waves struck the vessel and there were ominous scraping noises beneath their feet. Forcing their way aft through the crowd on the maindeck, Holt was somewhat relieved to see that Captain Brookes had assumed command once again, Higton being apparently incapable of dealing with such a crisis.

The rudder had been ripped off when the *Isabella* crossed the reef, but Brookes skilfully ordered the sailors to square the yards so that the vessel pulled clear of the first line of rocks and then scudded across a stretch of open water towards the shore, which they could see marked by a line of breakers. As they neared the land Brookes ordered the ship's carpenter to stand by the windward shrouds with his broad axe and as the vessel struck he shouted to him to cut the ropes which supported the mainmast. It took just three blows to sever the backstay and the windward shrouds, upon which there was a mighty crack as the mainmast broke and it came crashing down over the leeward side, fortunately without injuring anybody. The top came to rest on a rock and the butt on the gunwale, thus steadying the ship.

There was a popular myth on the lower decks of the period that once shipwreck was inevitable the master's legal authority no longer existed and it was then a case of every man for himself. Whether they had this in mind, or they were just reacting to the terror of the moment, the crew and the Marines of the *Isabella* now ran completely out of control, with Ansell and Mattinson the ringleaders. They careered about the deck cornering one passenger after another and demanding wine or liquor, drinking everything they could lay their hands on. They dashed the empty glasses and bottles to the deck, shouting, as they did so, that there would be no more use for them, as these would be the last drinks that any of them would ever have, either at sea or on the shore.

In the middle of all this pandemonium Mattinson, assisted by Lundin, lowered the ship's boat into the water in order, as Lundin thought, to take the females ashore. However, the cry of 'Women and children to the boat' was stifled as Sir Harry Hayes swept the women, including the heavily pregnant Mrs Durie, aside and tumbled down into the boat, followed by his friend Breakwell, the stowaway Mattinson and Private Bellingham, one of the Marines. Lundin stood on the deck, furious that he had innocently helped to prepare the boat, only for the four cowards to abandon them all, and he watched as the men cast off, quarrelling furiously among themselves over who was going to take the oars. After very nearly being swept on to the rocks they managed to get the boat under control and reach the shore, where they abandoned it and without a backward glance at the shipmates they had so callously abandoned, disappeared up the beach in the half light of dawn.[22]

Back on board the *Isabella* Captain Brookes seemed to be everywhere at once, controlling the efforts of the few crewmen who were not taking part in the apocalyptic binge. He had the kedge-anchor carried to the stern, made fast to a hawser and lowered in an effort to prevent the vessel being driven further onto the land. He also organized a gang to rig a bosun's chair forward and then oversaw them as the women and children were carefully lowered, one at a time, over the bow and onto dry land, with the pregnant Mrs Durie first over the side, followed by Mrs Holt.

Once the women and children were clear, Holt set about saving his goods, for which he had only the old and weak John Byrne to help him. Together they brought his trunks up from the cabin and lowered them down to the shore. There Holt placed the old man in charge, since even he could not control his other two servants, who were carousing with the sailors. Once all the trunks were ashore Holt followed them, where, on dry land at last, he joined Captain Durie and together they went to look for their wives.

They found Hester and Joanna-Ann comforting young Joseph Holt and Agnes Durie, the four of them sitting, cold and frightened on a hillock. Holt, who had a penchant for naming places, said he would call it 'Sorrowful Bank,' even though, sad as the occasion was, he was glad to see all of them safe on shore. Joanna-Ann Durie, always one for the social niceties even when sitting on an earthen bank on a deserted island on the morning after a shipwreck, held out a bottle of rum and offered him a drink, apologizing that there was no possibility of watering it down until the men found a stream. Holt, somewhat inconsequentially declaring that he had not yet broken his fast, elected to drink the fiery liquid neat.

The six of them sat there for several hours, thanking God that they were alive, but also apprehensive about what might happen next. As the sun rose, they looked about them and saw that the Falklands were indeed bleak. They appeared to be on a small island which was generally flat and featureless, but with a small hillock inland from where they sat. The ground was covered with short grass and some small plants, but neither trees nor bushes were to be seen. Mrs Durie remarked that it looked rather like parts of north-west Scotland, a resemblance heightened, she said with a touch of humour, by the fact that it was raining.

Holt rose to his feet and, ever the practical man, proposed to Durie that they should start to do something about shelter for the coming night, especially for the ladies and children. The two men set off for the wreck and on the way Holt spotted a hollow between two banks which would make a suitable site for a lean-to. They constructed a makeshift tent from some long lengths of timber and sails salvaged from the *Isabella* and then, using hatch covers as floor-boards, set up some beds.

Holt also collected his trunks, which were still being guarded in an apathetic fashion by old John Byrne, who was little help in all this activity, since he seemed quite devastated by the experiences of the last few hours. Nevertheless, he helped to carry the trunks to the bank-site, where they found that Mrs Holt had already started to prepare a very welcome meal.

Once they had eaten, Holt and Durie went aboard the *Isabella* where they found the sailors and Marines scattered about the deck in various stages of alcoholic stupefaction. Holt was particularly annoyed to see his two servants, Harney and Kilbride, stretched out asleep, the former bearing signs of having been involved in a fight. Going below decks they found that all the cabins had been ransacked and Holt was upset to find that a cask of his precious sugar had disappeared.

Nobody was very sure which island they were on, although Brookes guessed that they were at the southern end of Falkland Sound and that the small island they were on was probably off the easternmost of the two large islands, which was known then as Spanish Maloon. The *Isabella* was not actually too badly damaged at this stage, having been driven up on a smooth table of rock and quick, determined action could well have resulted in the brig being saved. However, the drunkenness of the crew and the total lack of any leadership or initiative from Higton prevented this.

Some days later when the men had recovered from their monumental binge, Brookes, Durie and Holt decided that, since Higton seemed disinclined to do anything, the time had come for them to bring some form of organisation to their little community in an endeavour to survive for as long as possible. Accordingly they called everyone together and proposed forming a council, which was generally agreed. The first to be nominated was Captain Durie, who was then unanimously elected, and he, in turn, proposed Captain Brookes and these two then named Lieutenant Lundin. One of the Marines then proposed Sir Harry Hayes, who was popular with them, while Durie and Brookes proposed Holt. Then finally, and with some reluctance, Higton and the mate, George Davis, were also elected, principally because the Master was legally still responsible for them.

The council immediately started its deliberations and produced a set of regulations, which were written in a book brought from the wreck. When they were completed a member of the council read them out so that all should understand what was being agreed before they voted on it:

'*First* – that no man should be exempt from work, till all our provisions are all landed.
Second – any man found guilty of stealing or robbing will be punished according to his offence.
Third – every man shall attend roll-call in the morning.
Fourth – that no man shall have more provisions than any other.
Fifth – that all private stores shall belong to the general store.
Sixth – that nothing shall be done without the voice of the majority.
Seventh – that the provisions shall be served out twice a week, to prevent waste in the first part of the week.'[23]

There was a silence when the reading had finished and taking this for assent each man was called forward in turn, those men who could write signing their name, the others making their mark. They had undergone the travail and dangers of shipwreck, but, astonishingly, without loss of life or even serious injury and now they could get on with sorting things out and planning for the future.

CHAPTER 4

Hoping that some discipline had been imposed at last, all the able-bodied men set-to and started to unload the wreck. First to be removed was the food, with bread, flour, peas and rice taking priority, followed by the salted beef and pork, and then the spirits and wine that the drunkards had failed to consume in their orgy following the shipwreck. Once all these were piled ashore, Holt and Sergeant Bean of the Royal Marines made an inventory, while the committee decided that they should base their calculations on surviving on the island for twelve months. This led to a ration per head of two pounds of biscuits, half-a-pound of flour or rice, and one pound of salted meat per person per week, plus a daily pint of wine or half-a-pint of spirits for each person, while water, fortunately, proved not to be a problem, since they had already discovered a number of clear streams on the island.

They had also observed an abundance of wildlife, especially geese and ducks, so Holt suggested that they should use such fresh meat to supplement their provisions. 'But,' he said, 'it ought to be proved who are the best shots among us: powder and shot are ten times more valuable to us on an island that is full of birds, than the biscuits, beef, or pork that we have landed. As long as our ammunition lasts we cannot want, and it is, above all, our particular duty to see that it is not thrown away and that every shot fired gives us full value for it.'[24]

He therefore proposed a shooting competition among the Marines and the prospect of such a martial event raised everyone's spirits. A wooden board was immediately set up with a piece of paper, marked as a target, pinned to it. The Marines were instructed to prepare to shoot and it was agreed that the man who obtained the best marks with three shots at one hundred yards would be appointed the sportsman. The distance was paced out, the line was drawn and then all was ready.

Private William Johnson fired first and missed the post completely, as did the next, and, to Holt's loudly expressed amazement, only two out of the ten competitors hit the mark at all with their first round. Their second attempts produced the same results – two out of ten hits – and the third, one out of ten. Fortunately, Private John Bellingham had scored a hit with each shot and was clearly the winner, but Holt stood in front of the chagrined Marines and told them that he was not surprised that soldiers were such bad marksmen as a vast number of shots had been aimed at him in the rebellion of '98 and not one had hit him. Then, turning to Captain Durie, he told him with mock seriousness that, 'the soldiers of the year 1798 in Ireland, would have picked a poor living if made fowlers on the Falkland Islands.' Everyone laughed at this sally and it was decided then and there that John Bellingham would be entitled to extra spirits in bad weather and that he could call for assistance in collecting the geese he shot, if he wished.

Protection of their stores proved to be a thornier problem, especially where the liquor was concerned. Not only was the stock ashore rifled, but some enterprising seamen had remembered the pipes of madeira in the hold and had gained access to them by breaking a hole in the ship's bottom. This act was truly scandalous as it killed any chance of the hull being refurbished and refloated, although such a prospect was, in any case, finally removed a few days later when a sudden storm drove the hulk further on to the rocks.

At Holt's suggestion a new appointment, that of store-keeper, was agreed and Sergeant Bean was elected. He immediately started to mount a sentry over the pile of stores outside the camp, but the following day a number of men, all either Marines or *Isabella's* sailors, had clearly drunk far more than their daily allowance. So it was decided to include passengers in the sentry roster, but even that failed to prevent the pilfering and drunkenness.

The next step was to move the store into the centre of the camp, but, to the annoyance of some members of the council, that still did not solve the problem and the drink encouraged Hayes, Mattinson and Ansell, sometimes abetted by Higton, to attempt to terrorize the others. Holt claims to have been one of the few to stand up to them but Durie, who had all the authority of both the King's Commission and his status as a Justice of the Peace to use if he needed them, kept quiet, as he was to do on several subsequent occasions.

Holt watched this with some indignation, especially the drunkenness, although, as he observed, 'you might as well expect to squeeze honey out of a blacksmith's anvil as to make an old sailor or marine honest.' Finally, the committee decided to dig a pit some four feet deep into which all the pipes of wine and spirit casks were lowered and then covered with earth. The only way now to obtain liquor or wine was to remove the earthen cover and then pump the liquid out with a small hand-pump, and this at last solved the problem, although, as Holt wryly commented, they now had to go to find the next sentry for duty, whereas previously he would have arrived without being called.

By now everyone had sorted themselves out into 'messes'. The Marines had their own mess, to which, as on board *Isabella*, Hayes, Breakwell and Mattinson had added themselves. Despite being a member of the council, Hayes continued to attempt to thwart any authority and took particular pleasure in seeking to repay old scores by arguing over any attempt by Captain Brookes to direct matters.

Higton, who, as the author of their disaster, was universally unpopular, had set up house with Mrs Bindell, the two of them having little to do with the others, except when absolutely necessary. He did nothing to exert any control over the passengers or his own sailors, although he occasionally appeared to be friendly with Mattinson and Ansell. He had periodic drinking bouts with them, but then, for no reason which the others could discern, he would suddenly become extremely hostile to them.

On one such drunken occasion a furious quarrel suddenly erupted between Higton and Ansell. They faced each other shouting and cursing, and Ansell challenged the ship's master to a fistfight, which Higton declined, but Ansell thrust his fist into the captain's face, shouting, 'Where's your quarterdeck now, then?' At this, James Hubbard, an American, stepped forward to prevent the threatened fight, whereupon Ansell turned towards him, paused for a moment, which caused Hubbard to lower his guard, and then delivered a haymaker to his head. This felled the unfortunate Hubbard and for several minutes the onlookers thought that he was going to die. He did, however, recover and his comrades bandaged his head, although on several occasions thereafter they noted him acting in a highly erratic manner and it was the general opinion that he had suffered a fractured skull. If the dispute was to affect Hubbard for a lifetime, however, the same could not be said of Ansell or Higton, who were happily drinking together again a few hours later.

Finally, there was Holt's mess, to which belonged the Holt family, the Durie family, Brookes, Lundin and Mary-Ann Spencer, who, despite her background, had become Joanna-Ann Durie's companion and helper. Mrs Durie was, in fact, nearing her time of confinement and had long remained cheerful, despite all the adversity.

On Sunday, 14 February, however, just one week after the shipwreck, the sky was grey, the temperature cool and it was pouring with rain. In Holt's mess they had just assembled to eat their midday dinner when the canvas roof suddenly collapsed under the weight of rainwater, which soaked them all. This was just too much for Mrs Durie who burst into tears and sat there, bedraggled, soaked to the skin, her belly distended by the baby so close to birth, and sobbing her heart out. As she wept she called down curses on the useless Higton, whose drunkenness and incompetence had brought all this trouble upon them. She knew that the baby must arrive within the next few days and all she had to look forward to was lying on the cold, wet turf, sheltered by a leaking canvas roof, helped by two very amateur midwives and with no surgeon anywhere near if things were to go wrong. Nor, indeed, was there any prospect of rescue for them all, even if her confinement should go well.

It was one of the very few occasions when this steely lady showed any weakness in public and everyone tried to comfort her, but it was Holt rather than her husband who came forward with a practical proposal. 'God has already been very gracious to us', he said, 'and has saved all our lives. Not just that, but He can and will provide for you in your necessity. With His help, madam, I will have a house raised for you by this time on Tuesday next'.

That evening Holt sought out a good site for the new hut and the next morning he was out and at work by five o'clock, assisted by the Marines who, at his request, had been detailed by Captain Durie to help. By nightfall the walls had been erected for a hut twenty feet long, ten feet wide and seven feet high. The next day Sergeant Bean was despatched to obtain two wooden yards from the wreck, one of which Holt cut in two to form the end-poles for the roof and the other he used for the ridge-pole. As the ridge was twenty feet long he took some deck planks from the wreck and mounted them at intervals as rafters, one end secured to a wall and the other to the ridge, and these then supported the roof, which was made from three overlapping sails, firmly pegged down to resist the Falklands winds.

Timber boards were then used to erect a platform, at one end of which a stove from the wrecked ship's galley was installed. Two days after he had started, and true to the deadline he had promised Mrs Durie, the new hut was finished by installing a table and some chairs from the wreck. Following this they all sat down for 'many a good bumper' and Mrs Durie, now very close to giving birth, was particularly grateful to the charming and resourceful Irishman.

The hut was finished none too soon because five days later while they were sitting at dinner Holt observed Mrs Durie's face strain and as an old married man he read the signs at once. Pausing only to fill his glass, he signalled to Brookes and Durie, and with the cryptic comment, 'A safe passage to all on their journey,' he rose to his feet. 'Gentlemen, we will take a walk,' he announced and with that the men beat a judicious retreat, leaving Mrs Durie with Hester Holt and Mary-Ann Spencer hovering over her, ready to serve as midwives. The men strolled about the camp-site for about an hour and a half, after which they judged it safe to return to the hut to see how things had progressed. They called through the door and on being invited by Mrs Holt to enter they went in to find that Mrs Durie had given birth to a daughter, and that, despite everyone's earlier fears, both infant and mother were in the best of health.

As is usually the case with men, they then decided to celebrate this momentous event, in which they had played no useful role whatsoever, and, pulling up their chairs, they drank well into the night. Holt declared that the newborn baby was queen of the island, being the first human to be born there, and the menfolk reached a consensus that she should be named Eliza Providence Durie.[25]

The celebration of Eliza's birth was also a farewell for Captain Brookes and Lieutenant Lundin, who were due to depart in the morning to seek rescue. A few days after the shipwreck Brookes had explained to the other members of the council that they were on a very isolated island and well off the routes normally used by shipping. Further, he told them, although American and British whalers and sealers sometimes used the islands off the west of the Falklands as bases, they seldom came this far to the east. He also said that he believed that there might be a small Spanish settlement somewhere on the northern coast, although it was very doubtful if any of their boats ventured this far south in the archipelago. So, the survivors had no choice but to send someone to tell the authorities where they were and to ask for a vessel to be sent to rescue them.

Faced with this sobering assessment of their predicament the committee instructed the ship's carpenter to set to work on the *Isabella's* longboat. This small, open boat was quite deep, but just under eighteen feet in length, so the carpenter fitted an extra strake to increase the freeboard by four inches and then, taking a number of thin planks from the wreck, he fitted a half deck, which stretched some thirteen feet aft from the bows, with a small hatchway in its roof to give the crew some protection from the elements. This left a small open cockpit, approximately four and a half feet in length, in the stern, where the helmsman and those controlling the sails would sit. The boat was rigged with a single mast, which carried a jib and a lug mainsail. The carpenter worked with a will, assisted by men who brought nails, ropes, rigging and spars from the wreck to help.

It was decided that six men should crew her and a general meeting was held to resolve who they should be. Captain Brookes, who had proved himself by far the best seaman in the group, was nominated to go by Captain Durie, seconded by Holt and then confirmed by a considerable majority. Sir Harry Hayes, seeing an opportunity to get off the island whose discomforts he detested so much, nominated himself, and six of the Marines voted for him, but the remainder of the castaways were adamant that he should not go. When it became clear that a communal selection of the men to go on the boat would go on for ever, it was agreed that, since Brookes would clearly be the commander, it would be best to let him choose his own crew.

Accordingly, Brookes announced his selections. George Davis, the mate of the *Isabella* and a good seaman was the first, followed by Lieutenant Lundin, since the presence of an officer holding the King's Commission might well lend weight to their pleas when they reached civilization. After that Brookes settled on Joseph Wooley, one of the Royal Marines, and two of the *Isabella's* sailors, Jose Antonio, a Portuguese sailor who could speak several languages, and an American called Ford.

So, on Monday, 21 February, sixteen days after they had been cast upon this deserted island and the day after Eliza Providence Durie's birth, they all went down to the water's edge, where the boat lay, loaded with provisions and as ready as she ever would be for her voyage. Holt, as always, felt that the occasion should be marked with a little ceremony and so he passed a bottle of rum around, inviting all present to drink to the prosperity and safe voyage for the boat, which he now named *'Faith and Hope'*.

Following the farewells, the sails were raised and with Brookes at the tiller the little boat sailed off into Falkland Sound. Brookes' plan, which he had agreed with the council, was to sail north up Falklands Sound to Port Egmont and, if that proved fruitless, to carry on in a north-westerly direction in an attempt to reach the mainland, a journey of some one thousand miles across open ocean. All the survivors' hopes were pinned on this voyage, but, despite their overt optimism, both the six men crowded into the little boat and those waving them farewell from the shore must have known in their hearts that it was a desperate and forlorn undertaking.

CHAPTER 5

The plight of those on the remote and desolate island was certainly desperate, but it was by no means yet hopeless. Their provisions were short, but they had deliberately planned on making them last a year and they had muskets and gunpowder, while there were considerable amounts of equipment and stores still in the wreck. The island had a plentiful supply of fresh water and although the vegetation was sparse, they had found several large patches of wild celery, which Brookes had suggested might have been planted by visiting American or British sealers and whalers in years gone by. In fact, their diet enabled many of *Isabella's* sailors, who had been suffering from scurvy at the time of the wreck, to be cured.[26]

The camp was on a bluff some two hundred yards from the wreck of the *Isabella* and no attempt was made to find a more sheltered site, even though it was on the windward side of the island and thus exposed to the prevailing winds. Holt, however, was very pleased with it and, with his never-ending delight at finding names, had christened their little settlement *Newtown Providence*, since it was the site of their salvation.

At the centre stood a square hut, which contained the stores, and covered the pit in which the spirits and wine had been buried. During the day this hut was occupied by Sergeant Bean or one of the Marines and it was guarded at night to keep marauders away from the alcohol. Around this were some fourteen other habitations, whose construction was of a quality and ingenuity dependent upon the skill, resourcefulness and enthusiasm of the occupants. The best was undoubtedly the hut occupied by the Holts and Duries, and most of the others also formed groups to provide themselves with shelter, the sides of their huts being constructed of earth and turf, with spars from the wreck serving as rafters, and bits of sail or even sealskins used for roofs. One or two of the less sociable, however, contented themselves with individual shelters consisting of a hogshead covered with turf, with a curtain of tussock grass to cover the opening. One way and another, all the castaways had soon provided themselves with reasonable shelter from wind and rain, and although the days were relatively mild, they found the nights to be extremely cold. As a final touch they erected a flagpole on a high spot several hundred yards inland and from it the Union Flag proudly fluttered.

The island, whose name they did not discover until later, was shaped like an inverted 'L'. The main part was some eight miles long and about four miles wide, with a long promontory at the southern end. At the northern end a narrow neck of land joined the main part of the island to another piece of land some three miles long by one and a half miles wide. The island's highest point was about one hundred and twenty-five feet above sealevel, but it was essentially as flat as a pancake. To the east they could see a huge mass of very low-lying countryside, from which they were separated by a channel a mile wide, and there was another, smaller island to the south. To the west all that could be seen was sea, although on a clear day they could see land, which Higton's chart told them must be the English Maloon.

The island itself was bleak. There was not a single bush or tree, although on some parts of the shore were great stands of tussock grass, which grew to some fifteen feet in height. The main part of the island was covered in close-cropped turf and Holt was quick to espy several peat-bogs, which, as an Irishman, he knew could be used for fuel, if the need should arise.

The island was inhabited by birds of many species, which Holt made it his business to examine and to record in his journal. He was astounded by the antics of the local geese, which, he noted, were simply incapable of taking fright. These birds tended to congregate in flocks and if one of the flock was shot they would gather round and stare at their dead comrade, which enabled the human hunters to approach and despatch many more. Sometimes, indeed, the geese would simply gather round the hunters out of curiosity, enabling John Bellingham, the elected 'sportsman', to kill them with a stick and thus save ammunition. Similarly, a species of flightless duck simply hid their heads in the grass when chased and could also be despatched with several blows from a stout stick. These two species were not only easy to catch, but they also provided very acceptable meat and soup, although the castaways discovered that several others, such as black shags and sea-geese, had a very fishy taste unless soaked in fresh water for at least ten hours prior to being cooked.

Holt observed many other birds on the island, including duck, teal, widgeon, snipe and dove. He also spotted many black-necked swans, magnificent birds with their glossy black necks and snow-white bodies, although he never managed to kill one since, unlike virtually every other species on the island, they had the good sense to fly away on the approach of a human. There were also several colonies of magellanic penguins, which lived in burrows in the ground, from which they peered myopically at any passing human.

Holt also saw several species of eagle and hawk, which caused him some

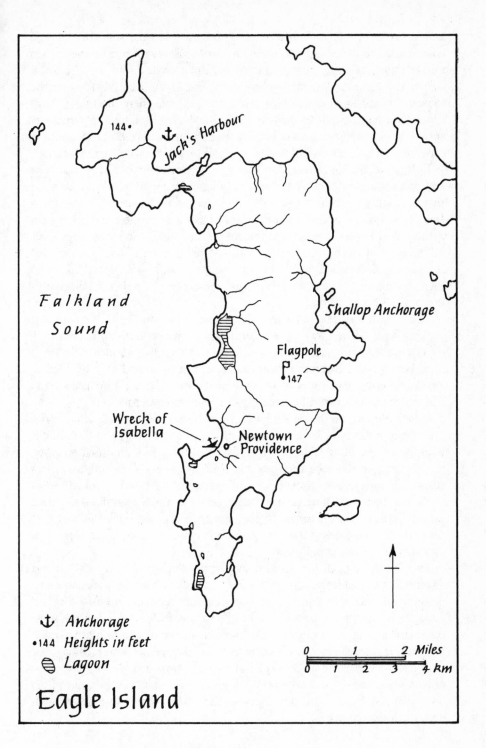

144•   Jack's Harbour

Falkland
Sound

Shallop Anchorage

Flagpole
⌐
•147

Wreck of
Isabella

Newtown
Providence

⚓ Anchorage
•144 Heights in feet
🐚 Lagoon

0   1   2 Miles
0   1   2   3   4 km

Eagle Island

annoyance at one point, when he made his own unusual and idiosyncratic contribution to the island's wildlife. He had brought with him on the voyage a large cage containing twenty-one parrots and a single cockatoo, which had cost him a great deal of money, no less than £63, in Port Jackson, but he looked forward to a considerable profit when he sold them in Dublin. Holt took a constant delight in the way they talked, the cockatoo, in particular, speaking a great deal, 'as much as any woman,' he observed acidly, and was especially receptive to swear words, which it picked up with particular ease.

Holt saved the birds from the wreck, but, faced with a biscuit ration of two pounds a person per week and nothing extra for livestock, he decided that he could not afford to feed them and so had no choice but to set them free. To his great annoyance, however, just as the newly-released birds were getting used to their unexpected freedom, some eagles and hawks appeared, killing most of the bewildered tropical birds in a matter of minutes. Four of the parrots fled back into the hut and sought shelter with Mrs Holt, who then insisted that they be saved, even at the expense of being fed on part of the family's bread ration.

The island was devoid of any quadrupeds, but one day Holt was out walking with Durie down at the south-east corner of the island when they discovered a colony of elephant seals. The two men had no idea what these huge beasts were, but managed to isolate one of them and Holt decided to attack, even though he was armed only with a stick. He went up close to the seal which reared up and he struck it a blow in one eye, followed quickly by a second blow to the other eye, which totally blinded it. Holt sent Durie, ever the bystander, to fetch two small rocks, and he then attacked, killing it with the second blow. The two men inspected their 'kill' and then returned to the camp to describe their achievement, whereupon one of the sailors rushed off to collect its tongue, which he brought back to be cooked on his mess fire, their first taste of fresh meat for some three months. After this, killing elephant seals became quite a popular 'sport,' although the only part they found a use for was the tongue, Holt claiming to have had no less than forty-five in his hut at one stage.

And so time slipped by, with life quickly settling into a routine. Holt was as busy as ever, adding constantly to his hut and keeping the stores account. Bellingham, the 'sportsman', was systematically reducing the island's bird population and many joined in killing elephant seals. Not even the most optimistic among them expected the longboat's departure to result in a quick rescue, but nevertheless they became increasingly anxious with each day that passed. The departure of Brookes and George Davis had left Higton as the only nautical 'expert' on the island, although, since he lived in a hut of his own with Mrs Bindell, his dealings with the others seemed to decrease with each week that passed.

When it was decided to start work on another boat, Higton had to be consulted and he decreed that a site somewhat distant from the water must be used. There was some surprise at this, since Holt, for one, could not understand how they would get the boat, if they ever finished it, into the water, but they accepted the 'expert' advice and made a start. It was an ambitious project, since the boat had to be large enough to take all forty-nine souls remaining on the island to Buenos Ayres and the *Isabella's* carpenter was given the task of constructing the vessel, assisted by another crewman, who had been a 'gimblet-maker' and was thus designated the blacksmith. Sergeant Bean constructed a makeshift bellows and one of the ship's cannon was dragged up to the site to be used as an anvil.

Everything for the new vessel had to come from the wreck and moving it all up to the site was laborious, causing some dissension. Timbers were taken from the *Isabella* and a large eleven-inch cable was pulled ashore and men set to unlay it to provide rigging. They had no proper tools, and neither tar nor pitch, and the prospect of success seemed remote, to say the least, but in their desperate situation it did at least give them some prospect, however illusory, of salvation.

As the days went by it seemed increasingly probable that the longboat had either failed to find any settlement at Port Egmont or that some accident had befallen it. Thus, morale began to suffer, and many of the weaker spirits began to despair that they would ever see their homes or loved ones again. Work proceeded with the new boat, but in late March Mattinson demanded that he should be allowed to take the jollyboat and make another attempt to find help. This jollyboat was even smaller than the longboat which Brookes had taken and the more prudent people in the camp thought privately that this was a hazardous undertaking. However the camp would be a quieter and more peaceful place without the objectionable Mattinson, so when volunteers were found to go with him, the project was agreed and the little boat set out at the end of the month, manned by four men: Mattinson, a marine and two of the youngest (and, thus, smallest) seamen from the *Isabella*.

On 4 April, their sixty-third day on the island, Holt and Durie took an afternoon stroll down towards the south of the island and suddenly spotted a sail to the west, heading towards them. As they hurried to the shore, Durie suggested that it was Captain Brookes returning in '*Faith and Hope*' but Holt was soon convinced that it was a much larger vessel. Holt took out a handkerchief and, attaching it to his walking stick, waved it in the air; to their delight the vessel hove-to off the shore and lowered a boat which was soon being rowed towards them.

Other people in the camp had spotted the vessel as well, and Holt and Durie were soon joined by a small crowd, all of them speculating wildly about the identity of the strangers. Their guesses were answered when they saw a flag being run up to the gaff, which was immediately recognized as the stars-and-bars of the United States, causing great excitement, as there had been some apprehension that the boat might be Portuguese or Spanish. They jumped for joy and threw their arms around each other as the rowing boat neared the shore and then they crowded around their rescuers as they stepped ashore.

The first on the beach looked at the cheering, laughing crowd and then caught sight of Holt with his beard under his chin. 'How was the settlement of the world'? the stranger asked and while the others were bewildered by this cryptic utterance, Holt's eyes opened wide with a hint of recognition. 'Very well', he replied and gripped the stranger's out-stretched hand in a brotherly greeting.

PART 2

Nanina to the Rescue

CHAPTER 6

To discover where the American rescuers had come from and why they were in the Falkland Islands we must go back to the previous year, 1812, and move to the United States of America, where hunting seals and whales had long been popular and profitable activities among New England sailors. Venturing ever further, the first recorded instance of an American whaling vessel crossing the Equator came in 1774 and within a few years vessels were regularly operating off the coast of the Spanish and Portuguese colonies in South America. Soon after the American Revolution a Lady Hayes financed a voyage by the sealing vessel *States* to the Falklands to obtain skins and oil from 'hair-seals'* and by the mid-1790s there were so many American ships operating around the islands that the seal population began to be seriously depleted. Unmindful of the effects of their operations, however, the hunters simply moved on to a new colony as they exterminated an old one.

Sealing was a profitable business, but became even more so when an enterprising skipper hit on a novel and advantageous scheme whereby the sealskins were taken to China and sold there for far more than they would have obtained in the United States. The Chinese were particularly keen to buy the skins, which they used to make both clothing and shoes, and the bristles, which had a role in opium smoking. The American masters then purchased Chinese goods, such as tea, silks and nankeen for sale in America at a great profit.† Only the seal-oil was not sold in China, being taken, instead, to the United States, where it was used as a machine lubricant in the burgeoning industrial revolution.

One of the first to conduct such a round-the-world operation was Captain Daniel Green of New Haven, Connecticut, who left in 1790, operated in the Falklands and South Georgia area for two years and then went to Canton, returning to the States around the Cape of Good Hope. This encouraged him to repeat the pattern, leaving New Haven on 29 November, 1796, taking

* Southern fur seal, *arctocephalus australis*.

† Nankeen was a hard-wearing, buff-coloured cotton fabric, the name being a corruption of its port of origin: Nanking.

50,000 sealskins in the southern oceans and returning, again via Canton, on 17 February, 1799, with Chinese goods that sold in New York for no less than $260,000.[27] Not surprisingly, this colossal sum encouraged many other businesses and captains to try their hands at such an extremely profitable undertaking.

By the year 1812 sealing in the distant south was a well-established trade and when a captain named Charles Barnard approached the New York firm of Messrs John B. Murray & Son with a proposal for such a voyage the latter was very pleased to participate. An agreement was reached whereby the Murrays would purchase a brig approved by Barnard, equip and victual her, and provide her with a small, prefabricated craft, known as a shallop. Charles Barnard would then find a crew and sail south to the Falklands where they would undertake a season of sealing, load the skins and oil into the vessel they had gone south in and send it back to New York, with a small crew commanded by his father, Valentine Barnard. The remainder of the party, under Charles Barnard, would stay in the Falkland Islands with the shallop and carry on sealing. The Murrays, in consultation with Valentine Barnard, would then purchase a rather larger vessel, equip and victual it as before, and then send it south to meet those who had stayed there. They would then load the entire stock of skins and sail into the Pacific where they would continue sealing until they felt that they had taken enough, when they would sail to Canton, sell the skins, buy other goods and then head for home. For this the Murrays would receive 52 per cent of the proceeds of the sale of skins and oil, while Barnard would receive the remaining 48 percent.

This was an ambitious and seemingly dangerous plan, but wintering in the Falklands held no fears for such hardened and experienced men. So, when the deal had been concluded to their mutual satisfaction, the Murrays had articles of agreement prepared and both sides entered into a bond of $5,000 for the satisfactory performance of their part of the undertaking. The only proviso was a standard 'war clause', which stipulated that, should a conflict break out, the agreement relating to the despatch of the vessel in the second part of the undertaking would be void.

These preliminaries having been agreed, Charles Barnard found the brig *Nanina*, which had been built in Pittsburg just eight years earlier. She had two decks, which provided ample accommodation for the crew, as well as a large hold, and 'measured' 132 tons, with a length of 73 feet, a beam of 23 feet 4 inches and a draught of 10 feet 2 inches when fully laden.[28] Although pitifully small by modern standards, she was a sturdy vessel for her day and considered well-suited for her long voyage to the southern ocean and back, and the Barnards were very satisfied with her. She had been bought from a Philadelphia owner by Anthony Chardon of New York as recently as 22

February, 1812, but she was so suited for Barnard's purpose that he was persuaded to sell her again.

Once the Murrays had completed the purchase, *Nanina* was registered at the Port of New York on 3 April, 1812, with John and James Murray shown as the owners, and Valentine Barnard as the master. The Barnards signed-on a crew on that same day and then obtained health clearance from the port medical authorities, together with customs clearance for a cargo of salt, which was needed for curing the sealskins, and empty casks to transport the seal oil.

There were, however, disturbing stories of an impending war. The United States' administration was becoming increasingly frustrated by the treatment it was receiving from the warring European powers, particularly Britain and France, and James Monroe, who had spent many years in the various European capitals, was appointed Secretary of State in April 1811, determined that, if necessary, the United States must resort to arms. The Twelfth Congress assembled in December, 1811, and on 1 April, 1812, President Madison proposed that a sixty-day embargo be imposed on the sailing of any vessel from a United States port, thus bringing commercial pressure to bear on Great Britain. Congress agreed, but extended the length of the embargo to ninety days.

The rights or wrongs of what was going on in a distant Washington did not concern Charles Barnard, except that it threatened his carefully nurtured plan. So, when a rumour reached him that Congress had passed the Bill he reacted at once, sailing *Nanina* out of New York harbour and anchoring off Sandy Hook. There he made some changes in the crew and then, all being ready and having evaded the embargo which had, in fact, been imposed on 7 April, he set sail for the Falkland Islands on 12 April, 1812.

There were thirteen men aboard the little vessel. According to the ship's papers the official master was Valentine Barnard, aged sixty-three. Born into a Quaker family in Nantucket in about 1750, he moved to Hudson on the Hudson River in 1773, and in 1812 he was still a sprightly and fit man, having been at sea for many years, even though, according to one of his crew, he had to wear no less than two trusses. He seems to have been somewhat elderly for such a voyage as this, but the most likely explanation is that his son needed to be absolutely certain that he could rely on the person who would take the *Nanina* back to New York to bring another vessel down the following year to collect him.

Valentine's partner in this business venture was his son, Charles, who was 29 years old in 1812. Charles was brought up as a Quaker but married a non-Quaker woman in 1804 and, as a result, was 'read-out' of his local group in January, 1805. Charles, nevertheless, retained much of the Quakers' stern

```
                           TABLE II

ABOARD THE AMERICAN SEALING BRIG NANINA ON HER VOYAGE SOUTH:
           SAILED FROM NEW YORK 12 April, 1812
        ARRIVED IN THE FALKLAND ISLANDS* 7 September, 1812


MASTER
Captain Valentine Barnard**

OFFICERS AND BUSINESS PARTNERS
Captain Charles Barnard **
Captain Edmund Fanning;
Captain Andrew Hunter;
Captain Barzillai Pease.

MATE
Henry Ingman, Mate

FOREMAST HANDS
Henry Gilchrist, Seaman; Jacob Green, Seaman; Andrew Lott,
Seaman; William Montgomery, Steward; John Spear, Cook;
Havens Tennant, Seaman; John Wines, Carpenter.

TOTAL. 13.

-----------------------------------------------------
Notes:
*  Of these 13 men, 11 went in the shallop to Eagle Island,
leaving Valentine Barnard and Barzillai Pease aboard Nanina
in Barnard's Harbour.
** According to the ship's papers Valentine Barnard was the
master of the Nanina, but his son, Charles Barnard,
exercised all the powers of master during the voyage down to
and around the Falkland Islands.
```

44

views on life and, like so many in that era, he was always moralizing and making appeals to the Almighty. He was, however, a humane and courageous man, and his beliefs were to prove the source of much-needed strength in the trials to come.

Because the British fleet had been hampering the activities of American merchant vessels there were few seagoing billets available and the industry was in a state of decline. Consequently, no less than three other qualified captains not only became business partners but also sailed in the *Nanina*. Captain Andrew Hunter, aged 39, was from Rhode Island, while the second, Captain Edmund Fanning, was from Massachusetts, and a nephew and namesake of the famous Captain Edmund Fanning of Stonington, a noted explorer and author. The third captain in this coterie was quite different. Barzillai Pease was born in Martha's Vineyard in 1773 and moved with his family to Hudson sometime in his youth. He ran away to sea at fourteen and sailed on at least one occasion under Valentine Barnard, who was the mate of a sealer at the time. Pease was familiar with the Falkland Islands and had even been to South Georgia, where he was shipwrecked. He was, without a doubt, the most complex character aboard the *Nanina* and kept a secret journal in which he recorded the daily events of his life.[29] This was not unusual as many seafarers of the time kept similar journals, but Pease's journal was highly personal, some of it in an elementary code, and he carefully documented every slight to which he felt subjected.

Nanina's mate was Henry Ingman, a young man of just twenty-two, who was, no doubt, somewhat overshadowed by the presence of five older and far more experienced captains. The foredeck hands comprised John Spear, cook; John Wines, carpenter; William Montgomery, steward; and four seamen: Henry Gilchrist, Andrew Lott, Havens Tennant and Jacob Green. Of these, all were black, except for the carpenter.

The most outstanding crewman was Jacob Green, who had been born in the State of Massachusetts, and despite being only twenty-six years old was a very experienced seaman who knew the Falkland Islands well. He was to show exceptional qualities of leadership and physical endurance during their later adventures, and Barnard thought very highly of him, a regard that was fully reciprocated.

Last, but by no means least, Charles Barnard took along his dog, Cent. This small animal, of no discernible breed, was one of those bouncy and gutsy dogs that add greatly to the quality of life and was to serve his master well during their coming adventures.

The voyage south was routed via the Cape Verde Islands, which they reached on 17 May. They took on more salt, as well as a large quantity of hogs, goats, fowls and vegetables, while the water-butts were also topped-up, and the ship's bottom was scraped and blacked. After ten days they set off again and soon crossed the Equator where, 'old Father Neptune came saucily on board and was received with the usual formalities. He was complimented with several bottles of the best from those novices who were even glad at so small a sacrifice to escape from the foam of his lather box, and save themselves from a ducking by his incensed majesty. Neptune is, indeed, an impudent fellow, but he is such a mighty water-drinker, that he ought to be pardoned for now and then demanding a hearty swig of grog from a novice, as the sea-water might otherwise disturb the tone of his thirsty stomach.'

Further south they experienced several heavy gales which delayed their arrival in the Falkland Islands until 7 September, 1811, one hundred and forty-eight days out of New York. They were in reasonable heart, although several of the men were suffering from scurvy, which was always a problem in those days, and there had been several disputes, which were also by no means unusual on such a long voyage.

CHAPTER 7

Nanina's destination was New Island, one of the westernmost of the Falkland Islands group. The island itself was shaped like a dog's leg, with the north-south leg being some six miles long and the top, east-west leg extending a further two miles. The western and northern shores, which faced the prevailing winds, were characterized by precipitous cliffs, while the eastern and southern shores sloped gradually down to the sea, with many, gently-inclined, sandy beaches. As a result there were some excellent harbours on the eastern side, which was sheltered from the prevailing westerly winds, which blew for most of the year, and also from the worst of the storms, which tended to come from the north and north-west. The island had consequently become a popular anchorage for whalers and sealers, Captain Edmund Fanning of Stonington describing it in a contemporary account as, 'the most convenient island for a ship is West Point or New Island in latitude 51° 41′ South, which is the most general for whalemen. At Little West Point Harbour there is good water and plenty of hogs and some goats. All the islands produce plenty of wild fowl, geese, ducks, teal, rooks*, curlews, etc, and plenty of eggs in October, November and December, the albatross beginning to lay about first to tenth of October.'[30]

Nanina entered Hooker's Harbour and dropped anchor at two o'clock on the afternoon of 7 September and no time was wasted in congratulations; they had been too long on the voyage for that. The Falklands' winter had just passed its peak and all were eager to get on with the task for which they had come, sealing. So, as soon as the anchor was holding and the sails furled, the yards and topmasts were sent down, while the long-boat ferried a small party of hunters ashore with their fowling-pieces and they shot twenty-eight geese, which made a welcome change to salted beef.

---

* Early nineteenth century sailors used the term 'rook' to describe what are now recognised to be quite different birds. In this case, Fanning appears to be referring to birds of the family *faclonidae*, of which three species are present on the islands: *phalcoboenus australis*, *polyborus plancus* and *falco peregrinus cassini*, known to today's Falklanders as 'Johnny Rook,' 'carancho,' and 'sparrowhawk,' respectively. To add to the confusion, sailors also used the term 'rook' to describe the Great Skua, *catharacta skua antarctica*, which belongs to a quite different species.

47

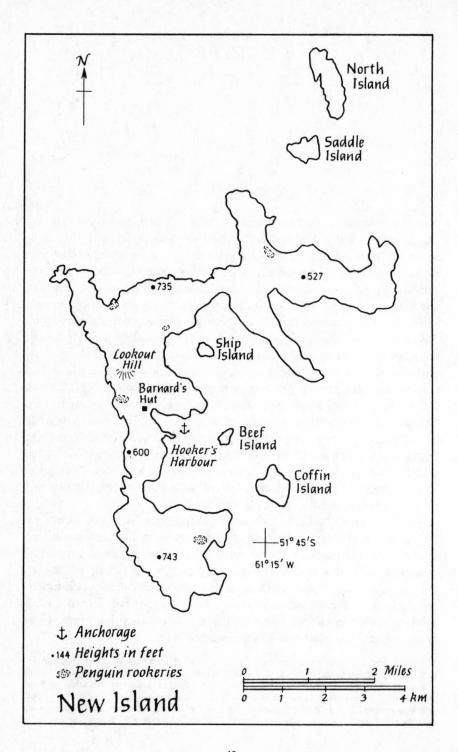

N

North
Island

Saddle
Island

•527

•735

Ship
Island

Lookout
Hill

Barnard's
Hut

⚓

Beef
Island

•600

Hooker's
Harbour

Coffin
Island

—51° 45′ S
61° 15′ W

•743

⚓ Anchorage
•₁₄₄ Heights in feet
🐧 Penguin rookeries

New Island

| 0 | | 1 | | 2 Miles |
| 0 | 1 | 2 | 3 | 4 km |

New Island was, like the rest of the Falklands group, barren, with no trees or bushes, although there were large areas of tussock grass. Nevertheless, it provided two facilities the Barnards needed, shelter and fresh water. Charles Barnard was fascinated by the strange lands he visited and he recorded a detailed description of the Falkland Islands as he found them. 'The climate,' he wrote,[31] 'is temperate and salubrious, free from the extremes of heat and cold; but there are frequent rains and stormy winds in all seasons of the year. The running streams are never frozen, and the ice on the lakes and pools is seldom sufficiently strong to bear the weight of a man above twenty-four hours in succession. Snow remains upon the tops of the highest mountains about two months in winter, but seldom above a day or two in the lower grounds. The hoar frosts in Spring and Autumn occasion no injury to the plants, but being thawed by the sun are converted into a refreshing dew. Thunder is seldom heard in Summer; but even during that season of the year, the winds are almost uniformly violent.'

Turning to the terrain, 'the surface is marshy, and the soil is composed first of a thick turf, then a black mould, from eight to twelve inches deep, and next a yellowish clay, resting upon a strata of slate and stone. The meadows, which are of considerable extent, and watered with numerous rivulets from the hills, afford abundance of excellent pasturage. The resinous gum plant is the most conspicuous and curious of the vegetable productions. It is of a bright green colour; but having neither stalk, branches or leaves, it is more like an excrescence from the earth than a plant. It is only about a foot and a half in height, but frequently more than six feet in diameter, and so firm in its texture as to bear the weight of a man without yielding to the pressure. A small shrub, creeping close to the ground, was discovered to possess the taste of spruce fir, and being made into beer with molasses, proved a powerful anti-scorbutic.'

'There are great quantities also of wild parsley, wood sorrel, and water cresses, which provide a valuable relief to those who are afflicted with the scurvy. The only fruits to be found on the islands capable of being used as food are the small berry the size of a pea, resembling the lucet of north America, and another similar to the mulberry, both of which grow upon creeping plants.'

Naturally, he was interested in whether the islands had ever been inhabited and in the wild life, but he recorded that, 'there is no appearance whatever of these islands having ever been inhabited previous to their discovery by Europeans; and the navigators who first landed upon their shores found the animals so unacquainted with man, that the birds suffered themselves to be taken in the hand, and even settled on the heads of the people when they stood still. Only one species of quadruped is observed on these islands, called the wolf-fox, from its resemblance to both these animals. It is about the size of a common shepherd's dog, with very long, sharp fangs, and barks in the same manner, but not so loud. It digs a kennel under the ground, and preys upon the wild fowl and seal.'

The lack of land animals was, however, more than compensated for by the abundant bird life, with land- and water-fowl being, 'found in great numbers and variety. The most remarkable are swans with necks of a velvet black colour, flesh-coloured feet and white bodies; wild geese, one species of which, similar to the Canada goose, feeds chiefly on dry land, and affords a wholesome and palatable food; ducks and teal resembling those of Europe; a species of grebe of the most beautiful plumage, and eyes like rubies surrounded with a circle of white feathers; a kind of guillemot, whose flesh is very good to eat; a species of penguin, distinguished by its stately gait and solitary habits; different kinds of petrels; small eagles; falcons, snipes, curlews, herons, thrush, etc.'

A curious feature of this list is that it completely ignores some birds which were to become very important to Barnard in his later adventures. The albatross, which had been specifically noted by Fanning, was a large and very graceful bird, which nested in large numbers on the outer islands. Also, Barnard mentions only one breed of penguin (and he seems to have been referring to the King Penguin) but there were also very large numbers of rockhopper, gentoo and magellanic penguins as well, together with the occasional pair of macaronis. He does, however, mention the seals, which were, after all, the object of his voyage, 'the coasts abound with seals, and walruses or sea-lions, many of which are of an enormous size, and also very formidable from their ferocity and strength.'

The whalers and sealers of the time had appreciated the lack of animals and vegetables in the Falklands, and there was an unspoken agreement to try to rectify this. Thus, many vessels, including *Nanina*, carried hogs to the islands, which were released in breeding pairs, and by 1812 there were quite large numbers in some places, especially on Beaver and Swan Islands. Goats were also released, although these do not seem to have survived so well. Unfortunately, but through no deliberate intent, rats had also found their way ashore from some visiting ships to a few of the islands and were very troublesome when encountered by man.

The birds and the hogs provided crews with a supply of meat, but sailors of the day were always worried about scurvy. The disease had first been encountered by the Portuguese explorer Vasco da Gama in the fifteenth century, but even by the nineteenth century was still not properly under-stood, although they did know that it was prevented and cured by fresh fruit and vegetables. There was no fruit on the Falklands and from the total lack of trees it appeared unrewarding to try to introduce any. Edible vegetables, as Barnard describes, did occur naturally, although only in very small quantities, and so celery had been introduced in places by visiting mariners and there were even a few potato patches.

The morning after their arrival Barnard and his companions started to ferry the pieces of the shallop ashore where John Wines, the carpenter, assisted by Pease and Fanning, laid the keel and then raised the stem and stern posts. This shallop was an auxiliary vessel and had been designed and assembled in New York, and then broken down into small elements for transportation in *Nanina's* hold. She displaced some 19 tons and was cutter-rigged, with a single mainmast, gaff mainsail, and a foresail set to a long bowsprit. She was fully-decked, with cabins below and a hold to accommodate the sealskins they intended to take; indeed, on one occasion in the coming months she would show that she could take large loads, sailing some forty miles with no less than twenty-six people on board. On that occasion Charles Barnard would find her difficult to manage, although normally she sailed well, being designed to withstand the Falklands' storms, while still being handy enough to be manned by a crew of two in fair weather.

Assembling the shallop took longer than expected, partly because some of the crew were still recovering from the scurvy, but also because the carpenter hurt his hand and nobody else was sufficiently skilled to take his place. As a result the boat was not launched until early October, when she was given the name *Young Nanina* by Charles Barnard.

Meanwhile two smaller boats, a yawl and a small sealing boat, were put to use for sealing on nearby islands, with early visits being made to Beaver and Staats islands. Once the shallop was ready, however, they were able to venture much further afield and on 26 December Charles Barnard led a group of ten men to the island of Steeple Jason, some fifty miles due north from New Island.

As with any trade, sealers had developed a language of their own and the fur seals, which were the crew's primary targets, were given special names. Mature adult males were called *wigs*; immature males, *bulls*; adult females, *clapmatches*; and the half-grown animals of both genders, *yearlings*. On the sealing beaches the adults lolled in family groups basking in the sun and were normally easy game for the hunters, whose main weapon was an oak or hickory club about five feet long, which was used to stun the victim, following which it was stabbed to death with a sealing knife. Barnard and his companions also took elephant seals when they could find them, which were killed in much the same way, despite their vast size. They had a fierce demeanour and roared loudly, but, except in the mating season, could normally be killed by a single, nimble man, even when armed only with a stick and a knife.

As soon as possible after being killed the carcasses were collected and skinned, with the skins later being scraped and pegged out, usually with ten wooden pegs, and left to cure. This process normally took about ten days, following which the skins were stacked to await the arrival of the shallop to be loaded and taken to the *Nanina*. Meanwhile, beeming knives were used to cut the blubber into 'horse pieces', each approximately twenty-four inches long, fifteen inches wide and up to four inches thick. These were then carried to a nearby stream where the sand and blood were washed off, following which the pieces were cut into strips about two inches wide and dropped through the bunghole into casks, which, once full, were sealed.

When a sufficient stock had been assembled a 'tryworks' was set up, either on the beach or on the deck of the *Nanina*. In the latter case, the casks were floated out to the shallop, which took them to *Nanina*, where the horse-pieces were removed. Each piece was then partially cut through laterally at approximately one inch intervals to increase the surface area before being dropped into a large, three-legged cauldron, known as a 'try-pot.' This was mounted over a roaring fire, fuelled either by wood or the remains of horse-pieces, although sometimes penguins were cut in half to be used as fuel, since their fat burnt well. At the end of the process the oil was poured into a cask and the scraps were put through a press to remove the final traces of oil before being used as fuel.

A tryworks with a one hundred gallon capacity could produce some nine hundred gallons of oil per day, but it was a very smelly and extremely messy business. It was, however, accepted by the men as being just part of their job and the financial returns were, of course, excellent.

Barnard left nine men hard at work on Steeple Jason and returned in the shallop with just one other man, reaching New Island on 3 January, 1813. There he found that another vessel, the *Hope* of New York, had called in for water and her master, Obadiah Chase, told him that war had been declared by Congress and approved by the President on 18 June of the previous year. Chase went on to say that he had also heard a rumour that the British were about to withdraw the orders-in-council, which were widely considered to be the root of the problem between the two countries, and thus the crisis might be short-lived.

Captain Chase then handed over some mail, which included a letter from Messrs Murray, the part-owners of the *Nanina*, which confirmed the outbreak of war and reminded the Barnards that their contract stipulated that this nullified the agreement to provide a vessel for the second part of the undertaking. The Murrays therefore advised the Barnards to make for the nearest United States port and take sanctuary there.

The most immediate problem facing the crew of the *Nanina* was that British whalers frequently called at New Island to take on water and it seemed possible that such a vessel, armed and issued with a Letter of

Marque could arrive at any moment.* The lightly manned and totally unarmed *Nanina* would be an easy prey to such a vessel, so it was quickly agreed to move to a less exposed site.

What to do in the longer term was a little less obvious, but they eventually decided that if they were to leave for the United States at once they would lose a lot of money and, in any case, would be liable to capture by a British vessel during the course of such a long voyage. On the other hand, if they stayed and carried on sealing they would stand to make much more money and if, on the return voyage, the war was still in progress, they stood just as much chance of being captured as if they left immediately. In any case, if the rumours about the withdrawal of the hated orders-in-council were correct, there was a good chance that the war would end soon anyway.

So they decided to carry on sealing, but, to be on the safe side, to move *Nanina* to a safer position. The shallop was, therefore, despatched to bring the sealing party back from Steeple Jason, fetching their equipment with them, but leaving the skins so far gathered to be collected at a later date. Pease, who had been on Steeple Jason but who had left separately in the longboat just before the shallop arrived, returned to New Island on 20 January. So, as soon as everyone was assembled, *Nanina* was rerigged and prepared for sea, but it was not until 26 January that a suitable wind enabled them to leave harbour, and the brig, followed by the shallop, left New Island.

Their destination was a long sheltered inlet, which some of them called Four Island Lagoon after the islands at its entrance, but which Charles Barnard preferred to call 'Barnard's Harbour,' since he claimed to have discovered it during a previous voyage.† Here the head of the inlet was hidden from the open sea and the steep hills either side meant that the vessel's masts could not be seen, so *Nanina* would be reasonably secure. Once again the brig was stripped down and, since they expected to remain there for at least twelve months, the spars were taken ashore and stored.

Having arranged matters at this new base, the shallop was despatched to Steeple Jason to recover the skins left there, leaving some men under Charles Barnard to catch seals locally. On the return of the shallop they decided to undertake a rather longer cruise and, having taken on board sufficient provisions for eleven men for three months, they departed on 16 February, leaving only Valentine Barnard and Barzillai Pease (who was suffering from one of his many illnesses) to look after her.

* Letters of Marque were a formal licence issued by a state to a private individual to arm a vessel and seize merchant vessels of a hostile nation. In the War of 1812 both the United States and British governments made wide-scale use of such documents, which, in effect, created additional warships at no cost to the government.

† A small inlet off Port Richards, it is now known as Double Creek.

The plan was to work their way through the channel between the English Maloon and Swan Island, and then to weather Cape Orford, but this proved impossible in the face of a strong south-westerly wind. So, they caught some four hundred seals on Barnard's Island and then ran before the wind in a north-easterly direction to Fox Island, where they killed some elephant seals before heading back to the brig, which they reached on the 28th. There they set up the tryworks on the shore and processed the blubber.

After a wait of a few days while contrary winds continued to prevent them starting their voyage to the Spanish Maloon, Barnard took advantage of a moderation in the weather on 4 March and they set off for a second time. This attempt proved more successful and, having weathered Cape Orford, they worked their way along the southern coast of English Maloon, reaching Fox Bay in early April.

While there they noticed a column of smoke rising in the east, and Barnard's initial reaction was one of alarm, since he thought it indicated the presence of Spaniards from Buenos Ayres, who were reputed to send a *garda costa* to the islands each year to assert sovereignty and to order off any foreign vessel, especially sealers. The Spaniards, so the stories went, were loath to see foreigners on islands they considered to be their property and would set fire to the tussock grass, which provided shelter for the seals.

When the pillar of smoke continued day after day, however, and the sound of what seemed to be a gun firing was heard at intervals, Barnard decided that it might, instead, indicate the presence of shipwrecked mariners, especially as he knew those particular islands to be surrounded by treacherous reefs. So, after some understandable hesitation, he decided to sail across the southern end of Falklands Sound and investigate.

They beat out of Fox Bay and then ran before a fine north-westerly breeze, arriving off the northern end of Eagle Island the same afternoon, where they anchored in Jack's Harbour. The more they searched for the source of the smoke and the gunfire the more inquisitive the crew became and the following day they set out again, running down the eastern side of the island, the shallop some distance offshore and the sealing boat closer to the beach, looking out for seals and also further signs of the smoke.

At one o'clock Barnard called the sealing boat alongside and as they raised it aboard, one of the crew drew attention to what looked like a ship's mast in the centre of the island. However, their midday meal was ready, so having decided to eat first and investigate afterwards, they went below. They had no sooner started to eat, however, than Havens Tennant, who was on watch, gave a shout from the deck and they went up again, where to their astonishment they saw a group of people standing on the shore, waving and gesticulating. They were close enough to the shore to see that at least one was a female and that several of the men were in what appeared to be military uniform.

As they steered close to the shore, Barnard ordered the American flag to be raised and shouted, 'What ship are you?' and '*Isabella* of London', came the reply.

Captain Fanning was despatched in the sealing boat to investigate and as he stepped ashore among the laughing and cheering people he quickly singled out a powerful-looking, bearded man as one of the leaders. He saw, however, that the man's beard was grown in a curious manner, similar to his own, which he knew to be one of the characteristics of the United Irishmen. He hazarded a covert greeting, 'How was the settlement of the world?' he asked and 'Very well,' came the correct reply. With that the two men left the group for a moment to establish each other's credentials and then, satisfied that they were both members of the same clandestine group, they rejoined the others.

CHAPTER 8

Charles Barnard watched from the shallop as the sealing boat went ashore and then put off again with several of the shipwrecked people on board. Some of the people on shore were so keen to come on board that the boat crew had difficulty in pushing off and he looked on with astonishment as they followed it until they were waist-deep in the icy water. There was great excitement as the first of the castaways climbed aboard the shallop, but as they chattered excitedly Barnard managed to ascertain that the ship's master was not among them, so he sent the boat to the shore again to fetch him. With Higton came Joseph Holt and Captain Durie, and the latter two explained carefully to the Americans what had happened to them and described their present unhappy situation.

Initially, Higton stood to one side, tightlipped and looking surly, but after a while he moved forward and joined in the conversation, telling the Americans that the castaways had already despatched *Isabella's* longboat under command of an experienced mariner. It had, however, left forty-one days previously and, since they had heard nothing further, they had come to assume the worst. Barnard, on hearing that the boat was a mere seventeen and a half feet long, could only agree, knowing that many such small boats had been lost in the dirty weather and tide-rips surrounding the Falklands.

Higton went on to describe the new boat they were constructing, but admitted that the carpenter was not very skilled and was, in any case, lacking in many essentials such as pitch, tar and planks. Barnard was astonished that they should be trying to build a boat to carry fifty people over a thousand miles of stormy water and reflected wryly to himself that, although he had often heard of building castles in the air, this was the first example he knew of building ships in the same manner! Despite this, when Higton asked for help, Barnard offered all that was in his power and said that, although they were unable to offer any timber, he would, nevertheless, lend them his carpenter, John Wines.

Realizing that sunset was rapidly approaching, Barnard then told the British that he must move the shallop to a safe anchorage for the night and so his guests went ashore to pass on the good news, leaving the shallop to tack up Eagle Channel to the cove opposite the flagmast. As they went Barnard and his compatriots discussed the situation, but came to no conclusion other than that the British people obviously had no idea that their two countries were at war, and they agreed to keep quiet about this until they had seen how matters developed.

At nine o'clock Barnard and Hunter went ashore, where they found Sergeant Bean and two Marines waiting for them on the beach, having been despatched by Captain Durie to guide them to Newtown Providence. On reaching the castaways' camp they were shown to the Duries' hut, where they were introduced to Mrs Durie and Mrs Holt, both of whom had not only made an effort to look presentable for such welcome strangers, but had also prepared the best supper their straitened circumstances allowed. The introductions over, Barnard asked if Higton, his fellow master mariner, was to join them and there was a moment of embarrassed silence, which was eventually broken by Holt observing flatly that this was unlikely, indicating that he would explain the reason to the Americans later.

Mrs Durie, playing the role of hostess, also covered the embarrassment by coming forward with a bottle of madeira and some glasses, inviting the Americans to join them in drinking a toast to their arrival. She was in sparkling form and told Barnard with much laughter that she and Mrs Holt had been cross with their husbands for not bringing their American guests straight back to Newtown Providence to meet them.

Barnard remarked that when he was younger he had heard reports of an Irish rebel called Joseph Holt and asked if there was any relationship? Holt replied that he had to admit that he was that man, but, with a quick sideways glance at Captain Durie, he quickly added that his days of rebellion were long past and that he was now on the way back to his beloved Ireland.

The atmosphere was very convivial, with Durie and Holt describing the events leading up to and following the shipwreck, while Mrs Durie interrupted regularly with highly entertaining and spirited, if somewhat scurrilous, character sketches of those involved. She described the drunkenness of Higton and Samuel Ansell, but reserved her most acid descriptions for Sir Harry and Mattinson, with her husband and the Holts nodding their agreement. The group then discussed the prospects of the *Isabella's* longboat and the more recent departure of Mattinson, but these sombre thoughts did little to dampen their merrymaking, which continued until well after midnight. Finally, Holt told the Americans that it was far too dark for them to return to their vessel and offered the two visitors bunks in their hut, which were accepted, and all went to bed.

The following morning the two Americans were up and about early, and strolled about the camp. They met other castaways, viewed their huts and also walked down to the shore to have a look at the wreck of the *Isabella* and her cargo. They then climbed the bluff to inspect the boat that was being built, wondering what had made Higton choose a spot so far away from the water's edge. As they stood beside the frame of the boat, the *Isabella's* master joined them and, after a few words about the boat, invited them to see his hut. There they were introduced to Mrs Bindell, who, Barnard noted, seemed very much at her ease, despite the fact that everyone knew that she and Higton were not wed.

Higton's conversation was limited and he confined most of his remarks to an abrupt and distant 'yes' or 'no' in answer to Barnard's questions. To the Americans' surprise he did not raise any questions concerning his crew or passengers, nor did he seem to wish to discuss his future plans; if, indeed, he had any. Barnard and Hunter were starting to feel a trifle uncomfortable when Higton suddenly remarked that he suspected that breakfast would be waiting for the Americans at the Duries' hut, and Barnard, reflecting that 'he knew a signal to weigh anchor when he heard one', nudged Hunter and they took their leave.

The two Americans breakfasted with the Holts and Duries, and then Barnard announced that they would leave that morning to continue their sealing among the islands off the southern shore of the Spanish Maloon. He told the British that he and Hunter had found it impossible to discover what Higton's intentions were, but he promised that they would return in a few days to see if the monosyllabic mariner had come to any decision. Barnard even said that if Higton persisted with his visionary scheme to build a vessel to take the castaways to South America then he would not only leave John Wines, his carpenter, together with such tools as they had aboard the shallop, but would also go to fetch some better tools and equipment from the *Nanina*.

After promises to meet again soon, the two Americans set off across Eagle Island and were about to hail the shallop to send the sealing boat for them when they heard shouts and turned to see Holt and Durie hurrying after them. So great was their rush that the Scotsman and the Irishman arrived out of breath and had to pause to recover before they could explain to Barnard that as soon as he had left their hut Mrs Durie had burst into tears of despair. She had begged her husband and Holt to go and use their best endeavour to prevail upon the Americans to take her and the children with them, and Durie added that his wife would prefer all the hardships and dangers she might encounter in the shallop to remaining on this barren island.

After a brief discussion Barnard and Hunter agreed to return to the camp, where they found Mrs Durie in floods of tears, with Mrs Holt trying to comfort her. Barnard, swayed, perhaps, by a combination of Joanna-Ann's despairing sobs and the sight of her two infants in the back of the hut, the two years old Agnes and the seven weeks old Eliza Providence, came to a quick decision. He told Mrs Durie that her condition distressed him and said that, since she was living in a state which a lady of her sensibilities must find most intolerable, he would take her, her family and all their effects on board the shallop at once. Also, rather than head east as they had planned, the Americans would, instead, work their way back towards the *Nanina* where the Duries could remain until the time came for departure. Then they would convey them to the United States, from where Captain Durie would be able to procure a passage to some port in the British dominions.

Holt immediately broke in to ask that Mrs Holt, their son and himself could be included in such an arrangement. Barnard was taken aback as he realized the implications of his offer and had a quick word with Hunter, following which he told Holt that they just did not have the space to make the same arrangement for his family.[32] But, said Barnard, he was very desirous of being of service to all; so, if Captain Higton would only state his wishes and reveal his plans, Barnard had no doubt that the Americans would be able to convey all the survivors to a port in South America, from whence they would be able to proceed direct to England.

Holt explained to Barnard that he had already sounded Higton out and the latter's only comment had been that the British must not appear too anxious to get off the island, because in such a case the Americans might 'take advantage' of them. Barnard was shocked by this ungrateful comment and replied that Captain Higton had formed a completely wrong opinion of the Americans, since their motive was not to take advantage of the Britishers' distress, but to relieve it to the full extent of their powers. He repeated that he was willing to fulfil his promise by taking them all, without remuneration, to South America or even to the United States, which would destroy totally the purpose of the sealing voyage, but simple humanity induced him to make such an undertaking, especially as winter was approaching.

He paused for a moment's thought and then suggested that as a small return for this favour, the captain and crew of the *Isabella* should abandon all claims to the wreck and cargo. It was, he said, impossible for the British to take any of it back to England and it would partly reimburse the Americans for the loss they would sustain by abandoning their sealing activities. Barnard was, however, quick to add that such an arrangement did not apply to private belongings, which would remain the sole property of the owners.

Higton had been standing nearby for the past few minutes, observing what was going on, but remaining just out of earshot, and Holt walked over to tell him what the Americans had offered. Higton seemed to be surprised by the liberality of the American demands, and, apparently now realizing the impracticability of completing the vessel on the bluff, he signified his agreement. At this, Barnard said that they must prepare written articles which would be signed by everyone, so that there should be no misunderstanding about what was being proposed.

While the document was being drafted, Barnard proposed some additional articles, the first of which was that the crew of the *Isabella* should be placed on exactly the same footing as that of the *Nanina* and thus would assist the Americans in assembling all the cargo from the wreck and in loading it aboard the American brig when she arrived. Also, he said, since everyone would then be on exactly the same footing, all of one company, as the sailors termed it, everyone should receive the same allowance of provisions. Holt, Durie and Higton quickly agreed to these, and they were added to the document.

A full meeting of the castaways was then called and since most had been hanging around anxiously watching the negotiations they were quickly assembled and the articles of agreement duly read out. To the surprise of many there was vociferous disagreement from Sir Harry, who advocated using force to compel the Americans to take them to South America, but rather than allow a public wrangle to start, Holt interjected and told the assembly, 'Now you have all heard the generous offer made by the American captains. Let all those who are inclined to accept it follow me, and step over on this side, and those who wish to remain on the island let them stand by Sir Henry Hayes'.

Captain Durie immediately stepped to Holt's side, followed by everyone else except for Higton and Mrs Bindell, together with Hayes and his friend Samuel Breakwell. After a pause, however, Higton decided to join the others and was, of course, followed by his paramour, leaving just Hayes and Breakwell.

Barnard felt that the moment had now been reached where he should reveal the news of the war. He had sworn his crew to silence, but there was always a possibility that one of them would let it slip during the proposed voyage, when such a revelation could well lead to misunderstandings. This might, in turn, lead to a take-over by the British, who were not only more numerous, but also, as Barnard had already noted, had the thirteen fully-armed men of the Marine detachment.

Barnard accordingly called Durie, Holt and Higton to one side and explained to them about the war, but adding that, in his view, it did not affect the situation for them in the Falklands. The three British nodded their agreement and then all returned to the assembly, where Durie passed on the news to the Marines, Holt to the passengers and Higton to his crew. It was generally agreed that this did nothing to affect the agreement, although Sir Harry, as was to be expected, raised objections.

After this, Barnard requested that all the British should either sign the articles of agreement or make their marks and all did so, the majority with obvious pleasure at the prospect of escaping from the island, but Higton with an ill grace. Hayes attempted to hold out, but Barnard pointed out that unless he signed he would be left on the island and so, muttering darkly, he signed, followed by the faithful Breakwell.[33]

This business finally completed, Barnard instructed his crew to bring some bread ashore from the shallop, and the survivors' rations were immediately increased from two-and-a-half to four pounds of bread a week, and from two pounds of salted meat to three. It was also decided to allow one fresh goose for every three persons per day.

In conformance with the agreement, the next step was to bring the *Nanina* round from Barnard's Harbour and here Barnard found himself faced by a dilemma. He needed plenty of men to send up the masts and yards, but he also needed men on Eagle Island to assemble the cargo scattered about the island and to recover as much from the wreck as possible. In addition, he found himself saddled with his promise to remove Mrs Durie and her family from the island, since that lady had declared that she could not bear to remain another minute in a place she so deeply detested.

After some discussion a plan was agreed. The Duries would go in the shallop, together with two women to help her with the children: Mary-Ann Spencer and Mrs Hughes, the Marine drummer's wife. In addition, five Royal Marines and seven of *Isabella's* crew would accompany them to help fit-out the *Nanina*. This large number of people left such a limited amount of room in the shallop that Barnard even had to put the sealskins ashore to make room for the Duries' baggage, and so he was only able to take four of his own crew: Ingman, the mate, and three foredeck hands, Tennant, Gilchrist and Green.

The Holts also wanted to go in this party, but Captain Fanning, who was remaining on the island with Captain Hunter, persuaded the Irish family to stay and provide them with a little company, as they had no desire to associate with either Higton or Hayes. Other members of the *Nanina's* crew to stay behind on Eagle Island were two seamen (Lott and Spear), the steward (Montgomery) and the carpenter (John Wines), together with the sealing boat.

Everything was ready at two o'clock on 8 April, four days after the Americans had first set eyes on the survivors' camp, and with the shallop loaded down with no less than nineteen adults, three children and all their baggage, Barnard set sail, heading up the Eagle Channel. The wind was very strong and with the sea getting rougher by the hour he decided that it would be imprudent to proceed into the open waters of Falkland Sound so he anchored in Jack's Harbour. They waited until the early hours of the 9th and then, with a light, favourable wind blowing, they set off again, but as the sun rose the wind suddenly veered and strengthened and they barely had time to take in a double reef before it was blowing a violent gale.

By mid-morning they were in the middle of the Sound when the lookout spotted a small boat running towards them at a prodigious speed. With consummate seamanship, Barnard brought the shallop alongside the jolly-boat, which contained Mattinson and his three companions, who had set out some ten days previously to seek help. The four men were in an appalling state and Barnard's inbred instinct to rescue those in peril overcame his reluctance to take *Isabella's* notorious stowaway on board.

The four had, in fact, already given themselves up for dead, believing that they would be drowned within minutes, so the sudden appearance of the shallop came as a total surprise and they did little to help themselves as they were hauled over the side of the bucking and heaving vessel. It was too rough to hoist the boat aboard the shallop, so it was streamed astern, while the Marine and the two boys were assisted below. Mattinson, however, remained on deck, lying motionless where he had been left by his rescuers and mumbling incoherently to himself.

A heavy sea struck the shallop and the icy water swept over the deck, soaking the crouching man yet again, and Barnard, his curiosity overcoming the doubts Mrs Durie's descriptions of the man had engendered, walked over.

'What would have been your fate if you had been left in the boat'? he asked. Mattinson looked up at him, as if stupefied, and replied, 'God only knows, but who are you and what am I aboard of'? 'The shallop of the American brig *Nanina*'. 'I cannot believe it', Mattinson mumbled. 'I had given all up for lost, when you appeared suddenly out of the sea to save me and it was only a few moments after that when I found myself aboard'.

Despite the gale and the high sea, the shallop arrived safely in Fox Bay on the English Maloon and Barnard was relieved to drop anchor after an eventful day. On going below, however, he was astonished to find Mattinson lolling at a table quite drunk, a full tankard and a cask of wine in front of him. One of his American sailors explained that Mattinson had been told that the cask contained only a small amount of wine, which he (Captain Barnard) had said was to be reserved for the three ladies, but the British sailor had taken no notice and helped himself.

The gale continued throughout the night and into the next day, so Barnard remained at anchor in Fox Bay, but to his indignation Mattinson found yet more liquor and by mid-morning was once again drunk. Barnard overheard the ex-naval man ask those within earshot 'how American prize money would drink'? but unfortunately thought it just the ravings of a drunkard. He was, however, anxious to get this appalling man off the shallop, and,

TABLE III

COMBINED AMERICAN/BRITISH PARTY THAT WENT IN THE SHALLOP TO
FETCH THE _NANINA_:
LEFT EAGLE ISLAND 8 April, 1813
ARRIVED BARNARD'S HARBOUR 12 May, 1813

NANINA CREW
Charles Barnard*; Henry Ingham*; Havens Tennant*; Henry
Gilchrist; Jacob Green.*

ISABELLA CREW**
Joseph Albrook*; Samuel Ansell*; John Babtist*; Joseph
Ellis*; James Hubbart*; James Louder*; William Robarts*;
John Servester.*

ROYAL MARINES FROM ISABELLA***
Private Robert Andrews*; Private William Catford*; Private
William Johnson*; Private James Rea*; Private James
Spooner*; Drummer William Hughes

ISABELLA PASSENGERS
Captain Durie; Mrs Durie; Agnes Durie (Infant); Eliza Durie
(Infant); Mrs Mary-Ann Spencer; Mrs Hughes; Mattinson****

TOTALS
Left Eagle Island in shallop   22
Rescued in Falklands Sound   4

Grand Total   26

Walked overland to _Nanina_   18
Remained in shallop   8

Notes
* Walked overland from Arch Island Harbour to Barnard's
Cove; others remained aboard the shallop.
** Two of these men were taken from Mattinson's boat in
Falkland Sound.
*** One of these men was taken from Mattinson's boat in
Falkland Sound.
**** Mattinson was taken from jollyboat in Falkland Sound.

discovering that Captain Durie felt the same way, they went below and sought to persuade Mattinson that it was now safe enough for him to continue his voyage in the jollyboat so that he could rejoin Higton and the others at the wreck. Mattinson's former companions in the jollyboat were, however, stunned to hear such a proposal, and their pleadings resulted in Barnard reluctantly shelving the proposal.

CHAPTER 9

By the following morning, 12 April, the westerly wind had moderated, so the shallop sailed at sunrise, reaching down the coast, but when the wind strengthened and shifted, Barnard was compelled to put the helm down and run through the narrow entrance into Port Edgar. They spent a quiet night, lying in one of the finest sheltered anchorages in the world, leaving next day to beat around as far as Arch Island Harbour, where they once again anchored for the night. Over the following week the weather continued to be very variable and Barnard made several attempts to weather Cape Meredith, only to be frustrated on each occasion. Finally, after yet another abortive attempt on the 20th, Barnard decided that the combination of wind and weather was such that he was placing the lives of the twenty-six people on board unnecessarily at risk. The hold was full of baggage and there was only limited space in the cabins, so the majority of people were obliged to remain on deck, which was not only uncomfortable for them, but also upset the vessel's natural trim, making her considerably more difficult to sail.

Looking at his map (which he had drawn himself) Barnard decided on a change of plan and returned to Arch Island Harbour, where he explained the problem. He told his crew and passengers that he now intended that the majority would walk across the island the following day to the inlet where *Nanina* was hidden, leaving only the Duries, Drummer Hughes and his wife, and Henry Gilchrist aboard the shallop.[34]

There being no objections to this proposal, the next morning eighteen men landed, each carrying a change of clothing and biscuits for two days, and then, with Barnard in the lead, they set off for *Nanina's* hiding place. The journey was a great trial for both the British and the Americans, the former having been confined to a small island on short rations for several months and the latter having scarcely set foot ashore for a year, apart from their sealing forays which were limited to the beaches. Nevertheless, they struggled across streams and over a hilly ridge, the rough, pathless moorland doing nothing to make the journey any easier. Consequently, when they reached the brig at six o'clock, they all agreed that they had undergone 'great fatigue and suffering' and, as people in such circumstances tend to do, they estimated that they had covered between thirty and forty miles, although it was, in fact, only fifteen.

Barzillai Pease was away on another of his lone sealing forays, so only Valentine Barnard was aboard when they arrived and he was more than a little astonished to see so many men arriving overland. As a result, his son had a great deal of explaining to do before the old man was clear about all that had occurred, how their sealing expedition had perforce been altered and what the new plan involved.

The following day Charles Barnard issued instructions to Henry Ingman, the mate, to supervise the preparation of the *Nanina* for sea. Then, leaving his father nominally in charge, he and Havens Tennant retraced their steps overland back to the shallop, arriving at four o'clock in the afternoon to an enthusiastic welcome. The strong winds continued, but now there were only Barnard himself, Gilchrist and Tennant to handle the shallop, assisted by the amateur Captain Durie and Drummer Hughes, so the American skipper was forced to await calmer weather.

At midnight on the 29th Barnard considered the conditions at last to be acceptable, so he weighed anchor and left harbour. They sailed along the coast towards Cape Meredith, but the American, being a wise and experienced sailor, gave that notorious headland a wide berth, which was just as well, because the wind strengthened and veered, and they had to take in two reefs before they could stand in towards the land. Then, as the weather was fair, Barnard decided that it would be pleasant to go ashore and so he brought the shallop into Two Island Bay (now Ten Shilling Island Bay) at the entrance to Port Stephens and dropped anchor.

Once the shallop was riding safely at anchor Barnard and Durie rowed ashore, accompanied by Joanna-Ann Durie, Mary-Ann Spencer, and Drummer and Mrs Hughes, to take some exercise. On the beach they encountered a small family of sea lions and Barnard, never one to let an opportunity pass him by (and perhaps not averse to showing his prowess before the ladies, either) attacked the bull with his lance, despatching it after some resistance. Durie then joined him in clubbing the young seals to death, but Barnard decided that he needed expert assistance in skinning them, which, in any case, was something the ladies might feel squeamish about, so they all went back to the shallop. Having seen Durie and the ladies safely back on board, Barnard returned to the shore with his crewmen to skin the seals and also to take the opportunity to shoot a few geese.

This enjoyable break completed, they raised anchor and ran before a following wind, weathered Cape Orford with ease and then turned northwards to beat up the channel between Swan Island and English Maloon, finishing an excellent day's sailing by anchoring in Canton Harbour on Swan

Island. Barnard was still concerned about the great increase in people to be fed aboard *Nanina*, so he spent a couple of days shooting hogs and geese on the well-stocked Swan Island, before going on to reach the brig on 12 May, after what was clearly a friendly and very relaxed cruise. On their arrival the Duries were introduced to Valentine Barnard, while Charles Barnard took over the supervision of the preparations of the brig for the forthcoming voyage. The oil casks were floated out and loaded into *Nanina's* hold, while special care was taken to ensure that the rigging was as secure as possible, since winter was approaching and the weather was likely to be extremely severe.

When Barzillai Pease came sailing up the inlet in the sealing boat he expected to see only old Valentine Barnard aboard the *Nanina*, so he was very surprised to see a large number of people working on the vessel. This surprise turned to astonishment when he spotted a British Royal Marine walking the deck with his musket slung from his shoulder, obviously on sentry duty. Coming alongside, Pease expressed his surprise with character-istic vehemence, whereupon Charles Barnard, who happened to be on deck, played a joke on the humourless sailor about why the Marines were present. When they had carried the joke far enough Barnard took pity on Pease and explained what had happened on Eagle Island and how he had contracted to take the British people to the mainland, but Pease was furious at having been teased and complained bitterly in his diary about '*the farse*'.

By 16 May the end of the work was in sight, so Barnard, having no further use for the shallop, despatched it to Eagle Island to help them move stores, and also to reassure them that all was well and that the *Nanina* would soon be with them. Henry Ingman, the mate, skippered the craft, assisted by two seamen, Henry Gilchrist from the *Nanina*, and John Servester from the *Isabella*, with two Marines, Privates Catford and Spooner, also on board. This must have seemed a logical move and one to which he probably never gave a second thought at the time, but unfortunately for Charles Barnard the consequence was that this left just four Americans on board the *Nanina* (three captains, Valentine and Charles Barnard and Barzillai Pease, and a solitary seaman, Jacob Green), but twelve British men.

The first hint of trouble came on the 19th after Barnard had failed for the third day running to work the *Nanina* out of the harbour, with the light north-north-west winds coming straight down the inlet making it impossible for him to beat out into the open sea. After the anchor had been dropped, a small group of British sailors and Marines came aft, grumbling loudly and headed by Mattinson, who claimed that he could get the brig round to the wreck, if Charles Barnard could not.

A furious altercation then developed between Barnard and Mattinson, with voices raised loudly on both sides, which shook Barnard greatly, and, perhaps for the first time, he realized the numerical weakness of his position. He enlisted Durie's aid in calming things down and the two men called a meeting of all the men on board, where, according to Pease, Barnard offered the men three choices: put Mattinson ashore, confine him aboard, or leave the brig stripped and laid up. After some argument, Barnard and Durie got the men to agree to follow Barnard's orders and Mattinson was confined below, guarded by a Marine sentry.

Next day Barnard, increasingly worried by both the weather and the attitude of the men, and with Mattinson still under guard below, managed to beat out of the harbour, despite reservations about the state of the weather. As with any sailing captain, he desperately needed to avoid finding himself on a leeshore, allied to which he knew from bitter experience that at that time of year Falkland nights were frequently accompanied by heavy gales. So he worked the brig along the coast, but when night approached, he headed towards the land, finding a somewhat dangerous anchorage just before sunset in the entrance to Carew Harbour. His alarm was heightened by the wind dropping to a dead calm as they gained the entrance and he had to launch the boat to warp the brig over the last few hundred yards.

They spent an anxious night, with Barnard dreading a change in the wind, since if it swung to the north there was little he could do to prevent the *Nanina* being swept onto the rocks. During the night (21 May) the clouds scudded across the skies from the south-west, but at four o'clock the wind swung to the south, reaching gale-force, and accompanied by hail and snow. Despite this Barnard decided to put to sea and with the sails heavily reefed the wind took them safely away from the shore, although it proved so strong that there was no hope of beating through the narrow channel between the English Maloon and Swan Island. This left him with no choice but to run round Loup's Head, the northernmost point of Swan Island, and then reach down to New Island, where they had made the initial landfall after the voyage from the United States.

The decision made, they reached Coffin's Harbour at New Island by midday after an extremely rough crossing, the ferocity of the weather having surprised even the most hardened of the mariners, and most of those aboard had been sea-sick. When they managed to come to anchor the wind increased to a full gale and they were all so frozen by the bitter cold that they had the greatest difficulty in doing any work at all. This appalling weather lasted from 22 May to 3 June without a break and they had to deploy three anchors to prevent *Nanina* being blown out to sea, reducing those aboard to a condition of abject misery.

Charles Barnard felt especially sorry for Mrs Durie and her two children, and suddenly recollected that he had once seen a patch of potatoes growing on the island, planted by some earlier visitor. So in a break in the weather he went ashore and, after some searching, managed to find fifteen fine potatoes, which he took back aboard the *Nanina* and proudly presented to the ladies, for which they thanked him profusely.

Barnard's major concern was that the lives of all those at New and Eagle Islands depended upon the safety of the *Nanina*, and the consequences of losing the brig were too awful to contemplate. Further, it was clear that the war had stopped all the normal maritime traffic around the Falklands, both British and American, so that if they did suffer an accident there was little prospect of another whaler or sealer appearing for a very long time.

Charles Barnard therefore called a meeting with his father and Barzillai Pease, with Captain Durie representing the passengers. He proposed that the situation in which they now found themselves left no alternative but to abandon any further attempts to reach open water and, instead, to send down the yards and sails, and then await the return of better weather, which, he thought, should come in a few weeks' time. This was agreed by the two Americans, and also by Durie, who observed with some feeling that he would rather wait three months than sail through another storm like the one they had just experienced. The decision was passed on to the crew and passengers, who seemed to accept it, so *Nanina* was warped into Hooker's Harbour, the sails unbent and the yards secured.

Despite Barnard's care in explaining his plan, yet another deputation came aft on 11 June to remonstrate about what Mattinson described as 'the failure' to sail to Eagle Island. The two Barnards calmed them down, or thought that they had done so, whereupon Charles Barnard, anxious, as ever, about their food supplies, decided to take one of the ship's boats and cross to nearby Beaver Island on what he regarded as a routine hunting trip to shoot some hogs, geese, seal, rabbits, or any other form of wildlife. So he called for volunteers to accompany him, and Jacob Green of his own crew plus three British sailors from the *Isabella* stepped forward: Joseph Albrook, Samuel Ansell and James Louder. The five men took to the boat and were soon lost to sight as they headed for Beaver Island.

Unfortunately, Charles Barnard's temporary absence was exactly what the evil Mattinson had been waiting for, because that left just three Americans aboard *Nanina*: Valentine Barnard, an old man; Barzillai Pease, who was recovering from being accidentally hit by a stone during a hunting trip ashore; and Havens Tennant. Then, the following morning, Valentine Barnard unintentionally added to the unrest, when his anxiety over the provisions led to him announcing a reduction in the issue of biscuits from seven per person per week to six.

Taking advantage of these favourable circumstances, Mattinson struck, leading a crowd of his fellow British to the quarterdeck, where he demanded of Valentine Barnard that, since the weather had now moderated, *Nanina*

TABLE IV

ABOARD THE *NANINA* AT THE TIME OF THE BRITISH
TAKEOVER 12 June, 1813*

CREW OF NANINA (American)**
Captain Valentine Barnard; Captain Barzillai Pease; Havens
Tennant, seaman.

CREW OF ISABELLA (British)***
John Babtist; Joseph Ellis; James Hubbart; William Robarts;
John Servester.

ROYAL MARINES FROM ISABELLA (British)
Private Andrews; Drummer Hughes; Private Johnson; Private
Rea.

ISABELLA PASSENGERS (British)
Captain Durie; Mrs Durie; Agnes Durie (Infant); Eliza Durie
(Infant); Mrs Hughes; Mrs Spencer; Mattinson.

TOTALS
American Males   3
British Males   11
British Females   3
British Infants   2

Grand Total   19

Notes.
* Four men had left Barnard's Harbour in the shallop to return
to Eagle Island on 16th May.
** On the day of the takeover two Americans were in the
party on Beaver Island catching hogs: Charles Barnard and
Jacob Green.
*** On the day of the takeover three British were in the
party on Beaver Island catching hogs: Joseph Albrook, Samuel
Ansell and James Louder.

should be prepared at once to go to sea and sail to join the other castaways on Eagle Island. The old man attempted to play for time, telling them that if they would wait until the boat returned with his son and their four comrades then, of course, if the weather continued good, they would run down to Eagle Island.

Valentine Barnard then turned to Captain Durie and asked him to use his influence to stop this aggressive behaviour, but to his dismay the British officer declined to take any action, as described by the Americans later. 'but capt. Drure (sic) refused to act on the occasion, notwithstanding he was one of the principle ones which requested the vessel should await a more favourable season'.[35]

This was, unfortunately, this officer's usual response in a crisis and it was all the encouragement that Mattinson needed for with a shout he ordered the men to set to and prepare the vessel for sea. Havens Tennant, the only American crewman present, stood by helplessly, while Captain Valentine Barnard fumed on the quarterdeck, but Barzillai Pease reacted in a quite different manner. He watched the British work all day and well into the night, raising the yards, bending the sails and taking in the stream anchor. He then approached Durie and said that, since the route to Eagle Island was complicated and difficult, and because it appeared that nothing would stop the mutineers, then he would undertake, for all their sakes, to direct the voyage, provided they called in at Beaver Island on the way to collect Charles Barnard and the four sailors.

This was agreed and the following morning (13 June) being fine the boats were hoisted in, the anchor weighed, and *Nanina* stood out for Beaver Island. Pease and Barnard prevailed on the British to pause at the entrance to Beaver Harbour on the northern side of the island, where they fired two shots from a light cannon, but after a very short delay the demands from the Americans that they anchor for a while and send a boat ashore were overruled by Mattinson, who lost patience and ordered the crew to sail on. So with complete disregard not only for the two Americans but also for three of their own shipmates, they sailed away, passing through the passage between Beaver and Swan Island, before heading along the southern coast of the English Maloon. By sunset Port Stephens was off the port beam and the following day they rounded Cape Meredith and out across the southern end of Falklands Sound, direct for Eagle Island.

As they sailed there was some doubt as to what to do when they arrived at Eagle Island. One possibility was clearly for the Marines to arrest the six Americans who had remained there and for the British to take the *Nanina* to South America, looking in again at Beaver Island for the missing men on the way. Alternatively, there could be a reconciliation with the Americans at Eagle Island, followed by a return of the *Nanina* to their control, although

Mattinson, as an ex-navy man, argued against it, as he was still thinking of the prospect of prize money.

The outcome was, however, quite different and totally unexpected. As they entered the Eagle Channel they spotted the shallop and a longboat heading towards them, while a lookout called out that he could see the masts of a strange vessel inside Jack's Harbour. There was no time to seek an explanation, however, because the longboat hove alongside, followed closely by the shallop, and to the astonishment of everybody aboard *Nanina*, British and American alike, instead of the Americans they had expected, a horde of British sailors and Marines, armed to the teeth and yelling loudly, scrambled aboard. The people on *Nanina's* deck reeled back in dismay and surprise, totally bewildered and at a complete loss to explain where these men had come from.

PART 3

HMS *Nancy* to the Rescue[36]

CHAPTER 10

The British sailors who erupted so violently over the side of the shallop had come from His Britannic Majesty's Gun Brig *Nancy*, whose masts had been glimpsed just before the attack on the *Nanina* began. But, to understand who these sailors were and why their vessel was in the Falkland Islands, we must turn to the Spanish colony of Buenos Ayres and return to the middle of the previous year.

21 July, 1812, was a typically cold and bleak south Atlantic day as HMS *La Bonne Citoyenne* swung at anchor in Buenos Ayres roads, an integral part of the ceaseless, world-wide effort by the Royal Navy to protect British interests in the war against the French. The officers on the quarterdeck watched as another and very minor part of that global system, the much smaller brig, *Nancy*, passed by and then came up into the wind, her crew swarming over the yards to take in the sails as the anchor fell.

Soon *Nancy*'s boat was lowered and headed towards *La Bonne Citoyenne*, bringing her commander to pay his courtesy call on the senior officer on the station. Or so it should have done, but it was not the expected Lieutenant and Commander Killwick who came aboard, but her Second Master, accompanied by the Assistant Surgeon*. These two looked rather anxious and when they asked to see Captain Greene on an urgent matter they were immediately ushered below to his cabin.

This was a curious breach of naval etiquette, since custom demanded that *Nancy's* commander should have come in person to report to the senior officer on the station. The reason became clear, however, when *La Bonne Citoyenne's* first lieutenant, Lieutenant William D'Aranda, RN, was called to join the captain in his cabin. There Captain Greene explained to D'Aranda that Lieutenant Killwick of the *Nancy* had been attacked by 'the mania' and was no longer fit to remain in command; indeed, he was in such a serious

---

* At that period there were only two commissioned ranks in the Royal Navy below admiral: captain (the more senior) and lieutenant. Where, however, a lieutenant was placed in command of a small vessel such as the brig *Nancy*, he was designated 'lieutenant and commander' in recognition of his appointment.

condition that the Second Master and the Assistant Surgeon had been forced to confine him to his cabin, trussed up in a strait jacket.

Immediate action was required and Captain Greene said that he was about to appoint another officer to command the brig when D'Aranda asked for the job for himself. Greene was initially a little reluctant, mainly because his own job required him to spend a lot of time ashore and he found D'Aranda a reliable 'first' to leave in charge of the ship. D'Aranda was, however, the senior lieutenant on board *La Bonne Citoyenne*, and, despite the fact that he had only joined her on 1 April, Greene felt he could not refuse the request, although, as he hastened to remind D'Aranda, this could only be a temporary arrangement. They both knew well that the custom and practice in the Royal Navy was that such appointments lay in the gift of the local commander-in-chief, which in this case was Admiral Dixon, commanding the Brazil station, who was located in Rio de Janeiro.[37]

Nevertheless, a sudden opportunity such as this was the dream of every junior officer and the same day found D'Aranda being piped aboard his new ship, where he was greeted with the proper formalities by the warrant officers. These comprised Mr Lutman, the sub-lieutenant; Mr Marsh, the midshipman; the Second Master and the Assistant Surgeon, both of whom he had met so recently in Captain Greene's cabin. Assistant Surgeon Brison explained that Lieutenant Killwick had formed the impression, for what reason nobody knew, that the Spaniards in Buenos Ayres were intent on murdering him. This had come to dominate his every waking thought to such an extent that he had eventually persuaded himself that an attempt had, indeed, taken place (although he had no physical wounds to show for it) and he lived in mortal fear of another. Lutman and the other warrant officers had become increasingly alarmed by this erratic behaviour and had eventually seen no alternative but to confine him in a strait jacket, which had been specially made by the leading sail-maker, a terrifying experience for the warrant officers who had been nurtured in a system in which the ship's captain was 'the first after God'. Thus warned, D'Aranda went below, where he found his unfortunate predecessor locked in a newly-constructed temporary cabin in the hold and one glance was sufficient to confirm Brison's diagnosis.

Captain Greene did not complete his despatches until 9 August, when D'Aranda was at last able to take his command to sea for the first time. He headed out of the Rio de la Plata and then turned north, following the coastline of the Portuguese colony of Brazil until he reached the splendid harbour of the capital, Rio de Janeiro, on 26 August. As she entered the bay *Nancy* sailed close-hauled past the Portuguese-manned Fort Santa Cruz, which protected the entrance, and then passed Admiral Dixon's flagship, HMS *Montagu*, which was lying at anchor in the roads. D'Aranda fired a 17-

gun salute in honour of the admiral's flag, and this was returned not only by the *Montagu* but also, with punctilious correctness, by Fort Santa Cruz.

As soon as *Nancy* was riding at anchor D'Aranda called away the boat's crew and set out to report to the flagship, where he presented the canvas bag containing the despatches to the Admiral's secretary. A little while later D'Aranda was summoned to the Admiral's cabin, where Admiral Manley Dixon allowed him to read the letter just received from Captain Greene. 'Lieutenant Killwick, Commander of the *Nancy*,' Captain Greene wrote, 'I am sorry to say, has fallen a sacrifice to the malacious spirit of some old Spaniards. Tho' not with loss of life, an attempt was, however, made to assassinate him about a month since, planned by some of them who reside at this place (Buenos Ayres). He has ever since been in a state of insanity from which I fear there is little chance of his recovering. I have therefore been under the necessity of superceding him and sending him to Rio with my first, Lieutenant D'Aranda, to whom I have given the command of the *Nancy* until further orders – He will more fully explain to you the particulars of this dark offence than I am able to do at present, and I beg to recommend him to your notice and request – if it does not interfere with your arrangements – he may be allowed to continue in the Nancy.'[38]

For D'Aranda the crucial part of the letter lay in the final sentence, but the Admiral's more immediate concern was with Killwick, as naval regulations required that there should be a 'survey' by a board of officers to make a formal record of that officer's state. D'Aranda explained to the Admiral that Killwick had no physical wounds from the alleged assassination attempt, and repeated Brison's theory that he believed that Lieutenant Killwick so worked himself up about this imagined threat of attack, and allowed it to prey on his mind for so long, that in the end he convinced himself that it had actually happened.

Next morning the Admiral, accompanied by two surgeons from the *Montagu*, went aboard the *Nancy*, where, joining D'Aranda and Brison, they visited the unfortunate Killwick. What they saw left them in no doubt as to what their verdict should be and so the Admiral was then able to take the opportunity to walk around the ship and examine her condition before returning to his flagship. Later in the day D'Aranda went aboard the flagship, where he was invited to sign the formal report of their 'survey'. 'We, whose names are hereunder subscribed, have been on board His Majesty's Gun Brig *Nancy* taking to our assistance the Surgeon and first assistant surgeon of His Majesty's Ship *Montagu*, and the assistant surgeon of His Majesty's Gun Brig *Nancy* and there taken a strict and careful Survey on John Arthur Killwick, Lieutenant and late Commander of the said Gun Brig, and find him affected with Mania and therefore deem him a fit object to be invalided. And we do further declare that we have taken this Survey

77

with such care and equity that we are willing, if required, to take oath to the impartiality of our proceedings.'[39] The formalities thus completed, a boat was sent to collect Killwick and the unfortunate man was removed to the flagship, where there were better facilities to look after him than in the confined space of the *Nancy*.

The Admiral did not, in the event, find it too easy to rid himself of Killwick, because when he instructed the master of the *Sceptre*, the next British merchantman to sail, that he was to convey Killwick to England, the master complained bitterly to the British deputy consul-general in Rio de Janeiro. The latter passed the protest on to Dixon on 3 September, as a result of which the exasperated Admiral issued a direct order for the *Sceptre* to accept the 'maniac,' but reduced the strain on the merchantman's crew by instructing D'Aranda to provide two marines from *Nancy*'s detachment to guard and look after Killwick on the voyage back to England.[40]

The demented officer's destination was the special naval ward in the mental hospital in Hoxton in north London, where he joined some fifteen other officer inmates.[41] It is astonishing to discover, however, that he was soon deemed to have been 'cured' and was back at sea by November, 1813, having been appointed First Lieutenant of HMS *Granicus*.[42]

Back in Rio de Janeiro, the Admiral handed D'Aranda a formal letter, appointing him to the command of the *Nancy*.[43] This came as a great relief to D'Aranda, since until this moment there was always the possibility that the Admiral had a favourite, or, perhaps, some political favour to repay in the squadron, especially among his own staff of flag lieutenants, to whom he could have given preference. However, the admiral dampened D'Aranda's enthusiasm somewhat by adding that he had been appalled by the state of the brig when he looked around her that morning and, as a result, he instructed her new commander to have her hove down and put to rights as best he could with the facilities available in Rio.

Nancy's story was a brief one. Some four years previously the (then) Commander-in-Chief of the Brazil station, Rear-Admiral Sir William Smith, had desperately needed a small man-o'-war to run dispatches between Rio de Janeiro and Buenos Ayres. The gun brig *Mistletoe* was expected to arrive from England to fill this task, but when she failed to appear Admiral Smith purchased the British-registered commercial brig *Nancy*, which happened to be lying in Buenos Ayres at the time.[44] The name was retained and His Britannic Majesty's Gun Brig *Nancy* was duly commissioned on 23 September, 1808, with Lieutenant Killwick, whom Smith described as a very capable officer, from his own ship, HMS *Foudroyant*, in command.

Nancy was a sturdy vessel, British-built, with an armament of eight guns and a draught of precisely ten feet, which was what was needed to clear the Ortis and Freshet banks in the Plate estuary. In naval service she had an authorized complement of forty-five,[45] of which only one was a commissioned officer: the 'lieutenant and commander,' who was in all respects the captain of the vessel. He was supported by four warrant officers, the senior of whom was the 'second master', whose principle tasks were to sail and navigate the brig, although he was normally the oldest and most experienced seaman in the wardroom and thus a close adviser to the younger commander. *Nancy* also carried a sub-lieutenant, an appointment (not a rank) created in 1804, specially to provide an extra officer in smaller vessels such as brigs and sloops. The officer concerned had to have passed the lieutenant's examination and was paid as a lieutenant, although only entitled to a midshipman's proportion of prize money. A sub-lieutenant did not, however, hold the King's commission and reverted to his rank of midshipman on moving to a new appointment unless he was selected for commissioning. There was also one midshipman and an assistant surgeon, while her foredeck hands comprised thirty-two sailors and a Royal Marine detachment of eight marines, commanded by a sergeant.

Nancy was not a large vessel, measuring some 200 tons, with a length of eighty feet and a beam of twenty-five feet, with eight six-pounder cannon mounted on the maindeck. She was a brig, a class increasingly popular in the Royal Navy, as they were small and handy, suitable for coastal work, but with a full sea-going rig, which enabled them to undertake ocean voyages if necessary.

As a brig, *Nancy* had two masts – the main- and foremasts – to each of which was bent three large square sails: the course, the lowest and largest; a topsail; and, highest of all, a topgallant. Unlike some brigs she did not have a yet further sail above that, a royal, but she did have studding sails which could be bent to yards extending from the topsail booms. The bowsprit jutted forward proudly at a sharp angle from the bows, carrying the main- and forestays to support the masts, as well as the stays for the two headsails. Aft there was also a large fore-and-aft sail, the driver, which was bent to the mainmast and loose-footed to a boom.

When new, *Nancy* was a smart, fast and handy vessel, but the rough weather of the southern latitudes had taken its toll. The constant need for her services, coupled with the parsimony of their Lordships of the Admiralty in distant London, meant that little money had been spent on repairs, and by the time D'Aranda came aboard she was in a very poor condition. In particular her rigging was showing its age and the sails were in a very parlous state, and neither were likely to stand the excessive strains of a violent storm. She was capable of some six knots close-hauled and nine knots when running before the wind, but even D'Aranda, who came to love her dearly, had to admit that she both pitched and rolled heavily, and was especially difficult in a head sea.[46]

The only recorded refit that she had been given was some four years previously, when, in one of his first endeavours, Lieutenant Killwick ran her aground in the Plate estuary on 23 November, 1808. A pilot was aboard at the time and the situation was made more difficult (as well as somewhat embarrassing) by the presence of two hundred Portuguese soldiers, whom Killwick had agreed to take to Colonnia in Uruguay at the request of the Viceroy of Brazil. The Portuguese authorities obviously acknowledged some responsibility for this mishap, as they repaired the *Nancy* at their expense.[47]

So, with all the enthusiasm of a 'new broom' and with the very active support of the Admiral, D'Aranda started to set his new command to rights. Work parties of sailors were sent over every day from the flagship and Portuguese workers were even engaged from the local shipyard, both groups combining with *Nancy*'s crew to restore both the standing and running rigging, recaulk the decks, repair the sails and generally prepare the ship for a further period of active duty.

A series of problems with the Second Master, who seemed incapable of doing his duty and who had made some surprising navigational errors on the voyage up from the Rio de la Plata led D'Aranda to ask for his removal. The Admiral promptly agreed, dismissing the man on 6 September and appointing William Shepherd, an experienced and senior seaman from the *Montagu* to take his place, although the new man did not actually come aboard *Nancy* until 17 September.

The reason for Lieutenant D'Aranda's Spanish-sounding name is not hard to discover, as he was, in fact, a direct descendant of Maitre Elie D'Arande, who had travelled to England in 1619 to minister to the Huguenots at Southampton.* The family produced a succession of business men and ministers until William's father, Benjamin, became a surgeon in Billericay, in the county of Essex. The eldest son was born in 1788 and, like his father, he too broke with family tradition, but this time by joining the Royal Navy in 1801. Thus, Lieutenant and Commander William Peter D'Aranda, RN, came from a thoroughly respectable family and, despite his Spanish-sounding name, his roots lay in England and he was as British as any other Royal Navy officer. He had been brought up in the shadow of his grandfather, a widely-respected cleric, and had undoubtedly been taught all the Christian virtues before going to sea.

He was taken aboard HMS *Powerful* (74) on 9 July, 1801, as a midshipman, and although he was only thirteen years old, this was by no means too young to start a naval career in that era. This also suggests that his family had some influential contacts, not least with *Powerful*'s captain, and it is probably no coincidence that Captain Sir Francis Laforey, RN, Bart, was

* A full description of the D'Arandas, including a family tree, is at Appendix B.

also from a Huguenot immigrant family (originally named Lafôret). D'Aranda spent a year aboard *Powerful*, where he served in the Baltic, the Mediterranean and the West Indies, and survived a mutiny in Gibraltar, an exciting, although by no means unusual, introduction to Service life.

When *Powerful* paid-off for what became known later as the 'short peace' D'Aranda, like many other sailors, was ashore for a year, but he found a new ship in April, 1803, when he joined *Diligence* (10) as a Volunteer First Class, although he managed to regain his midshipman status two months later. This small vessel served in the North Sea on trade protection duties, which was arduous without being very exciting, but he remained aboard for only a year and was then pleased to return to a large ship, joining *Atlas* (90) on 29 July, 1804. His four years aboard this ship included twice following the French squadron to the West Indies and an incredible twenty-two months on blockade duty off Cadiz, during which time the ship never once anchored.

D'Aranda was also at the Battle of San Domingo (6 February, 1806), where *Atlas* was part of a squadron which defeated an enemy squadron, the British losing no ships to the French five. Captain Pym of the *Atlas* was so pleased with the young man's conduct during this engagement that he took the unusual step of writing to the Admiralty requesting an early appointment to a Commission as a lieutenant, but the Admiralty declined to bend the rules as D'Aranda had not completed the statutory period at sea.[48] For his last two years in this ship D'Aranda served as Master's Mate, which meant that he was working directly for the Master and thus getting an excellent grounding in navigation and ship-handling.

He left *Atlas* in November, 1808, to return to England, where he received the long-awaited Commission on 15 December. He obtained an appointment fairly quickly and, a lieutenant at last, joined *Woodlark* (10) in June, 1809, serving in her for almost exactly two years. This time was spent in the Baltic where D'Aranda took part in numerous actions against gunboats, as well as a major 'cutting-out' expedition on the island of Bjornholm. In June, 1811, however, he was transferred to a 6th-rate, *Laurestinus* (24), in which he went to the Brazils* and after another year he received a further step up the ladder, being transferred to *La Bonne Citoyenne* (20) as First Lieutenant on 31 March, 1812, from where, as we have just seen, he was appointed to the temporary command of *Nancy*.

Thus D'Aranda had served aboard line-of-battle ships and taken part in a major fleet action, and had also served in several sloops, taking part in numerous small-scale engagements, many of them involving hand-to-hand

---

* At that time the Royal Navy referred to the entire South American station as 'the Brazils' and this term will be used throughout.

combat. Further, between joining *Diligence* in April, 1803 and taking command of *Nancy* in July, 1812 he had just one period ashore (4 January – 31 May, 1809), the entire remainder of the time being spent at sea on what would today be termed 'active service'. This service had taken him all over the western hemisphere: to the Baltic, the North Sea, the Atlantic, the Mediterranean, the West Indies and most recently the south Atlantic.

So it can safely be said that when William D'Aranda assumed command of the *Nancy* he was a thoroughly knowledgeable naval officer, with a breadth of experience as great as that of any of his contemporaries. He was only twenty-three years old, but he had eleven years of naval service, all of it at war, and his courage, resourcefulness and honesty were beyond doubt.

HMS *Nereus*, a ship of the line of which D'Aranda would soon see much more, sailed for the Rio de la Plata on 14 September, exchanging gun salutes with Admiral Dixon in *Montagu* as she passed and three days later *Nancy* herself was also almost ready for sea, and was warped out to the Outer Harbour. Among all this activity two of the ship's boys deserted on the 15th, a problem that concerned all captains in the Royal Navy when in port, and in *Nancy*'s case almost every visit to either Rio de Janeiro or Buenos Ayres was marked by at least one entry in the Muster Table under 'runners'.

On 20 September an American vessel entered the port and a few hours later Admiral Dixon informed all his officers that the United States government had declared war on Great Britain on 19 June. It had taken no less than three months for such important news to arrive at Rio de Janeiro and even then the British Admiral only found out from the chance arrival of an enemy ship!

Even in the remote Brazils they had, of course, been aware of the growing tension between Great Britain and the United States, one of the major bones of contention being that for many years British warships had been stopping American merchantmen on the high seas to 'press' sailors in their constant search for manpower. The men so taken were usually described on the Muster Tables as 'deserters', and while this might have been true in some cases it was frequently a fiction and at least some were American citizens with no previous connection with the Royal Navy.

So, in addition to the conflict against the French and their allies, the Royal Navy now found itself at war with the United States. This added to the threat which the navy had to face, but, on the other hand, it also had an implication much closer to the hearts – and pockets – of Royal Navy captains and their crews: prize money!

Under this centuries old system, enemy ships, particularly merchant ships, captured during a conflict were taken to a British port and, after certain legal formalities, sold and the proceeds divided among the crew. This could be a very lucrative proposition, some captains and their crews earning a great deal of money thereby. The system for dividing the spoils had last changed in 1808 and under this the captain received one quarter of the amount realized, of which one-third had to go to the Admiral commanding the area in which the action took place, regardless of how distant he was; in this case, that would be Admiral Dixon in Rio de Janeiro. Next came the middle-piece officers – naval lieutenants, captains of marines, masters and surgeons – who shared equally in a one-eighth share of the proceeds. Then the junior officers – lieutenants of marines, principal naval warrant officers and masters' mates – similarly divided a one-eighth share among them. That left a full half of the proceeds to be divided between the midshipmen ($4\frac{1}{2}$ shares), lower warrant officers (3 shares), able and ordinary seamen ($1\frac{1}{2}$ shares), landsmen and servants (1 share) and boys ($\frac{1}{2}$ share). This system could add a very considerable sum to the crew's meagre wages and served as a great spur in action – which is precisely what it was intended to do!

Admiral Dixon's first priority now was to pass the word on and he persuaded the Portuguese authorities to send one of their frigates across the south Atlantic to tell the commander-in-chief at the Cape of Good Hope. but for passing the message south to the Rio de la Plata he had, of course, the *Nancy*. Thus he instructed D'Aranda that he was to take despatches south to Captain Heywood of the recently-departed *Nereus* to tell him the news, and that *Nancy* would then operate from the Rio de la Plata under Heywood's direction.[49]

This was D'Aranda's first important assignment, but to his intense frustration the wind fell away and there was a virtual calm during the night. At 4am on the 21st, however, a light breeze arose and he gave the order to make sail and weigh anchor. *Nancy* ghosted out of the bay and D'Aranda cut in close by Fort Santa Cruz to save time, but as they came abreast of the fort a voice rang out in English asking what ship they were and one of the watch replied that they were 'His Britannic Majesty's Ship *Nancy*.'

Then to the utter astonishment of the unsuspecting British, there was a puff of smoke from an embrasure, followed by the sound of a cannon-ball whistling overhead and splashing into the water some distance to seaward. D'Aranda, faced with his first real challenge as a commanding officer, found himself in an unenviable position, with his ship barely moving in the light wind and well within the range of an apparently bellicose fortress.

To make matters worse, the fort's guns could seriously harm the lightly-constructed brig, while *Nancy's* cannon could inflict only the most minor damage in return. Nevertheless, D'Aranda ordered the marine drummer to beat to quarters, while he also instructed Sub-Lieutenant Lutman to go ashore immediately to resolve this case of obviously mistaken identity.

The boat's crew rowed the short distance to the shore and pulled up under the walls of the fortress, where Lutman's hails were met with jeering from the ramparts. A man signalled that the British were to go to the gate on the landward side of the fort and so the crew rowed the boat around the promontory, but when Lutman attempted to go ashore he was met with more jeers and eventually he decided to return to the *Nancy* and report.

Meanwhile, the fortress continued to fire slowly but steadily at the hapless ship, although fortunately for the British the shots passed overhead. After a long row Lutman managed to reach *Nancy* as the tide gradually pushed the brig out to sea and they all watched with relief as the final two shots from the fortress fell short.

D'Aranda was extremely perplexed by this action on the part of the Portuguese commander. His crew had answered the fort's initial hail, both challenge and reply had been in English, and the brig was flying British colours prominently. Nor did it seem possible that the fort's officers could have failed to recognise *Nancy*, since she was a well-known sight as she plied between Buenos Ayres and Rio de Janeiro. To cap it all, Portugal was a long-standing ally of Britain in the war against France and even if the fort commander claimed that he thought that *Nancy* was an American ship, that would make no sense either, since his country was not at war with the United States.

So, as the wind picked up and *Nancy* headed south, D'Aranda sat in his cabin to compose a formal complaint at this insult to the British flag, an act which was always taken seriously.[50] The complaint was subsequently forwarded to Admiral Dixon, who sent it to the British ambassador, Viscount Strangford, who forced the Portuguese authorities to make a written apology. Nor was that the end of the matter, since the fortress commander was not only dismissed, but was also compelled to call on Strangford to deliver a deeply humiliating personal apology.

Meanwhile, *Nancy* reached Buenos Ayres without further adventure and after several months lying in the roads was despatched north again, reaching Rio de Janeiro on Saturday 9 January, 1813. On arriving *Nancy* dropped anchor in the outer harbour, but on this occasion did not have to report to the Admiral as the latter had taken the *Montagu* to sea, following reports of an American frigate off the Brazilian coast.

The reports were, in fact, correct and, unbeknown to D'Aranda, he had just narrowly missed meeting USS *Essex*. This American frigate had spent Christmas and New Year off the Brazilian coast waiting to be joined by the remainder of the squadron commanded by Commodore Bainbridge, USN, and when they failed to turn up at either of two rendezvous *Essex's* commander, Captain David Porter, USN, decided to sail south and round Cape Horn into the Pacific. He gave the Plate estuary a wide berth, as he knew that there were Royal Navy ships-of-the-line there, but had he kept a little closer to the coast he would in all probability have met *Nancy* heading north to Rio. There can be no doubt that the larger, faster and much better-armed American frigate would have quickly disposed of the little British brig, but fortunately for D'Aranda this did not happen, although he was, nevertheless, to encounter Americans before too long.

CHAPTER 11

The morning following their arrival at Rio de Janeiro being a Sunday D'Aranda followed the invariable practice aboard every Royal Navy warship, wherever it might be, mustering the men by divisions at 11am sharp. Then, after the roll call, he read the Articles of War.

As always, he was plagued by a shortage of men and in the course of the afternoon, and despite having heard the penalties when the commander read the Articles of War in the morning, two more men 'ran'. D'Aranda waited for darkness and then sent a 'press gang' ashore to see what could be found and they came back with three men, one of whom claimed to be Danish, one admitted to being British, while the third proclaimed himself to be an American. The following night another nocturnal visit to the Palace Yard netted another American, but all four men's loud protestations were ignored, as 'pres't men's' complaints always were.[51]

D'Aranda then continued the never-ending work of maintaining his ship, sending down the fore topgallant mast to get at the crosstrees and repair them. Unbeknown to him, however, the United States Minister in Rio de Janeiro had got to hear of his press gang's activities and on the Tuesday morning General Sumpter penned a very strong protest to the Portuguese authorities. 'I have the mortification to tell your Excellency', he wrote, 'that a new outrage has been committed by the British in the Sovereignty of this Kingdom and on the Security of the Americans residing under its protection. A man whose name is Charles B. Paine was taken on the night of the 10th at the Palace Yard by a pressgang and carried on board the British brig-of-war *Nancy*. Another, whose name is Jeremiah Denis, was also taken at the Palace Yard on the night of the 11th and it is supposed has been lodged on board the same brig *Nancy*. I have the honour to demand of the Government in the name of my own the liberty of these two American citizens who have been made prisoners within this country and to require that their captors shall receive the punishment due for the commission of such offence under such circumstances'.[52]

This was followed by a much longer and more detailed letter two days later, and the two protests had the desired effect, as the Portuguese then complained to the British Minister, thus bringing the names of *Nancy* and D'Aranda to the notice of Viscount Strangford for the second time. D'Aranda must have been surprised at the row that ensued: 'pressing' was, after all, just a routine part of a British naval officer's life, and his country was at war with the United States. His mistake, however, was to conduct the pressing on Brazilian territory, as Portugal was strictly neutral in the war between Great Britain and the United States.

On 17 January, HMS *Racoon* arrived from England and her captain, as the senior British officer present on the station in Admiral Dixon's temporary absence, immediately became involved in the *Nancy*'s affairs. As always with the *Nancy* she required spares and *Racoon* was able to supply her with a new pump, even sending her Master Carpenter over to install it, a favour which was to prove invaluable in the months ahead.

Captain Black of the *Racoon* also became involved in the row over the two Americans, especially as it then became known that his ship also had no less than twenty Americans on board, who had been taken off the *Hope* earlier in the month. Although the British normally stoutly resisted any attempt to interfere with the activities of their 'press gangs,' on this occasion it seems to have been felt wise to give in to the pressure from the Portuguese authorities. Thus, on the 20th D'Aranda reluctantly agreed to the instruction from Captain Black to transfer the two Americans to the *Racoon*, immediately before *Nancy* sailed south on her way back to Buenos Ayres.[53]

D'Aranda's sub-lieutenant, Lutman, was left behind in Rio de Janeiro, having overstayed his leave, and when he reported back for duty he had to be taken on the Muster Table of the *Racoon* until he could rejoin the *Nancy*. In the event this never happened, which left D'Aranda with just two warrant officers to support him, the Second Master and the Midshipman, which was to increase the strain upon the brig's young commander in the adventures which were now to befall him.

As the *Nancy* sailed south D'Aranda was faced with his first serious disciplinary problems and he took the usual naval way out – the lash – awarding J^{no} Hanson, a sailmaker, eighteen lashes for neglect of duty on 23 January. Two days later the same sailor was given another twenty-four lashes for theft, a surprisingly light punishment for what was considered to be, especially by the sailors themselves, the worst of all crimes aboard ship. Nevertheless, a second series of lashes on wounds which had not yet healed from the previous punishment would have been extremely unpleasant for Hanson, not least because on this occasion the nine tails of the 'cat' were knotted, which was only done for theft. Not even mutiny warranted such treatment.

Hanson was, in fact, spared the even worse punishment of 'running the gauntlet,' which would have involved passing through two ranks of his fellow sailors, holding 'knottles,' which were made of plaited rope and, although relatively short, nevertheless inflicted very painful wounds. The term 'running' was, however, something of a misnomer, since in most ships the offender was preceded by the master-at-arms, who walked backwards holding a cutlass to the man's chest while another man followed, holding the point of a cutlass to his back; between them these two moved very slowly to ensure that the offender received the full strength of his comrades' fury over his crime.

Meanwhile, despite a steady deterioration in the weather, *Nancy* made fair progress and Wednesday, 3 February found her beating along the northern shore of the Rio de la Plata. D'Aranda was anticipating entering Buenos Ayres Roads the following day, but unfortunately for him, like all his other voyages aboard his brig, this was to prove very eventful.

Nancy was between Montevideo and Colonnia del Sacramento when, as was his usual practice in coastal waters with bad weather threatening, D'Aranda anchored for the night off Point Jesú Maria. Conditions worsened in the darkness and then, just before midnight, they were suddenly hit by a storm of quite exceptional violence; thunder roared, lightning flashed and the wind was whipped up to almost typhoon force within the space of a few tempestuous minutes. Mountainous seas made the vessel pitch heavily and then, with a sudden and loud snap, the bowsprit broke, initiating a catastrophic chain-reaction, which no human agency could then have stopped.

The bowsprit carried the stays for the foremast and foretopgallant mast, together with their 'preventers' and as soon as it broke the tension on these stays was so suddenly released that within a very few seconds the complete foremast had 'gone by the board', falling aft onto the mainmast. This, in turn, released tension on the main topmast stays, and the main topgallant mast followed almost immediately, while the top of the foremast hit the head of the mainmast itself, breaking off the first couple of feet. The gaff for the spanker also fell away with its jaws broken and at the same time both the foremast and mainmast chainplates were severely damaged. The damage was absolutely devastating and *Nancy's* deck was piled high with a chaotic confusion of broken masts and yards, cross-trees, tops and the gaff, together with masses of tangled rigging, amongst which the bewildered crew struggled to avoid being killed by falling debris.

All hands laboured throughout the night and the bitter Thursday dawn found them still trying to sort out the confusion. D'Aranda's aim was to clear the wreckage so that they could set up some form of jury-rig to enable them to get under weigh and reach Buenos Ayres. Herculean efforts eventually resulted in rigging a jury bowsprit, while a spare yard was used to provide a temporary foremast, but it was not until midday on the Friday that D'Aranda felt able to raise anchor and sail his sorry-looking ship a few miles along the coast until they anchored off Colonnia. More repairs continued throughout that day and into the following night, and it was only at dawn on Saturday morning that D'Aranda felt it safe to weigh again and limp the short distance across the estuary to Buenos Ayres.

In the afternoon D'Aranda went aboard *Nereus* to report to the new Senior Officer Rio de la Plata, Captain Peter Heywood, one of the best-known officers then serving in the Royal Navy. As a very young midshipman Heywood's first voyage had been aboard HMS *Bounty* on Captain Bligh's famous voyage, where he had been an innocent and astonished bystander during the mutiny. But, when Bligh and his loyal associates were crammed into the longboat, it became so overcrowded that Bligh refused to take any more on board and Heywood, together with another midshipman called Stewart, was forced to remain in the *Bounty*, which took them to Tahiti where, with twelve other sailors, they were dropped off to await rescue.

Eventually HMS *Pandora* arrived, having been sent specifically to look for the mutineers and her captain, Edward Edwards, had purpose-built accommodation ready for them. Without any attempt to identify the innocent or guilty, Edwards clapped all fourteen men he found at Tahiti in irons, and threw them into the prison. This consisted of an eleven foot long by five foot high iron box on the quarterdeck to which air and light were admitted through two nine inch square gratings, while the only access was through an eighteen inch square scuttle in the roof.

Five months later *Pandora* ran aground in the Endeavour Straits in the Dutch East Indies and as the crew abandoned the sinking ship Edwards forbade any attempt to release the prisoners, although fortunately the master-at-arms 'allowed' the keys to fall through the scuttle as he clambered over the stern. This enabled Heywood to escape, although Stewart and most of the others drowned.

The temperature in the prison had been so high that all the prisoners were naked and so the survivors who struggled ashore were without any clothing or shoes. Captain Edwards, who was nothing if not consistent, denied them any material with which to make a shelter and permitted them only the minimum of food, and that at irregular intervals.

The shipwrecked crew were eventually picked up by a passing Dutch merchantman which took them to Batavia, following which another Dutch ship took them on to the Cape of Good Hope. On both ships the prisoners continued to be treated with great severity, although they were treated rather more leniently when they were taken from the Cape to England aboard HMS

Gorgon. They were court-martialled in September 1792, where Heywood was the only officer to face the court and he was found guilty of mutiny and sentenced to death, but with a strong recommendation for mercy.

The First Sea Lord, Admiral the Earl of Chatham, was convinced of Heywood's innocence and obtained an unconditional pardon for him from the King. Despite his appalling treatment by the Royal Navy, Heywood was only too happy to accept reinstatement, being promoted to lieutenant in 1795 and to lieutenant and commander in 1800, eventually attaining command of *Nereus* in 1809.[54]

This was the officer who listened to D'Aranda's report of the storm damage and he promised to do all he could to help the unfortunate *Nancy*, but first, he told the young lieutenant, they needed a formal assessment of the situation. He was as good as his word and the following morning Lieutenant Vere Gabriel and four warrant officers from *Nereus* went aboard *Nancy* to carry out a 'Survey' of the damage and to decide what repairs were needed.

The report fully bore out D'Aranda's account and painted a very sorry picture. Lieutenant Gabriel stated that the bowsprit, foremast, mainmast, trysailmast, foretopmast, main topgallantmast, and the tops and crosstrees had all 'pitched away and broke on the evening of the 3rd instant' and in addition the foreyards, main topgallant yards and the jaws of the gaff had 'sprung by the falling of the masts.' But, in addition to all that, 'the stem and cutwater started, two beams defective, several deck planks require shifting, twenty chainbolts lost the planks being much decayed, her topsides and waterways much strained and leaky being too weak for her guns, two gun carriages useless and several breaching and tackle bolts broke and loose.'

In the face of such damage and defects, the opinion of the board was a foregone conclusion, 'that the expense of repairing her would far exceed the value of the said Brig'.[55] Captain Heywood accepted the survey report and forwarded it to Admiral Dixon at Rio de Janeiro, with the recommendation that 'she should be sold out of His Majesty's Service as being now quite worn out and in every way unfit for it. It will be impossible to procure the spars required to complete her, nor all the means, even at the most exorbitant expense, to make good her defects.'

Heywood did, however, decide to authorize some limited repairs to the brig, since *Nereus* was in urgent need of firewood. As a result 23 February was spent getting *Nancy* ready for sea and a jury rig was set up to enable her to sail across to Colonnia. There men from *Nereus*, who had come aboard for the purpose, spent some days ashore cutting wood and loading it aboard the brig, and on Sunday 7 March *Nancy* returned to Buenos Ayres, where her run of ill-luck continued when a heavy swell swept away her jollyboat; prompt action saved the boat, but the mast and sails were lost.

The remainder of the month was spent in continuing the repairs, with some sixteen men from *Nereus* employed aboard *Nancy*, while they awaited the final decision on the brig's future from the Admiral at Rio de Janeiro. On 9 March the principal task was undertaken and a pair of shears was constructed by lashing together two yards, which were then pulled upright and held in position by stays, while a pulley was used to unstep the butt of the damaged mainmast. This was a most delicate operation, since the foot of the mast had to be carefully controlled to ensure that it did not swing free as soon as it came clear, which would have allowed the heavy mast to crash to the deck and injure, possibly even kill, some of the seamen.

All was successful, however, and the replacement was stepped, following which the carpenters from *Nereus* climbed to the mainmast head, where they fitted new cheeks and fashioned fittings for the topmast housing. A new bowsprit was then stepped and the complicated task of reeving the standing rigging carried out, following which it was all tarred. Finally, the running rigging was replaced and at last *Nancy* was once more ready to go to sea, although her basic condition was still highly unsatisfactory.

The repairs had been a herculean task, taking many men more than a month of solid hard work to complete and while this was going on Captain Heywood's letter arrived at Rio de Janeiro where Admiral Dixon, who, of course, knew *Nancy* only too well, decided to endorse the recommendation. Accordingly, he wrote to the Admiralty that, 'the *Nancy* Gun Brig having met with several disasters and requiring more Repairs than She is worth, I have directed Captain Heywood to sell the Hull &c'.

But, both Captain Heywood and Admiral Dixon were quite wrong, as circumstances were to dictate that the weary and decrepit old brig was repairable after all. Indeed, after some very hurried fitting-out, she would soon be heading south into some of the stormiest and most dangerous waters in the world.

CHAPTER 12

Early on the morning of 1 April, 1813 D'Aranda was summoned aboard *Nereus* by signal, where, to his very great surprise, he was introduced to an Army officer, Lieutenant Richard Lundin, of His Majesty's 73rd Regiment of Foot, who was wearing a very dirty army scarlet jacket and black trousers, but with his feet bound in filthy bandages. With him was a weather-beaten merchant seaman, Captain Brookes. Both these men, Captain Heywood explained to D'Aranda, had just arrived from the distant Falkland Islands in a longboat.

Lundin and Brookes related to D'Aranda the story of the *Isabella's* voyage from Port Jackson, the drunken Captain Higton and the shipwreck on the remote Falkland Islands. It seemed like a story from another world, but D'Aranda knew from his recent experiences in the storm just how close sailing ships always were to disaster. The situation of the *Isabella's* survivors was brought even closer when Captain Heywood handed D'Aranda the letter which Lieutenant Lundin had brought with him from the Falklands:[56]

'Sir,
Falkland Islands
22nd Feby 1813

I beg leave to acquaint you that a merchant ship, the *Isabella*, Higton Master, bound to Europe from Port Jackson, from whence she sailed the 4th December last, struck upon a rock and went on the shore the 9th instant. There were 54 souls aboard including 14 marines placed under my Command by His Excellency Governor Macquarie.

The ship's boat was immediately fitted and has this day sailed to endeavour to find out a settlement, as the island we were cast upon, one of the most eastern, is uninhabited, and should she fail in the attempt will proceed to Rio. Lieutenant Lundin of the 73rd Regiment accompanies a Mr. Brookes in the Boat with four Seamen and one of the Marines, and will be able to give every further information respecting our present state.

To add to my personal affliction I have a Wife and Child, and Mrs. Durie expects to be delivered immediately.

Confident that you will have the goodness to order a vessel for our preservation.

Adm De Courcy, or	(signed) R Durie,
officer Commanding	Captain. 73rd Regiment.'
Squadron Rio de Janeiro	

22 February 1813 (Day 1)[57]

Brookes and Lundin started by telling the naval officers how they had left the other survivors at about four pm on 22 February, and had tried to head north in their longboat in order to reach the Spanish settlement, which was rumoured to be at Port Egmont.* Their immediate intention was to head into the Falklands Sound, whose entrance, they assumed, was between two headlands which could be seen on the horizon. The wind was, however, coming from precisely that direction and the inability of their short and overloaded boat to beat to windward made progress very slow. Thus, after some three hours they had only reached two small, tussock-covered islands a short distance from Eagle Island, so they anchored and went ashore, where they caught some geese which, together with a piece of salted pork and some wild celery, they made into a passable stew for supper. They then made camp on the beach, although their sleep was constantly disturbed by the snoring and snorting from the nearby colony of elephant seals.

23–24 February (Days 2–3)

The next morning the wind was even stronger and still dead against them, so they rowed over to the other island, where they were able to pull the boat up on the shore and rearrange the contents of the cabin. On the 24th they made a very early start and returned to the first island, landing among the elephant seals, which they forced to flee. Ford, an experienced sealer, reminded them that seal's tongue was very tasty, so they shot at one with a

---

* There was a British settlement at Port Egmont (present-day Saunders Island Settlement) from 1766–70 and from 1772–74, and a Spanish settlement at Puerto de la Soledad from 1767–1811. Thus, there was no settlement of any nationality anywhere on the Falklands at the time of their shipwreck but, as information travelled very slowly at that time, there was no way the castaways could have known this.

```
TABLE V

SURVIVORS OF THE WRECK OF THE ISABELLA WHO MADE THE VOYAGE
                      IN THE LONGBOAT:
        SAILED FROM EAGLE ISLAND 22 February, 1813
             ARRIVED BUENOS AYRES 1 April, 1813


Captain Richard Brookes        Passenger
George Davis                   Mate of Isabella
Lieutenant Richard Lundin      Passenger
Ford ("an American")           Isabella crew
Jose Antonio (Portuguese)      Isabella crew
Private Joseph Wooley          Royal Marine

TOTAL     6
```

musket, but when the ball failed to penetrate the animal's thick hide they decided not to waste any more valuable ammunition.

25–27 February (Days 4–6)

The next three days were devoted to beating slowly across the southern mouth of Falklands Sound, spending each night on an island, with their little boat either lying at anchor or pulled up on a beach. To their alarm they soon found themselves short of water, having assumed that it would be plentiful on the islands, which were by no means short of rainfall. Instead, they discovered that the rainwater simply drained away through the peaty soil, leaving no pools or streams from which to replenish their supply.

They eventually sailed between the two headlands late on the afternoon of the 27th, but found, to their dismay, that they were in a large bay and not in the entrance to Falklands Sound at all. Downcast by this discovery, they started to row ashore, heading for a beach under the lee of the eastern headland, but their problems were worsened when the rotting wood of one of the oars could take the strain no longer and broke, rendering the other one useless as well. When they eventually reached the shore, some of the men prepared a rather thin supper, while Brookes and Lundin climbed a nearby hill to see whether they could determine where they were, but ended up none the wiser.

28 February (Day 7)

The following morning they were surprised to find a fox had entered their campsite and was trying to steal Private Wooley's knapsack, but the animal ran away before they could catch it. Its visit did, however, lead them to guess (correctly, as it transpired) that they must be in Fox Bay on the English Maloon. Brookes and Lundin then climbed the headland again, where Brookes quickly realized that he had made an error in identifying the entrance to the Sound, which lay in the open expanse of water stretching to the north-east, rather than between the two headlands, as he had imagined. That conclusion quickly led to the realization that the wind of the past few days, which had been responsible for their slow progress to Fox Bay had, in reality, been ideal for heading up the sound. Chagrined, they hurried back to join the others with this news, but as the day was fine and they were heartened by at last knowing precisely where they were, they all agreed to spend another day in the bay, drying their clothes.

1–3 March (Days 8–10)

On the morning of 1 March they set sail once more and made good progress sailing north-eastwards, keeping close to the cliff-lined coast of the West Falkland Island. That night they camped on a small island and a foul wind then forced them to remain there for all of the following day as well. They set out again at 2am on the 3rd, but were blown to leeward, and, since their boat sailed so badly they were forced to run towards the Spanish Maloon, where they spent the night at anchor between two tussock-covered islands.

4 March (Day 11)

The eleventh day proved to be the best so far and by mid-afternoon they were abreast of Cape Fanning, which marked the northern end of the Sound, and when they were unable to see anywhere to land for the night they decided to carry on. As a result they blundered into the tidal race at the northern tip of the Cape, where their little boat was tossed about mercilessly among the boiling waves. In fact, the soldier, Lundin, was so frightened that he closed his eyes to shut out the alarming sights, only to have Brookes accuse him of falling asleep in the face of danger!

Brookes, ever the skilful sailor, put the helm down and ran before the wind, which, combined with the high sides of their little boat, enabled them to struggle through the race. Eventually the exhausted and frightened men were able to drop anchor off a shelving beach, from which they were separated by roaring surf, but they had only just started to nibble their supper of wet biscuit crumbs and a half pint of wine when the rising tide forced them into making a decision. The choice was stark: they could either run the boat ashore, which would save their lives (at least in the short term) but lose the boat, or they could attempt to fight their way out to sea. Even though the sun had already set, they unanimously chose the latter and with some trepidation they raised the anchor and headed north-westwards, parallel to the shore. So fearful were they of being driven on to the shore that Brookes piled on all possible sail, as a result of which they were constantly shipping water and thus had perforce to keep on bailing.

5 March (Day 12)

At about midnight they encountered a new hazard, when their boat suddenly slithered to a standstill, its progress impeded by a dense bed of kelp. This disheartened them even more, but they managed to work their way through the thickly-matted seaweed, but then, instead of running onto rocks, as they had expected, they found themselves in another tidal race. All these events were accompanied by thunderstorms, heavy rainfall and squalls and even the intrepid Lundin later described that night as being 'the most dreadful and tedious of my life, as during eleven hours we had reason to expect that every moment would be our last'.

When the sun rose they realized that during the night they had managed to work their way well out to sea and that the kelp bed that had delayed them did, in fact, surround the Eddystone Rock, which lay some five miles off Cape Dolphin.* Since then they had been blown back towards the islands and, as their spirits were now very low, Brookes ran before the wind, seeking a landing place so that they could recover and dry out. The day become quite hot, but frequent rain showers prevented their saturated clothing from drying out. Brookes steered parallel to the coast for some hours until the current eventually swept them into the entrance to a river and he ran the boat up towards the shore. Some were so eager to reach dry land that they jumped out and in the confusion the boat was swept up against a rock, where she was very nearly holed and sunk.

Quickly returning to their senses, they extricated the boat from its perilous position and once all were aboard Brookes steered further up the river, seeking a better spot for a landing. Suddenly, they were astonished to see some horses and cattle grazing on the far bank and their spirits rose instantly as they leapt to the conclusion that they had at last found the Spanish settlement, Port Egmont, that they were seeking. So, they were in a very cheerful mood as they landed for a second time, but on this occasion in a safer place and with the men showing more sense, and they soon had a fire going. A few minutes later, in the finest British tradition, they were able to celebrate with a cup of tea.

* The Eddystone Rock was given its name by British sailors due to its uncanny resemblance to the original Eddystone, which lies off the English naval port of Plymouth.

Somewhat refreshed, they then sailed further up the river and at six o'clock put into a pleasant creek where they ran the boat ashore and hauled it on to the beach. They managed to find a spring before dark and then constructed a shelter from the sails and, considering all this to be the height of luxury, went to sleep full of anticipation for the morrow.

6 March (Day 13)

They were up early the next morning to start the search for signs of human habitation, but met with no success and eventually held a meeting to discuss what to do next. The continued cruising in the coastal waters, especially after their adventures of the previous day, seemed to all of them to be very dangerous and when Brookes advised that the weather was deteriorating with each week as the southern hemisphere winter approached, they decided to set sail for South America. Their goal, they agreed, would be Monte Video, since they thought that the Portuguese would be more likely to help than the Spaniards in Buenos Ayres. The decision made, Brookes started work on resealing the planks of their little boat with oakum and tar, which he had brought along for that purpose, so Lundin and Ford, with nothing else to do, went for a walk to see what they could find.

They eventually saw the remains of a hut, which on closer investigation Lundin judged to have been occupied at some time by Spaniards. There were skeletons of several cows and horses on the floor, but the only thing of value they discovered was some wood in the roof, which they pulled down to take back to their companions. Before they left, however, Lundin took the castaway's traditional precaution of penning a scroll, which he then nailed to a beam inside the hut:

'Spaniards and Christians, should this ever meet your eye, know that fifty-two British subjects have been shipwrecked upon one of these desert islands, in latitude — and longitude ——; six of them, in order to obtain relief, have endeavoured to reach the main land in a boat. If they fail in this undertaking, their companions will, in all probability, be left to perish. If you find them there, the boat has been lost: if not, we have brought them relief. March 6, 1813.'*

Just as they finished this task Ford observed something in the distance that looked like a track and eager to grasp any chance of finding other humans on the islands, and despite the lateness of the hour, they set off at once.

* For some reason Lundin's account leaves blanks for the latitude and longitude stated in the notice.

When they reached the track they found wheel marks and the prints of cattle, so they pressed on with mounting excitement. Now they saw herds of horses and after some three hours they observed some cows and calves. The sun was setting and they were resigning themselves to a cold and wet night in the heather when they caught sight of what appeared to be the mast of a boat; then a single hut and afterwards an entire village came into view. Skipping with joy and full of anticipation of not only an imminent happy outcome to their search, but also of a warm and dry night, they started to run, but as they neared the village they began to realise it was all too quiet, and that there was neither smoke nor movement of people.

A herd of some eighty cattle observed their arrival from a nearby hill, and as the two men approached they charged down with apparent ferocity. When Lundin and Ford stood their ground (principally because there was nowhere for them to run for shelter) the stampede petered out some two hundred yards short of its target. This was repeated several times, distracting the men's attention, but even so, their spirits began to fall as they realized that the huts were not only empty, but were totally derelict, indicating that the former inhabitants had departed some considerable time previously.

The huts were constructed of wood and turf, but the best preserved building was a small stone chapel, near which they found a sign bearing the Spanish royal coat-of-arms, and a notice stating that the islands belonged to Ferdinand VII, King of Spain and of the Indies. It was dated February 1811, which Lundin took to be the date at which the settlement had been abandoned.

They sheltered for the night in one of the tumbledown buildings where they found two empty casks and, having knocked the ends off, they crept inside to sleep. Despite their tiredness, the bitter cold and the dampness of the casks kept them awake and eventually Lundin invited Ford to join him and the two men huddled together for warmth until dawn.

From Lundin's description it is clear that they were in the only Spanish settlement on the islands, Port Soledad, which had originally been established by the French as Port Louis. This means that when they left the Eddystone Rock two days previously they had run along the north coast of east Falkland, and that the 'river mouth' into which they had been swept was, in fact, Berkeley Sound, far to the east of where they had intended to be.

7 March (Day 14)

The next day was fine and they prowled around the village, which was well sited in a land-locked bay and defended by a fort at the entrance. There were abandoned bullock-carts, several gun carriages and a store containing a few pikes and knives, but no explanation for the evacuation of the place could be found. The only objects of any value they discovered were a garden filled with cabbages, some shoes and an iron pot. They also chanced upon an old, white, one-eyed horse, which they managed to capture after a hectic chase. Lundin christened the sad old beast 'Rosinante' after Don Quixote's faithful 'charger' and used her to carry their spoils as they wended their way back to their four companions, whom they rejoined at about four in the afternoon.

Not surprisingly, Brookes and the other three men had become increasingly anxious about the missing pair. At first, they had assumed them to be lost and so had lit fires on an adjacent hilltop, but had then decided that they had been charged down by wild cattle and, finally, that they had been killed by savages. Their imagination having run riot, they then concluded that the savages would turn on them next, so they relaunched the boat and sheltered in it through the night, in order to be safe from any attack.

In such circumstances of bewilderment, confusion and fear, the reunion was a happy occasion, although Lundin's tale of the abandoned settlement naturally caused yet further disappointment. Their course was, however, quite clear, since they now had final proof that the islands were abandoned and they spent the remaining hours of daylight re-stowing the boat in preparation for a departure the following day.

8–22 March (Days 15–30)

They raised anchor before dawn the following morning and, favoured by wind and tide, they made such good progress that by noon they were out of sight of land and well into their epic voyage: six men in a heavily laden and very vulnerable seventeen foot boat, seeking to cross a thousand miles of open and tempestuous ocean.

They started by heading due north to avoid the danger of being blown westwards on to the coast of Patagonia and found the first ten days the worst, partly because they were still adjusting to the conditions in the boat, partly because they were in dread of a voyage whose only outcome seemed to be certain death, but also because of the ever-present cold and wet. Indeed, for the first eight nights they never saw the moon through the ever-present clouds, but fortunately, they had brought a few candles with them, which were used from time to time during the night to illuminate the compass. During the day they hoped for a sight of the sun, especially at midday, when Brookes would use his quadrant to work out their position, which he then marked on the chart he had brought with him.

Steering required constant diligence. First, and most obvious, was the requirement to keep on course, since they were always aware of the possibility of being blown down on to the hostile shores of Patagonia.

Secondly, if the helmsman was inattentive, there was the danger of the sea suddenly overwhelming their little boat. But there were other hazards, too, as they discovered one evening when the three men on watch in the cockpit were chatting idly, when the American, Ford, glanced up, started in surprise and without a word grabbed the tiller from an astonished George Davis's hands. He threw the boat round as the startled men saw a huge whale right in their path and they barely escaped being lashed by the creature's tail as it proceeded, oblivious to their presence, on its way.

Cooking, not surprisingly, occupied a large part of their waking thoughts. They had brought a large iron pot from the *Isabella* and Lundin had found another, smaller pot in the deserted Spanish village. So in fine weather they lit a fire in the larger pot and used the smaller one to boil sufficient stew to last them for two days, in case the weather turned foul and cooking should prove impossible. The evening meal usually consisted of soup made from goose meat and cabbage, while breakfast was prepared by the night watch and consisted of fried salted pork and biscuit.

They had brought three casks of water with them, but eventually they began to run alarmingly low, due, in the main, to careless spillage in the early part of the voyage, especially when people helped themselves after dark, which led to a reduction in the drink of tea or cocoa, which accompanied breakfast. This problem was offset, however, by the considerable stock of liquor, which enabled them to issue a pint of madeira to each man at suppertime, while later in the voyage when the prospects of success were increasing and the weather was warmer they added a small amount of rum in a half-pint of water for each man as well.

Sleeping arrangements in the thirteen foot long cabin were unpleasant to say the least. Their numbers and the cramped conditions meant that there was a natural division into two three-man watches, the on-duty watch sitting or standing in the cockpit aft, while the others squeezed into the cabin. Brookes and Lundin took it in turns to occupy the space at the rear of the cabin, next to the bulkhead separating it from the cockpit. Each of them had brought a small trunk, both of which were placed in the bottom of the boat and then covered by a small mattress. This left so little room that the occupant had to turn and twist to get in, and once on the mattress the only position possible was to lie flat on his back, with his face touching the boards above and quite unable to move either legs or arms. The other two off-duty men then wedged themselves along the sides of the boat in similar discomfort. They had no protection from the cold and since the boat was constantly being covered in spray or it was raining – or both! – and because the cabin roof was by no means waterproof, the off-duty watch were usually well-soaked and freezing. But, despite the discomforts of the cabin, they found it such a relief to be off-duty that they all slept very soundly, the soldier

Lundin later declaring that 'I have experienced fully as much disinclination to turn out when my time expired, as I now feel at rising early to drill.'

23–25 March (Days 31–33)

Throughout this voyage the wind was fair, but, fortunately for them, although the seas sometimes became very rough, they did not experience any gales. They quickly learnt about the local conditions, one such discovery being that when the wind was from the south-east a strengthening was always signalled by an increasing swell, which gave them time to prepare. In fact, everything went so well for them that on 23 March they made landfall south of the entrance to the Rio de la Plata, almost precisely as planned by Captain Brookes. Thirty-one days had passed since they left their fellow castaways on Eagle Island, and sixteen days since they raised anchor off the Spanish Maloon. They had every reason to be very pleased with their success, but the fact that they had saved their own lives did not let them forget that they still had to arrange for their comrades to be rescued.

Brookes steered them parallel to the coast for two days and on Thursday 25 March they entered the mouth of the Rio de la Plata. Although they were still out of sight of land, they found that they were in only four-and-a-half fathoms of water, and decided to anchor for the night in case they ran aground in the darkness. This gave them an excuse for a small celebration and, as usually happened with all the groups involved in these adventures, the moment they relaxed their guard they came face-to-face with disaster.

They had kept their spirits high during the voyage by promising themselves a feast once their success was assured, which would consist of a 'regale' of cocoa, all that now remained of their stock, accompanied by a dish of fried pork. Accordingly, they were crowded into the cockpit, waiting for the pork to be ready when the boat lurched and the man holding the jug of boiling cocoa dropped it on Lundin's feet. The scalded flesh was immediately bathed in spermaceti oil and dressed in rags, which allayed the pain and inflammation somewhat, but the wound created a problem which was to remain with Lundin for many weeks – and, of course, they also lost their long-awaited feast!

Then, despite being tossed about by a heavy swell, they left only one man on watch during the night, and he failed to see the approach of a huge wave, which consequently swept across the bows without warning, rolling their little craft over on to its beam ends. The three men below were woken suddenly to find water pouring down the hatchway and, not unnaturally, they panicked, imagining the boat to be sinking, while the others in the cockpit received a rude awakening as they were given yet another soaking. Once again, however, all was eventually sorted out and they survived.

101

26 March (Day 34)

After the frights of the night and with success at last within their reach, they were keen to get started at first light, and by ten o'clock the northern shore of the Rio de la Plata was in sight. At about twelve they saw the first ship since they had left the Falklands, a Spanish schooner, but were unable to make contact, and sailed on. By two o'clock the mountain from which their destination takes its name – Monte Video – was in sight, but the wind and the poor sailing qualities of their boat prevented them from heading directly for it.

Instead, they made for the nearest shore where Brookes landed, leaving Lundin, who was very reluctant to walk because of his painful feet, to look after the boat. Brookes soon returned accompanied by some three dozen fierce-looking and heavily armed horsemen. The leader of this group demanded that the British flag, which Lundin had only just raised, be lowered and when Lundin enquired in Spanish whether or not the British and Spanish were friends, the leader snarled 'No!' The locals started pilfering, taking Wooley's hat and a pair of Lundin's trousers, and the British men's prospects were appearing to be bleak, when Lundin had an inspiration and digging out his trunk from the cabin he unpacked and donned his scarlet regimental jacket with its silver epaulettes, which proclaimed him to be a member of the elite grenadier company.

The attitude of the locals changed immediately to one of servile respect. The looted property was returned at once, and one of the band was despatched to find food for 'Senor Captain' and his comrades. Shortly afterwards some soldiers appeared, whose officer, Captain Antonio, explained to Lundin that the British sailors had arrived in the middle of a war, and that he and his men were members of the Buenos Ayres' army, which was attacking the Royalist forces in Monte Video.

Lundin was then taken off by Antonio and he was passed rapidly from one senior officer to another, rising steadily up the chain-of-command in search of someone sufficiently senior to decide what to do with them. Lundin suffered greatly in this odyssey, since when on horseback he could not put his feet in the stirrups, while if he was on foot it was agony to walk; nevertheless, he persisted, with his scarlet jacket still serving as his passport.

27 March (Day 35)

Just after midnight they arrived at the house of General Artigas, the commander of the revolutionary forces, to whom the story of the voyage from the Falklands was told yet again, with the general's English manservant acting as interpreter. Lundin was treated in a very friendly way and given good food, but he was somewhat downcast when he discovered that the problem was too difficult even for Artigas and that he had to progress yet further to meet a General Rondiou.

So he set off yet again to cover another three miles. Rondiou and his staff were very smartly dressed and treated Lundin with much courtesy. Having listened to the story and inspected the letter from Captain Durie Rondiou offered to send Lundin into Monte Video under a flag of truce in the morning, if the lieutenant wished it, but then added that there was a British frigate stationed in Buenos Ayres, which might be able to provide assistance more readily.

28 March (Day 36)

Lundin was desperately tired after this journey and his feet were giving him severe problems so he rested at Rondiou's headquarters, where Brookes and the others caught up with him on the evening of the 28th. Together they hatched a plan for Lundin and Wooley to go on to Buenos Ayres to meet the frigate captain, while Brookes and the others went into Monte Video to find a ship for England, but this was scotched by Rondiou, who insisted that they must stay together. So the party returned to their boat which, somewhat to their surprise they found safe and sound, and still with all their property aboard, all under the care of Captain Antonio.

29 March – 1 April (Days 37–40)

They departed early the following morning in their faithful boat and sailed all day and night with a good wind. They ran aground that night but were quickly under way again and early on the afternoon of the 30th they met some American ships riding at anchor in a small creek, who told them that they were sheltering from the Royal Navy, which would take them as prizes if they ventured out. Despite this, the Americans were well-disposed towards the men in the boat and even provided an interpreter to accompany them to the nearby Spanish fort.

The Spanish commandant welcomed them and did not seek to prevent them from proceeding, although they had to wait until four o'clock on the afternoon of the 31st before the wind was sufficiently favourable to enable them to start on the final leg. Thus, it was not until an hour after sunset that they anchored off the city of Buenos Ayres, and on the following morning (1 April) Lieutenant Lundin and Captain Brookes repaired aboard HMS *Nereus*, where they were conducted straight to the cabin of Captain Heywood.

Brookes has left no record of this epic voyage, but Lieutenant Lundin left two. The first was a rather laconic account, which he produced later in the year[58] and the second a much more detailed story which was published in the *Edinburgh Review* in 1846. The only contemporary record appeared in the '*Annual Register*' for 1813, which described how:

'On the 30th ult. a boat of about 17 feet keel arrived at this place (Buenos Ayres), with six persons on board. The following is the account they have given:- '. . . On the 23d February, having raised the long boat and decked her, it was agreed that a party of the unhappy sufferers should embark in her, for the purpose of arriving at some inhabited place, where the means might be procured of sending a vessel to bring away the other part of the crew and passengers. The six men who arrived here accordingly put to sea on the 23d of February and after a voyage of upwards of 450 leagues on the ocean, they arrived in this river, without having seen the land for 36 days. Nothing but the protection of the Almighty could have preserved them from the inclemency of the weather, considering the great fatigue they must have endured, both in mind and in body, and so long a navigation in seas almost proverbial for storms.'[59]

Their heavy and clumsy little boat was intended only for short trips in sheltered waters, transporting lumber and water, where a load of six grown men with their luggage and rations would have been considered unusually and dangerously excessive. On this voyage, however, that boat and her crew had covered 1,200 miles across some of the most dangerous seas in the world. That on this occasion those seas were less menacing than usual does not detract from the achievement, since at any stage one mistake by the helmsman would have consigned them all to a watery and unmarked grave. The only accident was that involving Lundin and the cocoa, but it is notable that there was no sickness during the voyage, not even the dreaded scurvy, which was almost certainly due to the supply of cabbage which Lundin found at Port Soledad. This must, therefore, rank as one of the more courageous and remarkable small boat voyages in maritime history, and one which was, in every respect, a complete success.

PART 4

HMS *Nancy* in the Falklands

CHAPTER 13

Captain Heywood immediately understood that time was of the essence: the survivors had sufficient food for the time being, but even though it was only the beginning of April, the weather was already very stormy and would get worse as the southern winter approached. Then, too, there was the problem of Mrs Durie and her children.

Heywood's first inclination, with his personal and never-to-be-forgotten personal experiences of shipwreck, was to go himself in *Nereus*, but that was impossible as she was the only major warship in the area and her presence was required for both military and diplomatic reasons. Nor was there any suitable merchantman presently in the Rio de la Plata, which might be chartered for such a potentially dangerous voyage. That only left *Nancy*, and, despite her acknowledged appalling state of repair, the worsening of the weather as winter approached and the hazardous nature of a voyage to the little-known Falkland Islands, she would have to go.[60] Captain Heywood's written instructions to D'Aranda were commendably brief and to the point:

'You are therefore required and directed to receive on board His Majesty's Armed Brig Nancy under your command as large a quantity of provisions and water as can conveniently be stowed, and using every possible exertion, as far as the same may depend upon you, to get the said Brig ready to proceed on this important Service, and you will report when this is so.

Then, having received such further instructions from me as I may see fit to give, you are further directed to put immediately to sea and proceed with all possible expedition to the Falklands Islands in search of the distressed persons wrecked in the late Ship *Isabella*. And having discovered them you will without delay rescue the whole of them with their personal effects and wearing apparel on board His Majesty's Armed Brig *Nancy* and bearing them as Supernumeraries for victuals return without a moment's loss of time to this anchorage.

From the information I have been able to obtain it appears that the *Isabella* was wrecked on one of the largest of the Anican Islands situated in the Latitude 52° 15′ south to the southward of the Falklands Islands, which I have marked on the Chart you will receive herewith . . .'[61]

For D'Aranda this voyage offered adventure and possible glory, as well as a release from the interminable voyages between Buenos Ayres and Rio de Janeiro. Captain Brookes was obviously the man who provided the latitude, which was quite sufficient to give D'Aranda a good indication of the whereabouts of the survivors, but when Lundin insisted that he would go back and serve as a guide, this solved the problem of actually finding the survivors in the Falklands, which were by no means well charted. D'Aranda's other concern was with his crew, but Captain Heywood offered to lend him twelve good men, in exchange for a similar number from *Nancy*, an offer the young commander gratefully accepted. Heywood did not, however, offer a replacement for the missing Sub-Lieutenant Lutman, who had failed to rejoin his ship before she sailed from Rio de Janeiro, which left D'Aranda very short of officers. In all other respects, however, Heywood proved most enthusiastic and in his subsequent report Lundin stated that he 'could not refrain from bearing testimony to the eagerness and activity Captain Heywood displayed', a most unusual tribute from a junior officer about an officer considerably his senior.

Having given all the information he could to Heywood and D'Aranda, Captain Brookes and the other civilian members of the longboat's crew went ashore at Buenos Ayres and then made their own way homewards. The only exception was the marine, Private Joseph Wooley, who had already been taken on the strength of *Nereus*' own Royal Marines detachment.[62]

Once back aboard *Nancy*, D'Aranda explained what was afoot to Shepherd, Brison and Marsh, and introduced them to their Army passenger. Even more furious activity than usual then commenced to prepare the battered ship for her journey south and they also took on extra supplies of meat, vegetables and water, which were needed not only for *Nancy*'s own crew, but also for the forty-eight extra, and almost certainly very hungry, survivors they hoped to rescue.

That night Second Master Shepherd must have wondered what the future held for them as he wrote his log, 'Came on board the Master Carpenter, one Midshipman and ten Seamen from HMS *Nereus* to fit us out for sea to go to Faulkland Islands in search of a wreck, by order of Peter Heywood, Esq, Senior Officer Rio de la Plata. At 3.30pm weighed and made sail into Outer Roads of Buenos Ayres. At 5 came to in 3½ fathoms water. Wait for weather.' And wait for the weather they certainly did, being prevented from sailing for no less than two weeks and it was not until 17 April that they

TABLE VI

ABOARD HMS NANCY ON HER RESCUE VOYAGE:
SAILED FROM BUENOS AYRES 17 April, 1813
ARRIVED FALKLAND ISLANDS 17th May, 1813

OFFICERS
Lieutenant & Commander William Peter D'Aranda, RN.

WARRANT OFFICERS
Acting Second Master William Shepherd; Assistant Surgeon
James Brison; Midshipman William Marsh.

NANCY CREW
John Cassantine; Anthony Daily; Cornelius Devon; Jonathan
Dodson; George Harrott; Matthew Lennon; Bryan McGowan, John
Marshall; George Pizadro; James Portee; William Proper;
Jonathan Turner; Robert Williams.

SUPPLEMENTARY CREW LENT BY HMS NEREUS
John Branson; William Brown; William Corby; James Curtis;
Anoch Gaskill; Peter Greame; William Green; Joseph Highwood;
J H Holmstein; Benjamin Lucas; William Simmonds; Richard
Sylvia.

ROYAL MARINES
Sergeant Joshua Nightingale; Private Hugh Caffrey; Private
Patrick Conway; Private William Hill; Private Edward Hollis;
Private Richard North; Private William Price; Private
William Rawdon; Private John Rawson; Private William
Shearman.

PASSENGER
Lieutenant Richard Lundin, 73rd Regiment

TOTALS.
Officers	1
Warrant Officers	3
Nancy Crew	13
Lent by HMS Nereus	12
Royal Marines	10
Passenger	1
GRAND TOTAL	40

managed at last to beat out into the Plate Estuary. Even so, they anchored nightly until the 20th, when at long last they were able to head out into the open sea.

The voyage south was a desperate affair. By the 24th they were beset by almost constant gales and the following day they had to take three reefs in the topsails, lower the topgallants and set a trysail. The phrase 'labouring much' was repeatedly entered in the Captain's Log, as were the efforts of the crew in the ceaseless work of repairing the ravages caused by the sea and the weather.

By the morning of the 27th the gales had become even stronger and a particularly violent squall split the main storm staysail, while just before noon a heavy sea struck the port quarter and carried away one of the ship's boats. The following day the foretopmast staysail split at five o'clock in the morning and four hours later the dolphin-striker was carried away, thus seriously weakening the bowsprit, which alarmed both D'Aranda and Shepherd, since it was the collapse of the bowsprit that had caused the disaster off Colonnia only a few weeks earlier. That particular gale continued without remission until 3 May, when, as so frequently happened in those latitudes, they were suddenly blessed with a brief period of light airs and D'Aranda immediately ordered the crew to repair the damage.

The respite was short lived, however, and next morning the gales hit them again. By now the pump, so providentially supplied by *Racoon* in Rio de Janeiro in January, was in full-time use, with a constant succession of men working in relays on the open deck in an effort to keep the level of water inside the hull under control. To add to their trials, the temperature dropped even further and on 6 May they had their first heavy fall of snow. Then came another period of light airs and D'Aranda seized the opportunity to order thirty-six lashes on a sailor for 'neglect of duty', one of the heavier punishments he awarded, indicating the severity of the offence.

The lull continued for a few days longer and as *Nancy* scudded through squally showers propelled by fresh breezes on the 10th the captain was able to order the crew to wash their clothing. The wind fell away again that afternoon and was followed by an almost total calm on the 11th which continued into the morning of 12th, but then, once again, the situation changed within a matter of a few hours and the gales returned with a vengeance. Indeed, the situation became so bad, with very high winds and a tremendous sea running, that D'Aranda was forced to heave-to under the forestormtopsail and a trysail.

D'Aranda's plan was to take a westward sweep around the Falkland Islands and on the late afternoon of the 14th excellent navigation resulted in a landfall exactly as intended off Cape Orford. Here a new hazard came into play – an impenetrable Falklands fog – and D'Aranda wisely hove to and dropped anchor. Next morning the fog had cleared sufficiently for them to weigh anchor and ran along the southern coast of the English Maloon, weathering Cape Meredith in thick and cloudy weather, before coming to anchor off Fox Bay at 3.30am on the 16th. The cutter was immediately sent to make soundings and on being told that all was well, D'Aranda took *Nancy* into the bay, where they anchored.

Close as they were to their destination and the castaways, D'Aranda was forced to take the opportunity to put things to rights and most of the crew were immediately set to work on essential repairs. The remainder were despatched ashore to seek fresh water, but the only streams they could find contained a brown and brackish-looking liquid, typical, had they but known it, of many Falkland Islands' streams, which Brison judged to be unfit to drink.

After barely a day in Fox Bay, they weighed anchor early on the 17th and set off on the final leg of their journey to find the survivors of the *Isabella*. Lieutenant Lundin had recognized Fox Bay as the place where the longboat had sheltered during her passage from the Falklands and so felt confident in guiding D'Aranda towards their goal. They sailed slowly across the southern end of Falklands Sound in a light breeze and by 10am were within sight of Eagle Island. By 11am they were close enough to the island to spot a group of people around a flagpole, from which they could see a British flag flying. D'Aranda hove-to and dropped anchor, following which the longboat was hoisted out and, accompanied by Lieutenant Lundin, he set out for the shore.

It was eighty-five days since Brookes and Lundin had left to seek rescue, and twenty-seven days since *Nancy* had sailed out of the River Plate. D'Aranda had shown the highest skill and determination in bringing his weary brig through almost continuous storms and violent seas, and had made such a precise landfall, despite a desperate shortage of officers and sickness among the exhausted crew. Lundin, the Army officer, was very impressed and later described their 'very boisterous passage in which Mr D'Aranda evinced the greatest perseverance.'

During their voyage Lundin had described the passengers and crew of the *Isabella* to D'Aranda and so, as their boat approached the shore, they sought to identify the small party awaiting their arrival. To Lundin's great surprise, however, neither the Duries nor his beloved Mary-Ann Spencer were there, and in addition there were others whom he did not recognise at all. As the two British officers stepped ashore Holt came forward to greet them and introduced his companion as Captain Hunter, an American. As soon as this nationality was mentioned there was a sudden cooling in the atmosphere and D'Aranda told Hunter curtly that he must consider himself a prisoner-of-war. If the others were surprised at this, Hunter himself seems to have taken it calmly, remarking philosophically that 'many a good man had been a prisoner.'

Despite this unexpected development, Holt invited D'Aranda and Lundin to accompany him to the camp at Newtown Providence, where they could take some refreshment at his hut and meet his wife. D'Aranda was uncomfortable on the land, as is any naval captain, whose mind must ever be on the safety of his ship, but he could not resist satisfying his curiosity about the survivors he had battled so hard to reach. As they walked along the shore Holt described how they had survived since Lundin's departure in the longboat and told them about the Americans' arrival. When they reached the hut Mrs Holt gave both Lundin and D'Aranda an effusive welcome and they sat down, talking the while, to drink a cup of tea, after which Mrs Holt withdrew, leaving the men to take a glass of wine together.

D'Aranda asked Holt if he needed anything for himself or his family, but the Irishman replied that he wanted for nothing serious, although his stock of sugar was getting a little low, while his elderly servant Byrne had had no tobacco for some time. D'Aranda promised to send over some of both the following day and also invited Holt to visit the *Nancy*, an invitation which was accepted with alacrity.[63]

Holt then described to the new arrivals how the Americans had appeared out of the blue on 4 April and explained that, since the survivors had come to believe that Brookes, Lundin and their comrades must have perished in the longboat, they had persuaded the Americans to agree to take them to a port in South America. So some of the Americans had left in the shallop on 8 April with the Duries, Mrs Spencer and a number of others, to fetch the brig and were expected back soon. Meanwhile, the remainder of the survivors, plus a number of the Americans, had remained on Eagle Island, where they had been engaged in sorting out the stores from the wreck and, inevitably, in the never-ending hunt for food.

Having satisfied himself about the number and state of the castaways, D'Aranda returned quickly to the *Nancy*, as he was unhappy about her exposed position on the windward side of Eagle Island. He decided to move her early the following morning to a more sheltered mooring in Jack's Harbour on the north-eastern side of the island and, on hearing of this plan, Higton offered to act as pilot, telling D'Aranda that he had sounded the passage. This was pure bombast, since Higton could not possibly have done so, but presumably nobody had the courage to inform D'Aranda that he was being misled. Thus Higton was aboard the naval brig when she weighed anchor early the next morning and once again he demonstrated his incompetence and despite standing well clear of the headland there was a heart-stopping moment as *Nancy*'s keel scraped on a hidden reef in the middle of the channel. Fortunately she had a considerable way on and, with a freshening wind and a rising tide, she forged over the obstacle without any apparent damage.

D'Aranda quickly became as disillusioned about Higton as the rest of the survivors, commenting acidly in a subsequent report that 'had I attempted the entry into Jack's Harbour under this Man's guidance we must inevitably have perished'.[64] He soon preferred to rely, instead, on Shepherd, his own Second Master, even though the latter made no pretence at local knowledge, and by four o'clock in the afternoon *Nancy* was safely anchored in the deep, sandy bay.*

Next morning Holt took up D'Aranda's invitation and went out to the *Nancy*, where he was entertained to a full meal and treated with great courtesy. Indeed, despite his misgivings about D'Aranda's actions to others, particularly the Americans, Holt had nothing but praise and gratitude for the consistent courtesy and consideration which the young commander showed to him and his wife. D'Aranda also spoke to Sergeant Bean, the Royal Marine who had been put in charge of victualling by the committee, and told him that, with *Nancy's* arrival, the weekly issue of bread could be increased from two to seven pounds for each person per week.

On 19 May the weather worsened and by midday there was a fresh gale, making D'Aranda glad that he had moved the brig. Then, at the height of the gale, Captain Fanning, who had been absent hunting geese on another island when *Nancy* arrived, returned and was at once made a prisoner, and, like the other Americans, confined to the area of the camp. Also on this day one of *Isabella's* crew was sent out to the *Nancy* for treatment by Brison, having been stabbed in the arm by one of the Americans in a quarrel, using a 'Malay dirk'.[65]

On board *Nancy* the crew worked as usual in repairing the vessel, particularly her sails and rigging, although D'Aranda was now experiencing trouble with his senior Royal Marine, Sergeant Nightingale, and the incessant problem of drink. These reached such a point that on 20 May Sergeant Nightingale had to be charged with repeated drunkenness and neglect of his duties, and D'Aranda reduced him to the rank of private. This was, however, only a formal prelude to his real punishment, thirty-six lashes, which was administered the following day, since Admiralty regulations stipulated that there must be a twenty-four hour delay between the award of such a punishment and its actual infliction.

The drill for such a punishment was well-known to all, and despite their isolation it was surrounded by a full and very formal ceremony. All crew-members, except for a very few on essential duties, were called aft by the bosun's pipe and stood, shivering, on the cold and windswept deck. The

* Present-day Phillip's Bay, but then called Jack's Bay or Jack's Harbour.

113

Marines formed up in single file on the poop and then the warrant officers fell in, wearing their full uniform, Assistant Surgeon Brison being responsible for ensuring that the punishment did not result in the offender's death.

When the ship's company was in position the bosun's mate had the prisoner brought on deck, accompanied by two escorts, and dressed only in breeches and a shirt. They halted in front of a hatch-cover which had been raised for the occasion and then waited for what was to come. All now being ready, D'Aranda came on deck, also in full uniform, a slim book in his hand. As he raised the book the officers removed their hats and then he read out the Article of War which the accused had transgressed, and announced the punishment.

D'Aranda's award of thirty-six strokes of the lash was, in fact, well in excess of the legal limit for the captain of a vessel, the actual regulation stating that if he considered the crime warranted more than twelve he should remand the man for court-martial. In the remote Falkland Islands, however, nobody was going to dispute the commander's right to award such a punishment and, in any case, no court could be assembled before they returned to Buenos Ayres, so there was a lot to be said for getting the affair over and done with quickly.

The preliminaries over, the escorts pulled the offender's shirt over his head and tied a heavy leather apron around his waist to protect his lower back. Following this Nightingale raised his arms so that the guards could tie his wrists to the grating and then, opening his legs, his ankles were similarly secured.

The bosun's mate stood to one side watching these preparations, holding a red linen bag containing the 'cat' which he had made the previous evening, no 'cat' ever being used twice. This implement consisted of a two foot length of one inch diameter rope handle, with nine tails, each some two feet long, made of plaited quarter-inch diameter rope and secured to the handle by a Turk's Head knot. Seeing that all was ready, the bosun's mate stepped forward and commenced the punishment, delivering twelve heavy strokes, slowly and regularly to the centre of Nightingale's back. At the twelfth he paused and glanced at the captain, who could, by custom, call a halt, if he wished to do so. But there was no signal, so the cat was handed on to one of the guards, who proceeded to deliver another twelve. By this time the victim's back was red and bloody, but Nightingale, like most offenders, prided himself on never making a sound. After the twenty-fourth stroke, the captain had another opportunity to call a halt, but, as he again remained implacable, a third man took up the cat and continued with the punishment.

When Nightingale's punishment was ended, a second figure was brought onto the deck, Robert Williams, a twenty-two year-old seaman, and the process was repeated as he received twelve lashes for neglect of duty. Only when he, too, had been released was the rest of the crew allowed to dismiss and return to their duties.

Meanwhile, the cutter had completed her soundings in Jack's Harbour and the *Nancy* was warped closer to the shore, so that repairs could continue. Some of the spars were sent down and taken ashore for repairs on 21 May and the next day the sails were unbent and also landed so that they could be properly dried and repaired by the sailmakers.

D'Aranda was considerably excited by the *Isabella's* cargo, which he quickly decided to take away from the Falklands for sale, and he ignored the Americans who told him that it belonged to them as a result of the agreement reached between Captain Charles Barnard and the *Isabella's* survivors. He had already mentally allocated *Nanina* to carrying most of the cargo, but as the *Nancy's* men started to bring the stores to their ship, four guns were lifted out of the hold and the remaining stores moved around to make room for *Nancy* to carry some as well.

On Tuesday, 25 May there was considerable excitement on Eagle Island when *Nanina's* shallop suddenly appeared and sailed into the bay. D'Aranda sent *Nancy's* longboat to tell the Americans that they were prisoners-of-war, although it transpired that there was only one actually aboard, *Nanina's* mate Henry Ingman, the remainder of the crew being all British. Once this had been sorted out, Ingman was taken aboard *Nancy* to be interviewed by D'Aranda, where the American, having overcome his surprise at being made a prisoner-of-war, told the British commander that when he left *Nanina* ten days previously she had been ready for sea and should arrive within the next few days.

On 29 May Lieutenant D'Aranda followed a long tradition by firing a twenty-one gun salute in commemoration of the restoration of King Charles II in 1660, and served slops* and tobacco to the Marines as part of the celebrations.† The disciplinary problems continued, however, and later in the day yet another man had to be punished for drunkenness, Matthew Lennon receiving thirty-six lashes, while on 4 June, after firing another salute of twenty-one guns, this time to mark the birthday of King George III, Anoch Gaskell, one of the men on loan from *Nereus*, was given forty lashes for neglect of duty, the heaviest punishment D'Aranda ever awarded.

Nancy's Marines were sent ashore daily to shoot for the pot, although, considering the friendly nature of the Falklands' Upland Geese, their 'bags'

---

* 'Slops' (or slop-stores), a naval term for officially-provided clothing. Although there was some measure of standardization, the items issued to the sailors were by no means identical, and only the Royal Marines were issued with uniform, as such.

† The log is quite specific about the reason for the salute, which appears to have been a carry-over from previous times and there is no evidence that it was general throughout the Royal Navy.

were remarkably low. Holt noted that they were as poor shots as their colleagues from the *Isabella*, four geese being shot on 26 May, ten geese and a duck on the 27th, and ten geese and two ducks on 11 June. It is possible, however, that by this time the island's wild-life population had been seriously depleted and there were not that many left to be shot, which may explain why Captain Hunter was away on another island at the time of *Nancy's* arrival.

Then on 15 June came the day that all on Eagle Island had been waiting for when at 9.13 am (the time is recorded precisely in *Nancy's* log) the lookout at the Camp excitedly reported a sail in sight. D'Aranda superintended the preparations on board *Nancy* and at midday he set out with *Nanina's* shallop and *Nancy's* whaleboat to meet *Nanina* as she entered the bay.

As described in Chapter Nine, there was no surprise among either the British or the Americans aboard *Nanina* when they saw the shallop heading towards them, although there was some puzzlement when they spotted the masts of an unknown ship further in the bay. This changed to alarm, however, as the whaleboat came alongside and the boarding party of British sailors rushed aboard, brandishing cutlasses and pistols, and yelling loudly, encouraged by D'Aranda's shouts and promise of prize money from the shallop.

The boarders' enthusiasm quickly changed to puzzlement, however, as they realized that not only was there no resistance, but that the vessel seemed to be already in British, rather than American, hands. Indeed, if anyone was in charge, it seemed to be the British Army captain, Robert Durie or the leader of the mutiny, Mattinson.[66]

The attack thus rapidly ran out of momentum in an atmosphere verging on the farcical, as everyone tried to sort out what was happening. D'Aranda quickly identified Captain Valentine Barnard, who was easy to spot since he was by far the oldest man on the deck, and told him that his vessel was a prize of His Majesty's Brig *Nancy* and that all the Americans were prisoners-of-war. Barnard and Pease, plus the only other American, Havens Tennant, were ordered to go below, where Valentine Barnard was phlegmatic about this sudden onslaught, although Pease was highly indignant, not least because he had navigated the *Nanina* from New Island to Eagle Island.

Lieutenant Lundin had followed close behind D'Aranda and his appearance caused great excitement with the British aboard the *Nanina*, since they had all assumed that he and the others on the longboat must have perished long ago during their voyage to South America. Thus, there was great interest as he explained to the Duries and Mary-Ann Spencer how Captain Brookes had safely navigated them to Buenos Ayres and how he, Lundin,

1. A goblet, one of several D'Aranda memorabilia in the possession of the Barker family, bearing the only known depiction of His Majesty's Gun Brig *Nancy*. (Photo: E.E. Currier, L.R.P.S.)

By Virtue of the P...
appoint you Lieut. R...
Nancy Willin...
you the Charge and Com...
Strictly Charging and C...
Brig to behav...
Employments, with al...
& Commander...
Instructions, and such...
receive from Us, or any o...
Hereof nor you nor any...
at your Peril. And for...
our hands and the Sea...
day of April 18...
Reign.

Seniority
16 Dec. 1808

By Command of their Lordships.

2. The commission under which 'Lieutenant Wil.
D'Aranda' was "appointed Lieutenant & Commander of
His Majesty's Brig the Nancy" which represents the
highpoint of D'Aranda's career in the Royal Navy. *City
Records Office, Southampton*

the Commissioners for Executing the Office of
High Admiral of the United Kingdom
Great Britain and Ireland &c

Val: D'Aranda hereby appointed Lt. &
of His Majesty's Brig the Nancy

Authority to Us given. We do hereby constitute and
ander of His Majesty's Brig the
iring you forthwith to go on board and take upon
Lieut & Commander in her accordingly.
all the Officers and Company of the said
es jointly and severally in their respective
espect and Obedience unto you their said
kewise to observe and execute the General Printed
Directions as you shall from time to time
Superior Officers, for His Majesty's Service
y fail as you will answer the Contrary
his shall be your Warrant. Given under
ffice of Admiralty this Twenty fourth
Fifty third Year of His Majesty

G. Warrender

R.J Hamerton Lith.

Day & Haghe Lith.^{rs} to the Queen.

Joseph Holt

From an original picture in the possession of Sir William Betham.
Painted in 1798.

London, Henry Colburn 13. G^t Marlborough Street.

3. Joseph Holt, an engraving based on a portrait painted in 1798 after the 'general' had surrendered and prior to his deportation to the penal colony in New South Wales.

had then returned aboard the *Nancy*. These explanations were interspersed with Captain Durie telling D'Aranda and Lundin how they had taken over the *Nanina* at New Island and brought her back to Eagle Island.

Their discussions were, however, interrupted because Joanna-Ann Durie and Mary-Ann Spencer, who had left the men to their talking, now returned laughing and shouting. They had been below to Captain Charles Barnard's cabin, where they had rifled the absent American's quadrant, a telescope, books and charts, which they presented to D'Aranda. Mrs Durie managed to look very winsome as she told the young naval officer that these were his by right of capture. The two women then hurried below again to return with clothes taken from Barnard's trunks and gave some to D'Aranda, before throwing the remainder onto the deck, telling the cheering British sailors and Marines that this was plunder.

This behaviour on the part of Joanna-Ann Durie is difficult to explain or excuse, especially as both the Barnards had been kind to her, particularly Charles, who had taken her and her children away from the hated Eagle Island and had shared a friendly and pleasant cruise round to *Nanina's* hiding place. But, worse was to come in the free-for-all which followed and the Americans had to stand by helplessly as their property was rifled: three quadrants were taken, three fowling pieces, many charts and books, and much clothing. Captain Valentine Barnard's journal, which like so many sailors he hoped to publish, was stolen, never to be recovered, but the most valuable damage, both financially and sentimentally, was their feather mattresses, and the owners fumed as the cheering British sailors and marines cut the mattresses open and threw the feathers to the winds.[67]

D'Aranda eventually restored some semblance of order and instructed that the shallop was to tow *Nanina* into a safe mooring in Jack's Harbour. He also announced that the *Nanina* would be used to accommodate those survivors that wished to come aboard, and, in particular, he allocated the master's cabin to the two Army officers and their ladies, Mary-Ann Spencer having by now become accepted as Lundin's 'wife', albeit without the benefit of a church service.

They were, however, unable to bring the *Nanina* into Jack's Harbour that evening as the wind and tide were both against them and so D'Aranda ordered that the anchor be dropped. They would, he said, complete the operation in the morning and, having moored the American brig, they all went ashore, where they found Sir Harry Hayes awaiting them.

As soon as he had been told of all that had transpired, the Irish knight turned to D'Aranda and, in his usual flamboyant way, claimed that, despite not having been there in person, the credit for the capture of *Nanina* should belong to him! His justification for this preposterous, but by no means uncharacteristic, piece of effrontery was that he had been opposed all along to the idea that British subjects should be carried aboard an American vessel and had been the first to advocate her capture.

Captain Durie interposed to say that the credit belonged to him, since he held the King's Commission and as the senior officer present, he had, therefore, been in charge of the capture. At this, Mattinson thrust himself forward and told D'Aranda that not only had he organized the takeover, but he had also supervised the preparation of the *Nanina* for sea. The two women stood slightly to one side as the men argued and it was clear to Holt that Mrs Durie, at least, felt that the real credit lay with her, since she knew from whence Captain Durie received *his* orders.

Eventually D'Aranda shouted them all down and told them that there was no way in which he could decide between these conflicting claims. He would, therefore, lay all their arguments before Admiral Dixon at Rio de Janeiro, and doubtless that gentlemen would communicate his decision to them in due course. There can be no doubt, however, that he had already decided that the credit for the capture of the *Nanina*, and thus, of course, the prize money, could rightfully only go to himself and the crew of the *Nancy*.

Holt stood a short distance away, watching all this, but keeping his thoughts to himself. He felt very sorry for the Americans who had undertaken to rescue the people of the *Isabella* only to find themselves declared prisoners, their ship taken as a prize and their cargo forfeited. He also felt deep regret that Charles Barnard, whom he had met earlier and taken a liking to, had been abandoned to a lingering death somewhere on the west of the English Maloon. But he could not help concluding that to a certain extent the Americans had brought this on themselves by deliberately evading their government's embargo on sailings at the outbreak of war. It was, however, none of his business and, muttering the proverb that 'a shut mouth denotes a steady head' (which was not a piece of advice that he always applied to himself) he set off on the return to Newtown Providence.

That evening D'Aranda, Durie and Lundin sat together, linked by the bond of the King's Commission, and told each other their tales. As they spoke, D'Aranda brought out the letter Captain Heywood had given him in Buenos Ayres and presented it to the Army captain who opened it and read:

'Sir,
As misfortune was one of my earliest Acquaintances, and having more than once borne, myself, the most painful privations incident to Shipwreck, I can therefore by experience and fellow feeling judge of, and sincerely commiserate, the distressing situation you have been reduced to by the loss of the Isabella on the Falkland Islands. Your misfortune is the more deplorable from the peculiar circumstances of a

Family Nature; deprived as your Lady perhaps is, of every comfort and convenience her situation so much requires.'[68]

D'Aranda explained to the Army officers that the powerful and dignified opening sentence concerned Heywood's early experiences with the *Bounty* and *Pandora*. Durie then read on, the rest of the letter explaining how Heywood would have liked to come himself, but that he was forced to send the *Nancy*, despite her poor state of repair.

Durie, with frequent interruptions and elaborations from his wife, then told D'Aranda about the events following the departure of Lundin and Brookes in the longboat. He related how the Americans had arrived and of their agreement. D'Aranda had, of course, already heard this part of their adventure from Higton, the Master, and Holt, the Irishman, but he was far more disposed to believe a fellow officer, even if he was only a 'redcoat'.

Durie described the agreement and their subsequent, short voyage in the shallop to reach *Nanina*. He also told his naval comrade about the takeover of the American vessel and it would not be surprising if he depicted his own role as having been rather more positive than had actually been the case. The two Duries also emphasized what they saw as the failure of the Americans to keep their part of the deal when they started to lay-up *Nanina* at New Island instead of hurrying down to Eagle Island to complete the rescue, leading D'Aranda to think the best of the British part and the worst of the Americans'.

He was, however, obviously disposed to support the British case, not only through national pride but because the *Nanina*, together with her sealskins and the cargo of the *Isabella*, represented the one thing that made all the hard work of routine naval patrols worthwhile: prize money. It might just have been possible at this stage for him to have restored the *Nanina* to the Americans and allowed them to sail away to search for Charles Barnard and the other missing men, but D'Aranda failed to take the opportunity.

Next day the combined efforts of the shallop and the longboat succeeded in warping *Nanina* into the shelter of the harbour, where she was moored close to *Nancy*. But, while this was going on, the atmosphere aboard *Nanina* became very strained, deteriorating as the day wore on, with Valentine Barnard and, more particularly, Barzillai Pease, becoming increasingly angry. Perhaps the greatest aggravation was the order to leave the master's cabin, but the British did little to endear themselves by what the Americans saw as their arrogant attitudes and their practice of referring to their captives, somewhat dismissively, as 'Yankees'. Pease, never an easy man to get on with, even at the best of times, managed to make himself so unpopular that some of the British threatened to 'string him up' from the yard-arm. Indeed, by late afternoon D'Aranda was so fed-up with the constant bickering that he ordered all Americans ashore to the camp and, with Pease complaining constantly and loudly, they made their way across Holt's road to the cluster of huts and lean-tos at Newtown Providence. Arriving wet, weary and not a little footsore, Barnard and Pease were invited by the Holts to join Fanning and Hunter in sharing their hut.

Meanwhile on board the *Nancy* D'Aranda and Shepherd made up their separate logs, the navy always insisting on two, one by the master detailing the sailing and the other, by the captain, giving not only a summary of the sailing, but also details of major events aboard. D'Aranda seems to have had some slight qualms about his action in making the *Nanina* a prize and chose his words with care:

'Brought the Nanina Brig in,' he wrote, 'belonging to New York, having taken possession of her in consequence of maltreatment experienced by every one on board of the infamous conduct of the master. Found a boat with part of late crew left behind but expected to follow.'

It would appear, however, that D'Aranda did not compare his entry with that made by William Shepherd in his Master's Log until some days later. Shepherd had given a purely factual description of the arrival of the American vessel and of the number of people aboard, and unfortunately for D'Aranda several subsequent entries had already been made. So, he instructed Shepherd to squeeze some additional text into the margin and at right angles to the rest of the entry for the 16 June, making it very obvious for all time that it was a later addition:

'Got intelligence from the passengers that the Americans had behaved to them in a scandalous, oppressive and fraudulent manner, and that this was the means of us seizing the Brig as prize.'

There was, of course, a major contradiction in both these entries, because *Nancy's* crew had actually taken *Nanina* by armed force *before* they had heard the stories from the British who had seized the American vessel at New Island. It is, therefore, clear that the question of the Americans' alleged bad behaviour was introduced afterwards to bolster what D'Aranda may, even then, have felt to be a weak case.

CHAPTER 14

By now the Falklands' winter was approaching and the weather deteriorating, which faced D'Aranda with three main concerns, the most important of which was to prepare *Nancy* for the hazards of the return trip. The second was to load as much of the *Isabella*'s cargo as he could, so that he could include this in the 'prize' and the third was to look for the missing men.

The work dragged on, with the carpenters and sailmakers carrying on with their unceasing task of making *Nancy* seaworthy, while many of the remainder of the crew were involved in bringing the stores and baggage over from Newtown Providence, both overland and using the shallop. All this took longer than expected, since the gales and snowstorms caused frequent delays, although several, including Lundin, thought that D'Aranda, for reasons which he did not make clear to anyone else, was not especially eager to set sail.

D'Aranda initially ordered that the Americans be confined to the camp at Newtown Providence, but after some eight days he allowed them to move to Jack's Harbour, if they wished to do so. Pease was one of those who did, but was soon involved in yet another argument, which arose because D'Aranda ordered the six American seamen (although not their officers) to assist his sailors in the work of transferring stores to *Nancy*. Pease stated loudly that since D'Aranda had made all the Americans prisoners-of-war, then by international custom they were not obliged to work for their captor and he made such a nuisance of himself that D'Aranda had him brought aboard *Nancy* to explain himself. A furious row developed, in which the commander, using a great deal of bad language, threatened to flog Pease and then throw him into irons, but fortunately, commonsense eventually prevailed and this did not actually happen.[69]

Meanwhile, drink continued to be a problem and, as always, those disposed to do so managed to find their liquor, no matter how hard the ship's officers tried to prevent it. Thus, on 24 June Matthew Lennon of the *Nancy*'s crew was given twenty-four lashes for drunkenness, while on 11 July D'Aranda considered it necessary to stop the 'allowance of spirits in consequence of their repeated drunkenness' for three of *Isabella*'s passengers, the notorious drinker, Mattinson, and two of the women, Mrs Connolly and Mrs Davis.

On 29 June a new hazard arose, when it was realized that *Nancy* had become overrun with rats. Ships of the period always suffered from these vermin, but this was something out of the ordinary and D'Aranda felt impelled to take unusual action. So he cleared the ship and battened down the hatches before 'smoking' the entire below-decks area by lowering iron baskets full of glowing coals with lumps of sulphur scattered on them. The crew shivered through the night because the hatches were not opened until 7.30 am the following morning, when every available man was put to work clearing out the ship and throwing many hundreds of dead rats overboard. The problem was not solved, but it was at least reduced to manageable proportions for a time.[70]

By early July the end of the work was in sight, so D'Aranda decided to make an effort to find the missing Charles Barnard and the four sailors who had disappeared with him, sending the shallop, skippered by the only man he could spare to command her, Midshipman Marsh, who was neither as young nor as inexperienced as his rank of midshipman suggests, having originally been in the merhcant navy. He had been shipwrecked on the coast of Brazil and found himself at Monte Video, where he joined the Royal Navy in December, 1810. His former service and experience enabled him to find a midshipman's berth straight away, initially aboard HMS *Porcupine* and subsequently, as we have seen, in the *Nancy*.

Despite this previous experience, the American captains attempted to persuade D'Aranda that one of their number who knew the islands on the west side of the English Maloon should accompany Marsh and initially he agreed that Pease would go, but just before she sailed he changed his mind, possibly because of his dislike of the argumentative American, and allowed only one of *Nanina*'s deck-hands to accompany the British crew.[71]

The shallop sailed on 10 July, but returned just three days later, having got no further than Port Howard on the other side of Falklands Sound. Whether this was by D'Aranda's order or due to Marsh's reluctance to stray too far did not matter, because it amounted to a most half-hearted effort and the shallop had ventured nowhere near where the missing men were thought to be.

Eventually the time came when no further delay could be countenanced and D'Aranda completed his plan, although in typical naval fashion he did not reveal it to his officers, simply giving out his orders for each step as it became necessary. In essence, he intended that the two ships should sail from the Falklands in company and proceed northwards, until, at a point to be determined at the time, they would part, *Nancy* heading for the River

Plate to resume her duties with the Brazil squadron, while *Nanina* would sail straight to England and the Prize Court. It seems extraordinary that D'Aranda should have planned that the heavily loaded and ill-equipped brig should head direct for England, and yet both Lundin and Holt state that this was his intention, the latter stating that the little brig carried sufficient food and water for no more than a quarter of such a voyage.[72]

Naturally, the continued effectiveness of the *Nancy* as a man-of-war was D'Aranda's top priority, but he also had to ensure *Nanina's* safe return with the people he had rescued and the American prisoners-of-war. Sub-Lieutenant Lutman having been left behind in Rio de Janeiro, he was faced with a serious problem, as there was only one warrant officer who could be spared as Prize Master to conduct the *Nanina* on a very long and hazardous journey, the 20 year-old and relatively inexperienced Midshipman Marsh, but D'Aranda literally had nobody else. This young man would be in the somewhat embarrassing position of being accompanied by four American captains, who were not only older and very much more experienced than him, but who were also the aggrieved and deprived former owners of the ship. He was given all thirteen remaining men of the *Isabella's* Royal Marine detachment, plus the majority of the *Isabella's* crew and most of the passengers, including Lieutenant Lundin.

Curiously, Captain Higton, accompanied by Mary Bindell and four members of the *Isabella's* crew, chose to go to Buenos Ayres with the *Nancy*. So, too, did the Duries and Sir Harry Hayes, although the latter's long-suffering friend, Breakwell, finally quit, electing to go straight to England in the *Nanina*.

D'Aranda was always very solicitous for Holt and his family, and invited them to come and live aboard the *Nancy* on 20 June. The American captains, who were still sharing the Holt's hut, helped the family to pack their belongings and then they all carried them down to the shore to see them loaded aboard the shallop, which had been sent round by D'Aranda for that purpose. The Holts left the Americans in their hut, together with old Jack Byrne, Holt's manservant, who always felt unwell in a ship and so the ever caring Holt insisted that he should remain ashore until the last possible moment.

On board *Nancy* D'Aranda regularly entertained the Holts to dinner in his cabin, although they were actually allocated the small cabin off the gunroom normally occupied by the absent Lutman. Holt messed in the gunroom with the Second Master William Shepherd, Midshipman William Marsh, and Assistant Surgeon Brison. The latter had little to occupy himself when not actually carrying out his limited medical duties, so he and Holt spent a lot of time together, Holt noting wryly that, like so many ships' doctors, he was 'a very hard-drinking man'.

123

In planning for the departure from Eagle Island D'Aranda was keen that the Holts should go with him aboard the *Nancy*, but the Irishman politely declined, setting out his reasons in a letter penned in his inimitable style:

'To Captain Dirlanda.

Dear Sir,
I hope you will pardon my impartnance to pursume to ask the liberty of going in the nannina brig as I hear she is to sail streight to England. my long apstence from my countery and the eager desire to imbrace a child dearly belove by her parens haiseings my wishes to go. your complying with this will ever obblige your very umble servant to command,

(signed) Joseph Holt'[73]

D'Aranda told Holt that, while he was prepared to agree to this, he still felt that the accommodation was not really suitable for him or his wife, but the Irishman thanked him for his consideration, saying that he really did want to get back to his beloved Ireland as soon as possible. He would therefore rather suffer the discomforts of a voyage in the *Nanina* in preference to the greater comfort of *Nancy*, but which would inevitably be followed by a delay at Buenos Ayres as he waited for a passage in a merchant ship. D'Aranda agreed with some reluctance and the Holts moved to the *Nanina* on 10 July.

The preparations for sailing now commenced in earnest. On 23 July the twelve Royal Marines and most of *Isabella's* crew and passengers were transferred from *Nancy* to *Nanina*. On the same day some 560lb of bread and 840lb of salted beef were also given to the Prize to sustain her crew and passengers on the voyage north.

After a series of farewells the *Nanina* sailed at 11.45am on 27 July, with orders to await *Nancy* in the Sound, but, just as she cleared Jack's Harbour a sudden squall prevented *Nancy* from following. As a result, the naval brig did not actually leave the harbour until just after 4pm, by which time the American vessel had disappeared from sight. Doubtless very annoyed by this early setback to his plans, D'Aranda had no choice but to set out for Buenos Ayres, hoping that he would catch up with the *Nanina* somewhere en route.

The *Nancy's* log was, however, soon recording similar problems to those encountered on the voyage down. On the 29th they were in the middle of a strong gale and just before four in the morning a heavy sea struck the larboard beam, damaging the side. Another heavy sea at 8.15am caused more damage, this time to the stern, and they were forced to take in the sails and proceed under stormsails. There was a slight lull in the following afternoon, but the wind soon picked up again, accompanied by a heavy snow storm. The brig was constantly shipping water in the heavy seas and relays

TABLE VII

BRITISH ABOARD HMS *NANCY* ON HER RETURN FROM THE RESCUE:
LEFT EAGLE ISLAND 27 July, 1813
ARRIVED BUENOS AYRES 19 August, 1813

OFFICERS
Lieutenant & Commander William Peter D'Aranda, RN.

WARRANT OFFICERS
Acting Second Master William Shepherd; Assistant Surgeon
James Brison.

NANCY CREW
John Cassantine; Anthony Daily; Cornelius Devon;
Jonathan Dodson; George Harrott; Matthew Lennon*; Bryan
McGowan; John Marshall; George Pizadro; James Portee;
William Proper; Jonathan Turner; Robert Williams.

SUPPLEMENTARY CREW LENT BY HMS NEREUS

John Branson; William Brown; William Corby; James Curtis;
Anoch Gaskill; Peter Greame; William Green;
Joseph Highwood; J H Holmstein; Benjamin Lucas; William
Simmonds; Richard Sylvia.

ROYAL MARINES
Private Hugh Caffrey; Private Patrick Conway; Private
William Hill; Private Edward Hollis; Private Joshua
Nightingale**; Private Richard North; Private William Price;
Private William Rawdon; Private John Rawson; Private William
Shearman.

PASSENGERS
Captain Robert Durie; Mrs Joanna-Ann Durie; Agnes Durie;
Eliza Durie; Sir Henry Hayes; Philip Harney; Captain Higton;
John Brown; Daniel Elrict; John Gordon; James Moss; Mrs
Bindell; Drummer Hughes, RM; Mrs Hughes.

TOTALS

Officers	1
Warrant Officers	2
Crew	25
Royal Marines	10
Passengers	14

GRAND TOTAL	52

Note
* Seaman Matthew Lennon died of the scurvy on August 19,
1813 as *HMS Nancy* entered the Rio de la Plata.
** Reduced in rank from sergeant to private on May 20, 1813.

of men kept the pump operating throughout the day and night as she continued to 'labour much.'

The next day things became very bad, with some rigging carried away in the morning and one of the boats lost in the afternoon, so D'Aranda ordered the hatches to be battened down. This continued, with *Nancy* pitching and rolling in the heavy cross sea, until 5 August when both wind and sea moderated, although, even so, towards evening they double-reefed the sails, possibly out of sheer force of habit. In the event, the mild weather continued and, their confidence increasing, they made all possible sail.

By now, however, there was a new problem as an increasing number of men were being taken ill. Assistant-Surgeon Brison was forced to spend more of his time with the sick and less with the bottle, but there was little he could do, as the symptoms of bleeding into the skin, swelling gums, dried skin, 'corkscrew' hair and offensive smell told him that they had been struck by the problem that dogged most long voyages of those days – scurvy. Like other naval surgeons of the time, Brison knew that fresh fruit and vegetables would cure the dreaded disease, although he had no idea of how or why this should be so, but, of course, he had neither aboard the little brig.

On 19 August the battered *Nancy* entered Buenos Ayres roads and exchanged recognition signals with HMS *Aquilon*, which was anchored in the outer roads. This arrival was, however, too late for Matthew Lennon, the twenty-five year-old able seaman who had been given thirty-six lashes on 29 May on Eagle Island, which may well have weakened his resistance to the scurvy, since one of its characteristics is that fresh wounds fail to heal. The captain's log stated that he *'departed this life'* and was *'committed to the deep with the usual ceremony,'* while his entry in the muster table was ruled through and marked with a laconic 'DD' (discharged, dead) – and that was the end of Matthew Lennon.

It was four months to the day since the *Nancy* had sailed southwards, but there was no time for celebration or congratulation and D'Aranda signalled HMS *Aquilon*, requesting that her surgeon come aboard immediately. This man confirmed Brison's diagnosis and he was followed the next day by two Spanish physicians, sent aboard by the port authorities, who were anxious to ensure that the crew were not suffering from any contagious disease. Once that clearance had been given *Nancy* sailed the short distance into the Inner Roads, where the sick (no less than twenty-seven men, well over half the crew) were sent ashore to recuperate. The remaining weary seamen set to, unbending and stowing the sails, while the carpenters and sailmakers started, yet again, on their endless task of repairs.

D'Aranda was, no doubt, perplexed by his failure to find *Nanina*, but there was nothing he could do about it and there were, in any case, two far more pressing problems than the whereabouts of the prize. The first of these was the shocking state of *Nancy*, which had been in an acknowledged state of bad repair for several years, but the battering she had received on the voyages to and from the Falklands was too much and when the captain of *Aquilon* came aboard he was appalled by what he saw. He quickly convened yet another 'Survey' which had no hesitation in once again condemning *Nancy* as unfit for further service.

This time, however, there was no reprieve and D'Aranda was given the sad duty of preparing the brig, which he had come to know so well over the past year, for sale, at which she fetched the somewhat derisory sum of 1,100 Spanish dollars. The end came on Sunday, 5 November, when, for the first time for five years when in port, there was no weekly mustering of the crew and reading of the Articles of War. D'Aranda filled in his time during the morning by completing a long overdue return which was required by the bureaucrats in the distant Admiralty on *Nancy's* sailing qualities – a particularly pointless exercise in view of her impending sale.[74] Then, the inevitable could no longer be delayed and, according to the log, at 11.50am:

'Discharged all crew into *Aquilon*. Hauled down pennant and colours with a gun as signal for the purchasers to take charge and possession of her.'

Punctilious to the last, D'Aranda could not resist one final, ironic – and somehow very touching – entry:

'at Noon moderate and fine weather'

and then signed his 'Captain's log' for the last time.

CHAPTER 15

Returning now to the Falkland Islands, it was *Nanina*, the former American brig and now a Royal Navy prize, which sailed first, on 27 July. D'Aranda, despite the isolation and the lack of any apparent need for secrecy, issued Midshipman Marsh with sealed orders, which the Prize-Master (as he now was) was not allowed to open until he had left harbour. Marsh must have been thrilled by the drama of it all and once out in the Sound he opened the envelope with considerable anticipation, only to discover that his orders were to proceed into Falklands Sound where he would await D'Aranda aboard *Nancy*, but that if they had not met within two days he was to return to Jack's Harbour.

Marsh had, in fact, been given a very poor deal by D'Aranda. None of the equipment which had been plundered from *Nanina* on her arrival at Eagle Island had been returned and she was completely lacking in even the most basic navigation aids such as a quadrant, a compass or even a chart. According to Holt they were so short of equipment that they had neither 'as much spare rope as would fetter a frog nor a second sail to put up, if we lost one', while Lundin records that *Nanina* was 'in a most miserable plight, with a leak in her bows, with neither sufficient sails, rigging, spars, or even provisions to last us one-fourth of the intended voyage'.

It can only be supposed that *Nancy*'s crew, knowing from bitter experience how ramshackle their own ship's sails and cordage were, had helped themselves to virtually anything that could be removed from the prize. It is, however, surprising that D'Aranda, considering the long voyage he was ordering him to undertake, failed to provide Mr Marsh with even the basic navigational instruments,

In addition to the people, however, *Nanina* also carried a substantial cargo. In their original sealing operations the Americans had taken the skins of 3,500 hair seals, 1,800 fur seals and 120 hogs, as well as eight tons of oil from elephant seals. Many items had also been saved from the *Isabella* by the Americans who had stayed behind on Eagle Island while Charles Barnard went to collect the *Nanina*, but these goods had later been claimed by the

British and loaded as part of the 'prize cargo'. This included twenty-five tons of whale oil, 1,030 skins from fur seals, five and a half tons of pearl shells, together with some cable, rigging and sheet copper taken from the wreck itself, all of which was, of course, intended to bolster the value of the sale when the prize reached England.[75]

The men of the *Nancy* had been so keen on this, however, that not only was *Nanina's* hold full, but there was also a considerable overflow on the maindeck, which made moving around very difficult, Pease recording acidly in his diary that they were sent out of the harbour 'with our Shallop towing and our decks lumbered up in A shocking manner for Sea'.[76] Despite this, and greatly to the Americans' indignation, much cargo had still been left behind, including a ton of pearl shells, three pipes of madeira wine, and some copper sheets and bolts, as well about five tons of iron from the wreck's ballast.

Marsh's crew was a very mixed bag. He had no Royal Navy sailors on board at all, a most surprising situation considering that the vessel was a prize, but D'Aranda either could not or would not spare anyone from *Nancy*. There were just nine seamen from the *Isabella*, but none of their officers, since Higton had left the Falklands on the *Nancy* and the first mate had long since gone with Captain Brookes in the longboat to Buenos Ayres and thence direct to England. Then there were eleven passengers from the *Isabella* – five men, five women and the Holt's child – and twelve Royal Marines of the draft that had been going home to England from Australia. Then, finally, there were eleven men from *Nanina's* original American crew, all of whom were considered to be prisoners of war.[77] The obvious problems of over-crowding were then made worse when Lieutenant Lundin requisitioned the largest cabin for himself and Mary-Ann Spencer, which greatly annoyed the American captains, who were forced to sleep in the hold.

The small vessel was thus loaded with no less than forty-four people, but, of these, only nine were actually the nominal crew. Fortunately for Marsh, however, the American captains decided to help rather than hinder him, despite their status as prisoners, and they joined in working the ship, as well as producing a quadrant and navigational books which the looters had failed to find.

D'Aranda's plan did not work out, because as soon as *Nanina* was out in the Falklands Sound a sudden gale, combined with the strong current, swept her quickly away westwards, thus preventing Marsh from following his instructions. Then, once his vessel was clear of the Falklands he had no choice but to head northwards on his own and at first he determined to head for Buenos Ayres, but when *Nanina* was within eight hours of the entrance to the Rio de la Plata the wind veered and the little ship was swept far out into the Atlantic. He then spent some days beating back towards the land,

TABLE VIII

ABOARD *NANINA* ON HER VOYAGE AS A PRIZE:
LEFT EAGLE ISLAND 27 July, 1813
ARRIVED RIO DE JANEIRO 23 August, 1813

IN COMMAND (PrizeMaster)
Midshipman John Marsh, RN

ISABELLA CREW
John Babtist; Hans Brockner; Joseph Ellis; James Hubbart;
Charles Lewis; Angus McCoy; James Read; William Robarts;
John Servester.

ISABELLA PASSENGERS
General Holt; Mrs Holt; Joseph Holt; Samuel Breakwell; Mrs
Bean; John Byrne; Mrs Connolly; Mrs Davis; Lieutenant
Lundin; William Mattinson; Mrs Spencer.

ISABELLA ROYAL MARINES
Private Robert Andrews; Sergeant William Bean; Private John
Bellingham; Drummer John Brind; Private William Catford;
Private Thomas Green; Private William Johnson; Private James
Rea; Private Richard Rowell; Corporal Richard Sargent;
Private James Spooner; Private Richard Walton.

AMERICAN PRISONERS OF WAR
Captain Valentine Barnard; Captain Edmund Fanning; Captain
Andrew Hunter; Captain Barzillai Pease; Henry Ingman; Henry
Gilchrist; Andrew Lott; William Montgomery; John Spear;
Havens Tennant; John Wines.

TOTALS

In Command	1
Royal Navy prize crew	0
Isabella Crew	9
Isabella Passengers	11
Isabella Royal Marines	12
American Prisoners-of-War	11
Grand Total	44

where he steered them too close to a rocky outcrop and Captain Valentine Barnard, partly out of a desire for self-preservation but also partly out of pity for the young midshipman, told him where they were, as he recognised the island. Realising that they were now much further north than he had intended, Marsh decided that there was no point in heading back to Buenos Ayres and so continued northwards.

There was considerable excitement on 14 August when a sail was seen to windward and, with a natural tendency towards assuming the worst, they took her to be an enemy. While the others lined the gunwale watching the other ship, the ever-prudent Holt dived below to extract his cash from the trunk where he had hidden it and then climbed down into the hold to place it in an even more secure hiding place. Meanwhile, Midshipman Marsh, with no cannon and only the marines' muskets for armament, decided that running would only encourage the other vessel, so he put the helm down and headed straight towards her, upon which she tacked about and was soon hull-down over the horizon.

Marsh soon realized that, despite his orders from D'Aranda, it would be extreme folly to attempt to sail direct to England. They were overcrowded, ill-equipped and, with so many people aboard, there was a strong possibility that they would run out of provisions and water, while there was also a chance that they might meet an American frigate or privateer, in which case *Nanina* would quickly be returned to her proper ownership. So he decided to put into Rio de Janeiro, a decision in which Valentine Barnard may have played a not entirely disinterested role. They sighted the Sugarloaf at the entrance to the harbour on 21 August and entered the harbour on the 25th.

Nanina had been through the same storms as *Nancy*, but was both newer and in a much better state of repair, and her only significant problem was the loss of the shallop which broke its tow and disappeared early on. Considering that this long voyage was completed with only the most rudimentary navigational aids and was conducted by a young midshipman, whose only help was a 64-year-old captain, and with a very large number of people aboard, eleven of whom were nominally his prisoners, it was a fine achievement. Lundin described it as:

'. . . a most trying voyage. The weather was excessively severe, and the people continually wet, with no change of clothing, or even common nourishment, and no spirits, excepting a dozen bottles of wine, which was soon finished. We were, in every other respect as ill-provided as possible, scarcely a sail-needle or piece of twine could be mustered in all the vessel, and, without the assistance of the Americans, we could not have made out the voyage'.

Even Barzillai Pease, who took advantage of his private diary to criticize virtually everyone else that he came across, whether American or British, managed to find some words of genuine praise:

> 'To do this Mr Marsh justice I must say he did every thing in his power for the comfort of us, for which I feel myself in duty bound to give it a place in my journal for he was sent in the Brig without a Quadrant book or Chart or even c(l)oths saving what he stood up in.'[78]

Marsh had certainly done a good job in successfully leaving the Falklands, but as it turned out he had, albeit quite unintentionally, done D'Aranda a singularly bad turn by putting in to Rio de Janeiro.

Having discovered that General Thomas Sumpter was their country's Minister Plenipotentiary in Rio de Janeiro the three American captains wrote him a letter, which Holt delivered on their behalf. The next morning, however, it was not the American who boarded the *Nanina*, but no less a personage than the British Commander-in-Chief, Admiral Dixon, himself. Marsh was ashore and so, having introduced himself to the Admiral, Holt called Barnard and Hunter on deck, and the old American captain told him the story of their adventures, ending up with the wry comment that their efforts to save the British had been a 'bad job'.

'I think not', replied the British Admiral, 'it was the hand of God that guided you there to save so many lives'. Then turning to Holt, Dixon asked, 'How long had you been on Eagle Island before the gentlemen arrived there'?

'From the eighth of February to the fourth of April, living on two pounds of bread and one pound of beef or pork', Holt answered. 'The Americans generously gave us plenty of food. It is my opinion, your worship, that a vessel taken up by British subjects and for the purpose of saving their lives ought to be considered as an exception to the rule respecting prizes. Although there was war between England and America at the time that the *Nanina* was seized, the conduct of the Americans towards us clearly showed that there was no enmity on their part'.

The Admiral agreed and told Barnard that he and his men could go ashore at once and should no longer consider themselves to be prisoners. Brushing aside their thanks at this surprising turn of events, the Admiral returned ashore, leaving the Americans to discuss what to do next, and there was no doubt about the first thing to be done, which was to mark the occasion with a little celebration. So Barnard, Hunter and Fanning, accompanied by General and Mrs Holt and their son went ashore to see the sights of Rio de Janeiro and they walked up the street until they came to a bar with the Union Flag flying at the door, and entering, Holt called for glasses of rum all round. The Irishman also found accommodation for himself and his family ashore and the next morning he returned to *Nanina* to fetch his goods, and for him that was the end of his association with both the Americans and their brig.

As so often in life, however, once the adventure was over the arguments started, and the lawyers and bureaucrats took over from the men of action, although the result in this case was to be something of a surprise. Having been released by Admiral Dixon, the Americans quickly found their Consul's office, where they had several long meetings with Philip Rutter, the acting Commercial Agent. The outcome of this was a lengthy and formally sworn 'public instrument of protest' in which the four captains, Valentine Barnard, Andrew Hunter, Barzillai Pease and Edmund Fanning, set out their full story. They described their voyage and the events on Eagle and New Islands, and pointed their complaints firmly at D'Aranda and Durie, although they took the opportunity to name all those who had taken part in the capture of *Nanina* at New Island. Having certified the document on 6 September Mr Rutter sent it off to Washington, DC, in the diplomatic mail.[79]

Then, in early October, the American vessel *Bingham* was given a safe-conduct to proceed to the United States and the master offered passages to *Nanina*'s crew, which was accepted by Barzillai Pease and two others, who arrived in Rhode Island in early December 1813. This left Valentine Barnard, Henry Ingman and six sailors in Rio, just enough to sail the *Nanina* to anywhere in the world, including, so they hoped, to the Falkland Islands.

The American Minister, General Sumpter, sent a formal protest to the Portuguese authorities, complaining that the British were illegally holding an American ship in Rio de Janeiro harbour, but the Portuguese politely and firmly declined to become involved. Admiral Dixon had, however, been thinking the matter over and was clearly concerned by what he had been told about the men left behind in the Falkland Islands, since he instructed the British Consular office to have informal discussions with the American master. As a result, Barnard sent them a list on 14 October, setting out the damage and deficiencies on his ship, to which Dixon replied two days later with an unexpected offer to return the *Nanina* to Barnard 'as she now stands' but having unloaded the *Isabella's* cargo, adding that 'the rigging and sails have now been completely put to rights for you.'[80]

Barnard thought about this for a few days and then replied on the 19th:

'I have had the honor to receive thy letter of the 16th inst within which thee purpose to deliver the brig *Nanina* and cargo to me as agent for her Owners, after taking out the Cargo received from the wrack^d ship *Isabella* and that thee will furnish me with such authority as thee

133

possesses to proceed to the Falkland islands and from thence to New York with hir cargo now on Board, which proposition will be agreed to. It is understood that the permission to proceed to Falkland islands and new york may be used or not at the option of thy
Well Wisher

(signed) Valentine Barnard.

10th Month, 19th, 1813'.[81]

This apparent agreement led the British to prepare a 'Bond of Acquittance' which the Consul asked Barnard to sign on 27 October, but the stubborn old man, thinking, perhaps, that he had gained the upper hand, refused. Instead, he countered with a proposal to sign for *Nanina* and her contents, but reserving the right to a future claim for all losses and damages sustained during the previous months in the Falkland Islands.

The British baulked at this and matters rested there for over a month until 6 December when HMS *Hermes* sailed into Rio de Janeiro harbour, with a sick Lieutenant D'Aranda among her passengers. His feelings when he espied *Nanina* riding at anchor can only be imagined, since up to that moment he must have been convinced that his prize was well on her way to England. As soon as his presence was known, he was summoned to Dixon's office, where he gave the Admiral his version of the events in the Falkland Islands.

Although Dixon believed that D'Aranda had done a good job in difficult circumstances, this conversation did nothing to alter his views, and he decided on another effort to reach an agreement with Valentine Barnard. As a result, on 9 December D'Aranda and Valentine Barnard made their separate ways to the British Consul's office, where the two men, who had parted four months ago as captor and captive, now found themselves meeting as equals in a neutral country. D'Aranda, on instructions from the Admiral, made a new offer, saying that the Americans could have *Nanina* back on one condition, namely that they must pay all the harbour dues, which had accrued since the vessel's arrival at Rio de Janeiro. Barnard firmly refused, partly because the dues amounted to some 400 Mil Reals (which he obviously did not have), but also because this did nothing to recompense the owners for the damages and losses.[82]

This finally tried Admiral Dixon's patience too far and he immediately broke off all contact with Captain Barnard, ordering that *Nanina* be prepared for the voyage to England. This not only left the remaining Americans high and dry in Rio de Janeiro and with no alternative but to make their own arrangements for a return to the United States, but also, of course, removed any possibility of rescue for the five men so cruelly abandoned in the Falklands.

Nanina's adventures were still not quite over. She left Rio de Janeiro on 6 February, 1814 in a convoy, with William Marsh still the Prizemaster. He had, however, been given a scratch Royal Navy crew from HMS *Akbar*, the flagship of the convoy and, as usual when a ship was required to give up men in this way, some of the men were reasonable, but others were definitely not.

One of the latter was Seaman Edward Grimmit who had been a member of the crew of the transport *General Hewitt*, which was taking convicts to the penal colony of New South Wales. Grimmit, however, caused so much trouble on the first part of the voyage that when she called at Rio de Janeiro the master persuaded the captain of the *Akbar* to take him off his hands. *Akbar's* crew were equally eager to be rid of this troublesome man and he was, therefore, a natural selection to be passed on to *Nanina*, where he caused trouble from the moment he came aboard. He refused to obey orders, started fights, ignored people who spoke to him – even his own shipmates – and swore loudly, violently and often.

The evening of 28 February began pleasantly enough aboard *Nanina*. The weather was calm, there was a bright moon, the convoy was about half-way home and William Marsh was relaxing in his cabin. Suddenly, he heard a violent altercation taking place and he went on deck to find three sailors arguing loudly in the waist. Observing that Grimmit was at the centre of yet another disturbance Marsh went up to him and ordered him to go to the quarterdeck and, after a great deal of cursing, the sailor eventually obeyed. Perhaps unwisely, Marsh followed, repeating his order to 'be quiet', whereupon Grimmit lost his temper, swore violently and took a swing at his superior, hitting him in the face.

Marsh grabbed a rope starter and hit Grimmit, who then went for'ard, but Marsh was not content to let things rest there and sent two sailors to fetch him back. This resulted in more shouting and cursing, culminating in Grimmit hitting Marsh for the second time. The midshipman now considered his authority to be in jeopardy, so he ran below, grabbed his midshipman's dirk and rushed back to the quarterdeck, where he brandished the short sword and shouted at the sailor: 'If you hit me again, I'll run you through!' This was too much for Grimmit who was now beyond reason and, breaking free from the two men restraining him, he hit Marsh twice in the face, screaming 'Let drive, you bugger, let drive!'

Unfortunately for Grimmit, Marsh was as good as his word, stabbing the dirk through his groin, but the force of pulling it out made the sailor spin round so that Marsh's second blow landed in Grimmit's back. The sailor collapsed to the deck, screaming and bleeding profusely, while everyone else was suddenly sobered by the violence and the blood. Two sailors carried the badly wounded Grimmit down to Marsh's cabin, while a signal for urgent medical assistance was sent to *Akbar*, which happened to be nearby. A surgeon was rowed across and after dressing the wound took Grimmit back to the flagship, where he died of internal bleeding four days later.

When the convoy arrived in England Marsh was warned for court martial, the trial duly taking place aboard HMS *Gladiator* at Portsmouth on 31 May, 1814. The midshipman found himself faced by a court comprising no less than twelve captains, supported by a deputy judge-advocate-general. The charge of 'stabbing Edward Grimmit from which he died' was read out and then three sailors gave evidence on the events of the night.

The verdict of the court was that Marsh's mind had been 'considerably irritated at the time by the highly mutinous conduct of the deceased and by his [Grimmit's] having struck the said William Marsh a second time...and that the crime of murder has not therefore been committed.' Midshipman Marsh was no doubt very relieved both by this and by the fact that his long and unhappy involvement with *Nanina* was now at an end.[83]

CHAPTER 16

D'Aranda's voyage home was by no means uneventful, either. He sailed as a
passenger in HMS *Hermes* on 19 January, 1814, bound for England. He was,
no doubt, keen to return home, but the circumstances were not happy: his
ship had been taken from him and he may well also have felt the pangs of
the loss of privilege and status that went with command. He had been
dismayed to discover that Admiral Dixon did not fully support his action in
capturing the *Nanina* and, on top of all that, he was feeling very ill after all
his exertions.[84] Now, to cap everything, he discovered that *Hermes* was a
most unhappy ship, where the officers, led by the first lieutenant, were
bitterly opposed to their commander, Captain Philip Browne.

There was a series of rows, both private and public, between the first
lieutenant, Letch, and the captain, which increased in seriousness as the
voyage progressed. Letch accused the captain of paying illegal pilotage fees
to *Hermes'* master while they were in Buenos Ayres, but what followed was
worse. On 21 January the captain called Letch a coward in front of the ship's
company, then on 14 February he gave an order to the master gunner, which
Letch publicly challenged, and this was followed two days later by an
incident on a punishment parade when the captain took exception to the fact
that Letch was wearing a hat and publicly ordered him to remove it. Finally,
on the 28th, Letch accused the captain of ordering him to sign an illegal
certificate for money and Captain Browne immediately confined the first
lieutenant to his cabin.[85]

It was in this troubled atmosphere that D'Aranda, too, became embroiled
with the captain, in one of those incidents that start innocuously enough.
D'Aranda had been writing his reports during the voyage, a task which he
completed on 30 March when they were just one day's sail from Plymouth.
He no doubt felt a sense of relief as he summoned the ship's sailmaker and
instructed him to sew the papers in a canvas cover for their journey by stage-
coach to London. This was a very routine request, but the sailmaker
declined, politely telling D'Aranda that he was under very specific orders
that no canvas was to be used for any purpose without the captain's personal

authority. D'Aranda was considerably taken aback by this and endeavoured to browbeat the sailmaker who refused to budge, so D'Aranda sent for the Master. When that warrant officer fully supported the sailmaker, D'Aranda, incensed by what he took to be impertinence and influenced perhaps by the bad atmosphere aboard, became very angry and wrote out a statement for the illiterate sailmaker to sign, in which the unfortunate man declared that he had refused to obey a superior officer's order. D'Aranda then ordered the sailor to 'make his mark', which, with great reluctance, he eventually did.

Meanwhile, the Master had hurried to apprise the captain of what was going on and Browne immediately summoned D'Aranda to his presence on the quarterdeck, where he berated the junior officer, accusing him of interfering with the crew in the performance of their duty, which as a passenger he had absolutely no right to do. When D'Aranda attempted to dispute the issue Captain Browne lost his temper, accusing D'Aranda of cowardice and villainy, and threatening to let him loose among the ship's company who would 'sort him out.' In his later letter of complaint D'Aranda described 'a volley of the most opprobrious language which was ever uttered in the hearing of man' and the 'unmerited opprobriums and passionate insults of Captain Browne, whose language would have disgraced the veriest vagabond in St Giles' and nothing but the most ungovernable temper would ever have uttered'. (All of which makes a fascinating comparison with Barzillai Pease's description of the occasion back in June when he was berated by D'Aranda on the quarterdeck of the *Nancy* in the Falklands, the American writing in his diary that he 'received such foul and abusive language as I never before heard from any low-bred Carracter.')

Aboard the *Hermes* Browne summoned all those involved in the dispute to his cabin, where the master, sailmaker and D'Aranda's servant related their sides of the story. The sailmaker felt particularly aggrieved and told his captain that he had been very reluctant to make his mark on a statement which he could not read, but that he had been persuaded to do so by D'Aranda. At this Captain Browne lost his temper again and immediately changed D'Aranda's status aboard from that of a passenger to being on the strength of the ship's crew as a supernumerary, which immediately gave him the legal authority to confine him to a cabin under arrest.

The Commander-in-Chief at Plymouth must have been somewhat surprised the next day when *Hermes* anchored in the River Tamar and the captain came ashore to tell him that his first lieutenant and a former passenger were both under arrest, and should be court-martialled. The Admiral's surprise increased even further when Lieutenant Letch sent in seven specific charges against his captain and requested that he, too, should be court-martialled, while D'Aranda satisfied himself with two requests for redress.

The Commander-in-Chief moved rapidly to resolve this tangled web of charge and countercharge, the first court martial taking place on 21 March, where Lieutenant Letch, having been charged by his captain, was found guilty and 'reprimanded and admonished to be more circumspect in his future conduct'. This extraordinarily light punishment was followed on 30 March by the court martial of Captain Browne himself, where he was found guilty and sentenced to be 'dismissed His Majesty's Service.' Not surprisingly, Browne felt very hard done by and his crew rallied to his support, producing a very touching appeal to the Admiralty Board on his behalf, which was signed by the warrant officers and the entire crew, but with the unsurprising exception of the lieutenants. Browne took legal opinion and was informed that the sentence was 'informal, irregular and illegal', as a result of which he appealed, and both finding and sentence were completely reversed later in the year, Browne being fully reinstated in the navy on 20 April, 1815.

Browne's charges against D'Aranda were for:

' – *Treating me with disrespect and contempt on the quarterdeck of HMS Hermes.*
– *Attempting to seduce part of the crew of HMS Hermes under my command to join in a confederacy against Mr Hodges, Acting Master of Hermes in conjunction with Lieutenant Charles Letch and Lieutenant John Kennedy'.*

These were, however, quietly dropped shortly after Browne had been sentenced by the court martial to be dismissed the service, presumably because the principle witness could only have been Browne, who was now no longer serving and thus ineligible to appear. Had the court-martial gone ahead, however, there would seem to be little doubt that D'Aranda would have been found guilty. Captain Browne may have over-reacted, but no junior officer, let alone a passenger, could expect to get away with seeking to persuade members of a ship's company to go against their captain's orders. Nor, worse still, should a junior officer have argued openly with a captain on his own quarterdeck. Once the charges had been dropped, however, D'Aranda, who, on this occasion at least, was rather fortunate, was released from arrest in Plymouth and allowed to make his way to London.

In all these lengthy and complicated return voyages, most of the people involved seem to have gradually forgotten that there was still one small group of people unaccounted for. As the reader will doubtless remember, when *Nanina* was captured by the British on 11 June, 1813, they had sailed from New Island for Eagle Island, abandoning five men – Charles Barnard and four sailors – and their fate had never been established.

The British aboard *Nanina* had made a perfunctory attempt to look for the missing men on their way to Eagle Island, and later Midshipman Marsh had made a brief and not very enthusiastic voyage to look for them in the shallop. Then, in Rio de Janeiro, Captain Valentine Barnard had wanted to sail to seek them out, but in the end the commercial and financial aspects of the deal he was offered had proved insufficiently attractive, the British Admiral withdrew the offer, and Barnard was forced to return to the United States.

So, now, with the others all safely home, we must return to the Falkland Islands to discover what happened to those five men who had been so cruelly abandoned.

PART 5

The American Crusoe[86]

CHAPTER 17

Day 1: 11 June, 1813*

On 11 June, 1813, the day before the British takeover, *Nanina* was lying at New Island with her combined American and British crew, when a break in the wintry weather, coupled with a shortage of food, led Charles Barnard to decide on a brief trip to nearby Beaver Island to supplement their fresh provisions. He called for four volunteers and when all was ready he collected his faithful dog, Cent, asked his father to take charge in his absence and set off in the small boat for Beaver Island. There had been a number of previous such trips and during the short voyage Barnard chatted idly to the crew, but without taking any real notice of them, apart from observing that there was one of his own American sailors, Jacob Green, and three British, Samuel Ansell, Joseph Albrook and James Louder, all formerly of the *Isabella*. The trip to Beaver Island did not take long and when they arrived Barnard decided to go on to the weather side of the island (ie, along the south-west coast) and once there he ran the boat onto a convenient beach and they all set off to hunt.

Day 2: 12 June

They spent the night on the beach and continued hunting the following day until the afternoon when their ammunition ran out. Then, with enough hogs to fill the boat, they set off for New Island despite the darkness, rather than spend another night in the discomfort of an open beach. The night crossing caused them no problem, but as they came around the headland guarding the entrance to New Island's South Harbour they noticed that they could not see any lights from *Nanina*. Then, to their alarm, they realized that she was not there at all and although they were completely mystified, and not a

---

* The count of days has been added to help the reader to keep track of the length of time these five men spent on the islands after they had been abandoned.

little annoyed, by this they were left with no choice but to head for the shore and spend a second night on a beach.

Day 3: 13 June

None of the five got much sleep, as they waited for first light, so that they could start searching for the message which they were certain must have been left for them. When dawn came it did, indeed, confirm that *Nanina* was nowhere to be seen, but frantic searches along the shore failed to reveal any indication which would explain where the brig had gone, or why; not even the mariner's traditional message in a bottle. The five men felt confused and increasingly angry, but they still found it difficult to persuade themselves that they had really been deserted.

Their hopes were temporarily raised by Barnard's suggestion that the brig might have had to leave early for reasons which they did not yet understand and that it could then have gone to Beaver Island to pick them up, but on the leeward rather than the windward side, where they had been. Buoyed by this hope they quickly returned to the boat and rowed back across to Beaver Island, although their thoughts were naturally, if very reluctantly, turning to the possibility that they had been deserted.

Barnard tried to cheer the worried sailors by telling them that it was highly unlikely that the people they had left aboard *Nanina* could be so devoid of humanity as to abandon them to the horrors and sufferings they would inevitably endure in this inhospitable climate. So, buoyed by a degree of optimism, they sailed round to Beaver Harbour, convinced that they would sight the brig at any moment. But, it was not to be and they felt totally cast-down as they searched the foreshore for any sign that *Nanina* had been there; as on New Island, there was not a trace to be found.

They could now only assume that *Nanina* had gone to Eagle Island, which left them no course other than to go there themselves; the alternative, to stay where they were, was just too awful to contemplate. Even if *Nanina* only stopped at Eagle Island long enough to pick up the other people, Barnard argued to himself, they must surely leave some written messages together with the necessities of life for the five men they had so barbarously deserted.

Barnard planned their passage with care, knowing that it would be difficult to weather Cape Orford in such a small boat, having had considerable difficulty in the much larger shallop only a few weeks earlier. But, even if he succeeded in rounding the Cape, he would still have to be wary of the southern shores, which were generally very rocky and fully exposed to the prevailing westerly winds, affording little shelter for a boat as small as theirs. This, combined with tide-rips, made that route too dangerous to attempt.

So he decided to take the longer route around the northern side of Swan Island and then to head south past Barnard's Island and across the South Harbour to McCockling's Lagoon. From there they would drag the boat across a two-mile-wide neck of land to Port Stephens and sail in easy stages around Cape Meredith to Fox Bay and thence cross the southern end of Falklands Sound to Eagle Island. Even this route would be dangerous at that time of the year, but in their desperate circumstances there was no alternative. So, having resolved to undertake the hazardous journey, they calculated that they only needed four hog carcasses to sustain them for long enough to reach their destination and they lightened the boat by throwing the other four carcasses overboard, an act they were to regret in the coming days. Thus prepared, they set off on a north-easterly course to head round Swan Island.

Day 4: 14 June

They had to row for most of the night and eventually sought shelter in a bay on the eastern side of Swan Island, landing in the early hours, very cold, soaked to the skin and extremely hungry, since they had been unable to eat during the passage. The four sailors complained bitterly of the cold and, as was to happen so often in the future, they looked to Captain Barnard to find some way of alleviating their misery, although there was little he could do. As dawn came, however, he helped them to kindle a fire and together they managed to cook some pork, their first food for twenty-four hours. Thus fortified, they relaunched the boat and continued their voyage, although, since the wind was fresh and from dead ahead, they could not set the sail, which left them with no choice but to row into the head sea. With waves breaking over the bows every few minutes they were soon soaking wet again and they were very thankful when a favourable tide enabled them to work their way into the lee of Barnard's Island.

Barnard had neither compass nor map, having taken only the bare essentials for an overnight trip when he left *Nanina* four days previously and he thus had to base all his decisions upon experience, memory and local knowledge. At this point, however, everything, from lack of a compass, through poor visibility, strong tides and the bitter cold, to indignation with whoever had caused them to be abandoned and sheer anxiety about their predicament, combined to make things even worse than they already were. Thus, unnoticed by Barnard, they were swept eastward by the tide and when they put ashore, well after sunset, he thought they were much closer to the narrow entrance to McCockling's Lagoon than was, in fact, the case.

Day 5: 15 June

The five men spent another unpleasant night on an open beach, huddled under the upturned boat, which, while it gave them no warmth, did at least keep most of the snow off. Dawn showed them that they were at the head of a small bay from which a valley ran gently up between two hills, and on walking up to its head they saw that it then sloped equally gently down to another stretch of water. They leapt to the conclusion that the distant water must be Port Stephens Bay and, since the crossing looked much less arduous than they had expected, they decided to haul their boat across here rather than sail on to McCockling's Lagoon. So they set to with a will and spent the day carrying the sails, mast, oars and stores across, finishing at dusk, when they fed and then rested, looking forward to the next day with some anticipation.

Day 6: 16 June

The whole of the next day was spent in dragging the boat across the neck of land, since it was too heavy, and they were too weak and too few to carry her. Nevertheless, they succeeded and by nightfall she was in the water once more, loaded and ready to continue the voyage, but they were so keen to proceed that they were unable to wait for the dawn, and foreseeing no danger in enclosed waters, they pushed off and set sail confidently towards their goal. After some hours, however, Barnard was astonished to discover that waves were breaking over the bow and, with increasing alarm, he realized that they were not in a sheltered bay, as he had imagined, but had somehow returned to the open sea.

Barnard quickly realized that he had made an error, but with neither chart nor compass to help him, he was unable to work out what had happened, or where they were. So he put the helm down and headed for the nearest shore, where, after a somewhat hazardous landing, they pulled the boat up onto the beach and turned her over to serve as a shelter for the rest of the night.

There were some eight inches of snow on the ground when they landed and the men had to clear a space under the boat before scrambling underneath and huddling together for warmth. There was only one blanket between the five of them and the sailors used it to cover their bare feet, because they had no shoes. One after another the four sailors started to weep from a mixture of terror, frustration at their inability to make progress in the appalling conditions, and fury at their comrades for placing them in such a position. Seeing their despair, the dog Cent crept in among them and licked their bare legs and feet, as if aware that they were in need of comfort, but Barnard was more practical and scraped a hole in the bank against which the boat was resting so that he could light a fire and cook some strips of pork.

Days 7–9: 17–19 June

The 17th dawned cold and bleak, and as it grew light they crawled out from under the boat to look about to discover where they were. Barnard was at a complete loss to explain what had happened, but he knew that there was no point in giving way to despair and so, remarking that they were very short of both firewood and drinking water, he sent Green and Ansell along the beach to see what they could find. Some hours later the two men returned frozen, very miserable and empty-handed, so, after chewing at the inevitable pork and drinking some heated snow, Barnard set off with Albrook in the opposite direction. They had walked about a mile when they stumbled upon a frozen pond and when they broke the ice they discovered fresh and clean water underneath. Then, a little further on they found four sealions and quickly killed the smallest. They were not after its flesh, however, but its blubber and having hacked off as much as they could carry they hastened back to the boat, where they were in time to throw a lump on the fire and prevent it from going out.

Now that they had both water to drink and fuel for the fire, Barnard sent the men back along the beach to kill the remaining sealions and bring back more blubber, because he was worried that the storm might last for days, if not weeks. They spent the rest of the day huddled under the boat, cold and wet, while their faces began to turn increasingly grey from the fumes given out by the evil-smelling blubber fire.

Day 10: 20 June

The weather was calmer on the 20th, so they launched the boat and rowed all day in the direction in which they anticipated land to be, pulling into a small beach under a rocky headland just before sunset. Barnard still had absolutely no idea where they were, but when they saw and killed a fox, he guessed that they must be on the Spanish Maloon, since, to the best of his knowledge, that was the only habitat for such animals.

That he came to such a conclusion indicates how disoriented he was, since to have reached the Spanish Maloon (East Falkland) they would have had to cross Falkland Sound, when clearly they had not done so. Then, on top of everything else, while it proved to be the only life in that bleak spot, they found the fox's flesh to be totally unpalatable, but, as a very small consolation, one of the men did at least manage to make a hat out of the pelt.

Day 12: 22 June

They had discovered that they were in some sort of bay, and despite a strong westerly wind they were able to launch the boat and run some six miles across to the opposite shore. Once there, Barnard cast about to see if he could recognize anything which might enable him to solve the overriding problem of just where they were, but there was no clue at all. By this time they had no food left, so, in the now-established pattern, they split into two pairs, each going along the beach in opposite directions, while the fifth man remained by the boat.

Barnard and his partner returned empty-handed in mid-afternoon and were reduced to tearing out the tussock-roots to see if there was anything edible in them. Barnard became increasingly anxious about the other pair, but they struggled back just before dark, almost completely exhausted. They had, however, stumbled across a flock of skuas feeding on the putrid carcass of an elephant-seal.[87] They had managed to kill seven of these carrion birds and the five men managed to eat them, even though, as Barnard remarked in an unusual display of 'gallows-humour', judging by their smell the elephant seal must have been dead for a very long time.

Day 13: 23 June

Next morning Green and Ansell set out to see if there were any more skuas still feasting on the elephant seal carcass, while Louder remained with the boat, and Barnard and Albrook went in the other direction once more. The latter pair had not gone far when they found a newly landed young elephant seal, which stood no chance against two experienced and, what was perhaps of rather greater significance, very desperate hunters. The unfortunate creature was soon despatched, but it took them two journeys to carry all the flesh and blubber back to the boat, where they found that the other pair had only been able to catch five more of the nauseating skuas.

Day 14: 24 June

They christened this site 'Pinch-Gut Camp' from the extreme hunger they felt there and were not sorry to leave it on the morning of 24 June, landing some hours later further along the shore. They immediately got the fire going and boiled some blubber, which was all that they had left to eat. The

4. Sir Henry Hayes from a miniature in a private collection in Ireland. His serious demeanour belies his tempestuous behaviour both in New South Wales and during his enforced stay on the Falkland Islands (via A.H.P. Crosbie, Esq).

5. An engraving from Barnard's book published in 1829, showing the survivors' camp at Newton Providence on Eagle Island, with *Nanina's* shallop (left), the wreck of the *Isabella* lying on the beach and the frame of the boat being constructed for the proposed voyage to South America. It appears to be generally accurate, although according to the written descriptions the huts had turf walls and were neither as neat nor as substantial as shown here.

6. New Island showing the shed now standing on the site of Barnard's hut. The penguin rookery from which Barnard obtained so many eggs is up the valley to the left. Photograph taken by the author.

smell was appalling and they were very averse to eating the noisome substance, but they had no choice. Unfortunately, the strong smell attracted a large number of skuas, one of which swooped in and then flew off with their last remaining seal-hook firmly gripped in its beak.

Somehow sensing the men's desperation, the birds became braver and started to tear at the pile of blubber, but they became so intent on this task that the five men were able to kill no less than eighteen, using stones and their bare hands. Nothing typifies the true horror of their situation during this period so well as this episode in which the exhausted, starving and terrified sailors were reduced to tearing at half-cooked blubber, for which they competed with a crowd of screaming, vicious skuas.

Days 15–20: 25–30 June

By now the combination of near starvation, being lost on an extremely hostile coast, constant bad weather and the sense of appalling injustice was sapping both their strength and their willpower. The prospect of a very unp'easant and lingering death was becoming increasingly real, but, encouraged as always by Barnard, they never quite gave up. On the 25th they went out singly to increase their chances of finding something to eat, but at the end of the day their total haul was one small seal and two skuas, all of which were eaten that night.

The following day they found themselves reduced once again to tearing at tussock roots, even though they all developed alarming symptoms of dizziness and vomiting, with Louder and Green being especially badly affected. Their miserable state was not helped by the weather, which continued to be so bad that there was no prospect of launching the boat, leaving them no choice but to remain where they were.

Day 21: 1 July

The following day the weather eased a little and Barnard decided to risk putting to sea, but the waves were bad and they were so weak from hunger that they almost suffered two simultaneous disasters. As they launched the boat a wave threw it against a rock, splitting one of her bottom planks and, if that was not bad enough, Jacob Green was suddenly knocked down by a wave and almost swept out to sea, but fortunately one of the others managed to grab him before he disappeared to a certain death. After hasty repairs to the boat, they managed to put to sea, where they ran along the coast for some ten miles in very rough conditions and with everyone bailing constantly to prevent the boat from sinking under them.

Ansell became more agitated than the others because he could not swim and suddenly reached the conclusion that all was lost. As a result, and to his companions surprise, he suddenly confessed that his surname was not Ansell at all, but Stone, and insisted that the others should promise that if any of them escaped they would inform his widowed mother at Lutondon, near London, of the death of her son.* Fortunately, Ansell's fears proved misplaced and they eventually managed to land, where they spent yet another miserable night, with only two foxes, three geese and some seal flesh to eat.

Days 22–24: 2–4 July

Once again the weather confined them to the beach for three days and as they approached what they thought to be the extremity of endurance, it was Ansell, the bully and blackguard, who was the first to crack. On 2 July he suddenly broke down and started to cry like a child, confessing to Barnard that he had been a member of the conspiracy to take over *Nanina* and that the gang had only been waiting for a suitable opportunity to offer itself. His greatest regret, he told Barnard bitterly, was that he had foolishly volunteered for the expedition to Beaver Island, which, unintentionally on his part, had been the occasion of offering his fellow conspirators the opportunity they had been looking for. Not surprisingly, Barnard was angry at this and told the sobbing sailor that he had earned the awful fate he was now sharing with them. Indeed, of the four sailors, Ansell's behaviour throughout this period was by far the worst. Whenever he felt secure he acted the bully, swearing and cursing at the others, which enabled him to achieve virtually total domination over the two other British sailors, although his influence over the American, Green, was rather less. But, despite all this bluster and bravado, when danger threatened Ansell was always the first to shrink back.

Days 25–27: 5–7 July

Eventually, Barnard was forced into deciding that the only course remaining to his little group was to retrace their tracks with the aim of returning to Swan Island, where they would not only know where they were, but would also be able to catch some hogs. So, on 5 July they set out again and coming to a bay sailed up it, where, when they reached its head, they realized that by the sheerest chance they had returned to the neck of land over which they had dragged the boat. Relief at finally re-establishing where they were was tempered by the knowledge that they must cross the land once again and if

* Ansell was known in the Royal Navy as John Stone, but his real name was Samuel Stone. He was most probably a deserter, since most such men changed their name to protect themselves from being court-martialled if the navy managed to arrest them.

hauling the boat over nineteen days previously had been bad, it would be even worse this time, because they were so much weaker through continuous exertion and starvation.

Nevertheless, they knew that the effort had to be made and in two days of unremitting toil they got the boat, her equipment and such stores as remained across into South Harbour. Consumed with impatience, they set sail as soon as they were ready and by three o'clock on the afternoon of the 7th they landed on Swan Island, where Cent knew full well what was expected of him and rushed into the undergrowth, soon catching a hog. They were so hungry that it was more than they could do to wait for the meat to cook properly and so the five desperate men grabbed the semi-cooked flesh from the fire and tore at it ravenously.

Once they had some food inside them they felt strong enough for a more deliberate hunting expedition and soon had six carcasses lying beside the boat. Then, so rapidly does the human spirit recuperate and so soon does hope return, that they decided to make another attempt to reach Eagle Island in case *Nanina* had not yet left for the mainland, abandoning them to a lingering death.

Days 28–29: 8–9 July

They sailed from Swan Island at two o'clock on the morning of 8 July and this time they managed to reach the real entrance to McCockling's Lagoon, arriving as the sun rose and the wind veered to the south, strengthening and bringing with it heavy snow. In what was by now a well-practised drill, they hauled the boat out of the water, removed the rigging and equipment, turned her over and got a fire going underneath to give them some feeling of warmth. They were, however, extremely anxious to confirm that they had arrived at the right place this time, so Green and Ansell set off across the neck into the driving snow.

Once down on the far shore Green immediately recognised several landmarks and was quickly able to confirm that it was, indeed, Port Stephen's Bay, because he had been there several times in the past. The knowledge that they had at last found the correct place was, however, more than offset by their discovery on the way across that the distance was considerably greater than Barnard had told them it would be, being more like four miles than two. On top of that, the going was much more severe than they had expected and so the prospect of dragging the boat across was a very daunting one.

This depressing conclusion may well have distracted the two men during their return journey. They were very tired, and the tall grass and heavy snow combined to make their progress even more difficult than usual, so they did not return to the shore of the bay where they had left the others until after dark. All this combined to disguise the fact that they were veering to the right and as a result they ended up by going down the eastern shore of the bay. Fortunately, a chance sighting of the distant fire glimmering from under the boat on the western side of the water showed them that they had made a serious mistake and they then had no choice but to retrace their steps to the head of the inlet before going down the western side, which they should have done in the first place.

They did not reach their anxious comrades until midnight and then they all crouched under the boat, holding a council on what to do next. Eventually, Green, Louder and Albrook told Barnard that they did not feel that any of them had the strength to drag such a heavy boat over the four miles to Port Stephens, but Ansell, despite his tiredness, was for going on. Barnard tended to feel that it was possible, too, despite the difficulties, but he knew that he would need the unstinted support of everyone for such a major physical exertion. He also felt that a three-to-two vote would be too close, so he sided with those who wanted to go back, putting Ansell into a minority of one, and that settled the matter.

The next day the weather continued to be so severe that they could not set sail and to add to their problems they had run out of fuel, so that they could not even cook the small bits of pork that remained. Realizing that lying under the boat doing nothing could be fatal, Barnard relentlessly drove them out to seek fuel and when they returned with some withered grass and dead vines, they managed partially to cook some meat, which at least assuaged the very worst of their hunger.

Days 30–31: 10–11 July

The next morning the weather was better and they set out once again for Swan Island, passing Barnard's Island and then reaching northwards up the eastern shore of the island they were now beginning to know so well, heading for Loup's Head. Their attempt to reach Eagle Island had lasted some twenty-eight days at the very worst time of the Falklands winter and during that time there had been only brief periods of clear weather and calm seas, and for the rest there had been high seas, heavy snowfalls and piercing winds.

They had left *Nanina* on a two-day foraging trip, so they had taken only the minimum clothing and equipment with them and they were thus singularly ill-prepared for what turned into a major expedition. Barnard at least had a change of clothing, but the four sailors had only what they stood up in and, as was usual with sailors of the time, wore neither shoes nor stockings.

Despite all this, and even though they had neither map nor compass, they had travelled a prodigious distance. The effort of dragging a heavy boat across a two-mile wide neck of land and back again in bad weather at a time when they were starving had taxed them to the very limits. During most of the time they spent lost they were perpetually on a knife-edge of survival, faced by dangerous seas, lee shores, high cliffs, narrow beaches and only a very few animals and birds to be hunted for food.

Barnard, Green, Albrook and Louder managed to get on well together, but Ansell was always the weak link. For all five of them, however, the worst aspect was the continuing uncertainty of what had happened to *Nanina* and even Ansell's revelation about the conspiracy could only suggest a possibility of what might have happened. They guessed that *Nanina* had headed for Eagle Island but, even if that was correct, their prospects of getting there before she left for South America seemed very slim indeed, but there was no alternative to making the effort.

It was, by any standard, an epic journey, exhibiting great bravery and endurance. That Barnard made a navigational error which led to a lot of suffering was certainly not his fault; indeed, it is astonishing that he made only the one mistake and it is to his great credit that he kept his head and ensured that his men stayed together until they had all survived these exceptional privations. Their problems were, however, only just beginning and as they sailed along the shore of Swan Island Barnard's mind was already turning to the future.

Ironically, and totally unknown to the castaways, they had reached the furthest point in their struggle to get to Eagle Island at almost the same time as Midshipman Marsh was making his half-hearted search to reach them. Thus, Green and Ansell were on the shore of Port Stephens Bay on 9 July, while Marsh reached Port Howard on 13 July, but the two groups were still four days and forty miles apart. Had Barnard and his men been capable of keeping going, they might well have reached Eagle Island before *Nancy* and *Nanina* sailed away, but there is no way in which they could have known that.

CHAPTER 18

Days 32–44: 12–24 July

They spent the night of 12 July on a beach just south of Loup's Head and the following morning rowed around the headland, across the mouth of Chatham Bay and on into Quaker Harbour. There they found a comfortable campsite and pulled great armfuls of tussock grass to give them their first comfortable night after four weeks of the most acute discomfort. The next day they caught more hogs, but their anxiety about the brig inevitably led them to want to return to New Island and they set off in that direction on the 14th, anxiously searching each inlet and beach as they passed. But, as before, they found absolutely nothing.

Days 45–51: late July

Eventually the weather improved sufficiently for them to be able to sail across to Beaver Island where they established a campsite below Quaker Hill, from which they could keep New Island under observation, just in case a ship called in. Their plan was to spend the rest of the winter there, since Beaver Island boasted rather more wild life than New Island, and they developed a routine, with one pair of men going daily for hogs, a second pair for seals and the fifth man remaining on his own by the boat. This man's jobs were to cook, keep the fire going and to treat the seal skins, while also keeping close observation on New Island, which was some seven miles distant. These duties were shared absolutely equally, including Captain Barnard, and rotated daily, so that nobody had any grounds for complaint.

Unfortunately, the hogs tended to be on the far side of the island, which involved a round trip of some twenty miles, floundering through snow drifts and wading through deep creeks. The hogs were lean, mean and fast, the boars being particularly hard to catch and their tusks could inflict an unpleasant wound on the intrepid Cent or an unwary hunter. Once killed they were heavy and awkward to carry, but the sailors found that by gutting

154

the animal, cutting off its head and tying the legs together they could carry it round their necks. Arduous as the task was, however, it was worth the effort, since they found the flesh to be pleasant to eat and easy to digest.

They were also close to a fur-seal rookery, where the seals sheltered among great piles of rock. The blubber was used to keep the fire going, but the skins were also invaluable as the men's clothing was in a very bad state, having been worn constantly for two months and badly in need of replacement. The seal skins were pegged-out and dried, following which they were rubbed vigorously until they were reasonably pliable and then made up into outfits, comprising jacket, trousers, shirt and hat. Fortunately, they had some sail needles and a ball of twine, although this, too, eventually ran out and they had to cut a piece of cloth out of a sail and unpick it to provide a substitute. These new suits were, in fact, so comfortable and warm that Barnard was eventually persuaded to make one for himself, even though, at that time, he somehow still had an adequate supply of proper clothing.

They named this campsite 'Rat Camp,' as it was infested with the rodents, with which the five men were in constant conflict, Barnard remarking acidly that 'in general, their sagacity in committing their felonies was greater than ours in preventing them'. Hog carcasses proved to be especially attractive targets and several had been lost before the men eventually outwitted the rats by raising three oars and tying them together to form a shears. The carcass was then suspended by a rope and both oars and ropes covered with seal blubber to make them unclimbable, and all this, at last, defeated even the most determined of the rodents.

On 27 July, quite unknown to the five desperate men, *Nanina* sailed from Eagle Island, followed by *Nancy* a day later. Both brigs headed westwards, but were then swept far to the south and thus passed out of sight of New Island before being able to achieve any progress northwards up into the Atlantic. So, now Barnard and the four sailors were truly on their own in a totally uninhabited archipelago and one which, due to the outbreak of war, would be devoid of shipping for a long time to come.

Days 52–123: 1 August–11 October

Although ignorant of their comrades' departure, by the beginning of August they had come reluctantly to the conclusion that their chances of being found by the shallop or the *Nanina* (they did not, of course, know of the existence of HMS *Nancy*) had disappeared. As a result, when the weather began to improve they decided to move their camp to New Island on the off-chance that a visiting whaler might call in and find them, and on their arrival they made their camp at the foot of the valley at the northern end of South Harbour and, as usual, set about finding food.

Barnard, recalling that it must be time for the albatrosses to start laying their eggs, sent the men off with sealskin bags to see what they could find and they returned some hours later with six eggs, which made a delightful change to their diet of endless pork. Not surprisingly, Barnard had become confused over dates during the course of their recent adventures, but knowing that albatrosses start laying about the first week of October, and since the eggs looked a week or so old, he arbitrarily set the date of their discovery as 10 October, which was as good a system as any.

The men were so hungry that they had no compunction about raiding the nests of the albatross, although actually obtaining the eggs was not particularly easy. Each pair of albatrosses constructed a nest from a small mound of earth, on top of which was laid just one egg, which was then constantly guarded by one of the pair. The albatrosses were large birds with a wingspan of some twelve feet and a very sharp beak which could seriously wound the hands of a human predator, although the ever-watchful skuas were a greater danger to the eggs. These vicious birds patrolled the rookery alert for the slightest opportunity, when they would pounce, diving down to break the egg and devour the contents.

Day 124: 12 October

One morning Barnard decided to go down to the southern end of New Island to kill a hair seal, as he needed to make himself a pair of moccasins. He went over to where the sailors were chatting beside the upturned boat and asked if one of them would accompany him, but they all made excuses. Green and Albrook told him that they were about to set off to find vines for the fire, Louder that he was the duty cook, and Ansell that he needed to mend his trousers. This lack of response did not particularly concern Barnard and he went under the boat to finish sharpening the knives he would need to kill and skin the seal. Emerging, he called for Cent, but Louder told him that the dog had already left with Green and Albrook, so the captain remarked casually that, since he did not intend to go alone, he would await their return so that he could at least take his beloved dog for company.

At this Ansell leapt to his feet, saying that he would leave mending his trousers until later, and offering to accompany the captain. So they set off southwards together, chatting as they went and walked round the shoulder of the hill, where they descended into a valley full of tussock grass. This was so high and dense that Barnard lost sight of his companion and on emerging at the other side he stopped to wait for Ansell to catch up.

But after a couple of minutes had passed and Ansell failed to appear an awful suspicion occurred to Barnard and, abandoning all thoughts of catching seals, he hurried back to the campsite. As he rounded the hill hurrying northwards, his worst forebodings were confirmed as he spotted the boat running out of the harbour under full sail, propelled by a fair, following wind. He raised his hat on his walking stick, waving and shouting to his crew, but to no avail.

In desperation he rushed up to the campsite to see what they had left him, but when he got there he found that they had taken everything. His first thought was for the fire, because without that he would be in desperate straits indeed, but although it looked dead he managed to coax it back into life, using some dry straw. This achieved, he looked around but found that they had taken quite literally everything: his clothes, sewing implements, fowling piece, tinder, sealskins, the last flint and even his dog had all been systematically collected and removed. He was now truly on his own and he could not escape the conclusion that, for whatever reason, they wished him dead.

Days 125–132: 13–20 October

Barnard watched the boat's sail disappear towards Beaver Island, but wasted no time in senseless recriminations or anger, since he realized that he had to act quickly to ensure his survival. The first priority was to preserve the fire, because, since they had taken his last flint, the small piece of tinder he had left was useless and he developed a method of using pieces of tussock grass, which he found could retain the fire for several hours. Then, since he no longer had the upturned boat as a shelter, he made a crude lean-to out of tussock grass, but when it was finished he decided that he could do better, so he took it down and rebuilt it, ensuring this time that it would keep out the rain.

Scavenging along the shore he found an old tin pot which they had used as a bailer in the boat until the bottom fell out, after which they had thrown it away. In his new extremity, however, it had a value it previously lacked, and he managed to bend and hammer it into a shape suitable for use as a cooking pan for his eggs. He also found a twelve-foot sapling lying on the beach and dragged it up to the top of the nearby hill where he raised it as a mast, with some pieces of sealskin flying from the top as a distress signal. The mast also served as a talisman, giving him some hope, as well as a calendar, since he cut a notch in it to mark each day as it passed. Apart from losing count of the date, which he had resolved by means of the albatrosses, he had also lost track of the days of the week, so he arbitrarily declared the day of the desertion a Friday, which enabled him to keep track of Sundays, which he scrupulously observed as his days of rest.

At the head of the valley where he was camped was a penguin rookery and as the laying season had now started he was able to gather eggs, although this involved him once again in a severe conflict with the skuas. These birds are virtually fearless and sometimes when Barnard was in the penguin rookery they would fly at him, even to the extent of actually hitting him on the head. They also demonstrated an insatiable appetite for other birds' eggs, particularly those of penguins and albatrosses, and they took great interest in the store of eggs he began to accumulate in his crude shelter. He placed the eggs in groups according to when he had collected them, first covering them with tussock grass to keep them dry and warm, and then overlaying this with turves to keep the marauding skuas at bay. Despite this he would sometimes return to the shelter to find that the skuas had clawed their way through to the eggs and on occasions he became so angry and frustrated that he would spend the better part of a day just throwing stones at them.

Day 133: 21 October

The skuas also caused Barnard another problem during a trip to an adjacent hill to gather vines for the fire. Once there he placed his club on the ground while he got on with the work, but when he had collected enough for his immediate needs and went to recover his club, he found that it had disappeared. Not unnaturally, this gave him a considerable shock and he began to wonder whether he really was alone on the island.

That night he lay awake puzzling and worrying over the mystery of the disappearing club when there was a sudden and ghastly shrieking noise from just above his head. Thoroughly alarmed, he rushed out into the darkness to find an owl sitting on the roof of his shelter, but he was so upset by the fright it had given him that he immediately attacked and killed it. Returning to bed after this incident, his mind returned to the mystery of the club, which was no nearer a solution and it took a long time for him to get back to sleep.[88]

Day 134: 22 October

On the 22nd, the weather was quite pleasant, so Barnard occupied himself with light jobs around the shelter. He had found a new club lying in the tussock, where it had presumably been mislaid by some visiting sailor in years gone by, and this, coupled with the spring weather, and the songs and antics of the birds, cheered him somewhat, although it also made him nostalgic for his distant New England home. In this thoughtful mood he ascended what he now referred to as Fairy Hill to gather some more vines for the fire and he carefully laid his new club where he knew he could find it again. Once more, however, when he had gathered enough vines for his requirements and went to pick up the club he found that it, too, had vanished. He was stunned by a second such inexplicable disappearance and searched the entire hilltop for some clue as to what was going on.

Not surprisingly, he began to think that there must be some form of 'evil genius' at large, but just as his mind was starting to envision all sorts of diabolical explanations the mystery was suddenly solved when he espied a skua flying above him, carrying the club, with the ring firmly clasped in its beak. Fortunately the thief was close enough for him to be able to bombard it with stones which succeeded in making it drop the club, which he then retrieved. So, as he returned to his shelter Barnard was able to reflect, with some relief, that the solution to the loss of the clubs was physical rather than metaphysical, although there can be no doubt that these incidents, coupled with his loneliness and the general uncertainty of his predicament, were beginning to prey on his mind.

Day 136: 24 October

Next day Barnard walked to the top of Rookery Hill, some 600 feet above sea level, to maintain his watch for a passing vessel. Being in a reflective mood – he did not have much alternative! – he sat there meditating on his situation, which led him to compare his lot with that of Alexander Selkirk. That Scottish sailor was marooned from 1704 to 1709 on one of the Juan Fernandez Islands in the Pacific, some 600 miles off the coast of Chile and his story had inspired Daniel Defoe to write the book *Robinson Crusoe*. Barnard knew the story well, although his meditations on New Island led him to conclude that Selkirk had many more advantages than he, having been put ashore on a semi-tropical island, fully equipped with clothing and stores, whereas he was on a wild, wind-swept, rocky outcrop, having been abandoned with only what he stood up in. Barnard did hope, however, that they would have one thing in common: a happy deliverance from their fate!

Day 137: 25 October

Barnard's 32nd birthday did not seem at first to give much cause for celebration and his early thoughts turned naturally to his home and family, as he went for a somewhat morose walk along the beach in an effort to cheer himself up. Being, as always, observant for anything which might alleviate his plight, he first noticed a small rock from which he could obtain a spark to ignite his tinder, thus replacing the stolen flint. The next discovery was even more important, because, taking a new route up the hill to the north of the bay, he discovered some large holes, caused by some earlier, natural fire. Examining them more closely, he observed that the sides were composed of peat, a substance he recognised from a visit he had paid to Wales on an earlier voyage.

In a state of some excitement he dug out a couple of lumps by hand and hastened back to the shelter, where he found, as he had expected, that they burned well, giving off considerable heat and a very pleasant smell. Greatly elated, he rushed back up the hill with a large sealskin bag which he filled to the brim and returned to the shelter confident that his problems with the fire were now largely solved. So, as he ended his birthday with a meal of freshly cooked eggs, he felt much better than for some time past, so much so, that he resolved to take a longer term view and to build a proper stone hut, with a decent sealskin roof.

Days 144–173: November

As the Falklands spring turned to summer the weather became more pleasant and one day Barnard was sitting outside his hut when he suddenly remembered the potatoes he had gathered for Mrs Durie in those far-off days aboard the *Nanina*. Full of hope he strode off down to the spring at Coffin's Harbour, but the most minute search only revealed three small roots, each the size of a pigeon's egg. Meagre as this find was, it still elated him and, having marked the spot, he left them growing, hoping that he would be able to use them as seed potatoes in the following year.

He had no doubt that the four sailors who had so cruelly deserted him had set off for Eagle Island, and as he wandered over his desolate kingdom he worried about their fate. During their earlier and almost disastrous, joint attempt to reach the site of the wrecked *Isabella* he had tried his best to educate them in navigation and sailing, and had pointed out such hazards as lee-shores and tide-rips. Now all he could do was to hope that they had listened to him and that they would profit from the knowledge and experience which he had tried so hard to pass on to them. As he well realized, despite their shabby treatment of him, those four men now remained his only hope of a release from the enforced and depressing solitude, which he was finding increasingly hard to bear. Indeed, in spite of everything, he told himself that he wished them no ill.

Meanwhile, the penguins had been returning to their island rookeries since September and were now present in vast numbers. There was a large rookery of rockhoppers at the head of the valley in which his shelter was situated and he regularly went there, sometimes to collect eggs, but at others just to watch the birds.[89] Occasionally he used to climb down the cliff at the southern end of the rookery, following the path beaten by the penguins, to the gully where they entered and left the sea. Barnard watched fascinated as the rockhoppers waddled down the track, jumping from rock to rock and then threw themselves into the sea to go out to search for food. He also saw them return and observed how when a marauding sealion blocking their way back to the beach the penguins would wait until a large group had assembled and then make a concerted dash for the shore, tacitly accepting that one or two must be sacrificed for the survival of the many.

Days 180–181: 7–8 December

By the start of the second week in December, Barnard decided that he had enough penguin eggs to last him for four months, which was as long as he could expect them to remain edible, so he resolved not to take any more. He also noted at about this time that Macaroni penguins had joined the rockhoppers, although in much smaller numbers.[90]

Next day he observed a new phenomenon, which excited his curiosity, when a strong south-south-west gale was followed by an exceptionally low tide, enabling him to walk out almost to the point where *Nanina* had been moored. He could think of no explanation for this, however, and so he continued working on his hut, whose internal dimensions were some nine feet in length and seven feet wide, while the tapering walls were three feet wide at the base.

His work was interrupted in the afternoon by a loud bang and looking up he saw that his flagpole had broken near the top and, somewhat mystified, he went over to investigate. There he found a dead shag lying on the ground and he could only conclude that the bird must have failed to see the pole and flown straight into it with such force that it not only broke the pole but also killed itself into the bargain.

Day 187: 14 December

Barnard was amazed and delighted to see smoke, which appeared to be rising from Beaver Island, and which he presumed to be man-made. Full of eagerness, he hurried down to the hill at the southern end of New Island and from its peak he confirmed that the smoke columns really were coming from Beaver Island. Such smoke signals were commonly used by sealing parties to communicate with each other and he hazarded a guess that it might indicate that at least one of his errant sailors was trying to make contact with him. It might, his desperate mind suggested, even be the shallop or *Nanina* trying to find him. He remained on the hill for some time, but, as there was a strong westerly wind blowing, he concluded that whoever it was would not be able to sail to New Island that day, so he went back to his hut to carry on with the building work.

Day 188: 15 December

He was up very early the next day and after a quick breakfast he laid a great pile of peat on the fire, which generated a huge column of smoke. That done, he set out for the hill to await developments, but nothing happened and eventually he fell asleep, only to be rudely awoken by some skuas, which were trying, with great impudence, to drag his sealskin moccasins off his feet and he lunged at them with his club. When he had recovered, he looked towards Beaver Island, but there was nothing to be seen and so, somewhat despondently, he returned to his hut where he remained sitting in the entrance watching the eastern approaches until darkness fell. Then, sick at heart, he turned in.

Day 189: 16 December

Despite the previous day's disappointments, Barnard was up early again the next day and, the wind being from the right direction for a quick passage from Beaver to New Island his anticipation grew as he rushed to the hill. Once again there was nothing to be seen and by now his mind was turning to suspicions of dark and evil plots against his life. After all, he told himself, the *Nanina's* people had to all intents sentenced the five of them to death by abandoning them back in June, while his four sailors had even more clearly tried to ensure *his* demise by leaving him in mid-October with virtually nothing upon which to survive. The trouble was that his spirits had been so raised by the sight of the columns of smoke, which, he told himself repeatedly, could only have been manmade, that the subsequent disappointment was all the harder to bear. By nightfall Barnard had convinced himself that an attempt on his life was intended by someone, so he started to take serious precautions, determined to defend himself to the last. Indeed, his fevered imagination led him to believe that they might have crossed secretly to New Island and could already be watching him.

CHAPTER 19

Day 190: 17 December

As a result of his fears, Barnard slept little that night and on the following morning his worst fears seemed to be correct when, as he was engaged in cooking dinner, he heard a sudden snapping noise, which he thought was that of a fowling piece being cocked. Thoroughly alarmed, he searched the surrounding area, but could find nothing and eventually returned to his meal. Then the sound came again and he searched once more, but again to no avail. On the third time, however, he happened to be looking at some spoons he had made out of shells, when he noticed that when the wind caught them they were blown against a board, and thus made the noise which had so worried him!

Barnard cursed himself for having frightened himself in such a way, but he could not, nevertheless, shake off the feeling that someone else was on the island. To set his mind at rest he took a walk down to the southern end of New Island and searched it minutely, but found no trace of humans. Somewhat reassured he returned to the hut and, it being late afternoon, he started to cook some supper. The eggs were sizzling in the frying pan when a movement attracted his attention and looking up he saw a rowing boat coming around the headland some eight hundred yards away.

Who could this be, he wondered, as he watched the approaching boat with a mixture of surprise and hope tinged with suspicion. He saw it draw into the beach about a quarter mile distant and then a couple of men went ashore, paused for a moment and then re-embarked, following which the boat was rowed into deeper water, where some sort of discussion took place. Then, at last, it headed towards him and as it approached he realized that it was, indeed, the missing boat and these were his erstwhile companions, who, for whatever reason, had decided to make contact with him once again. When they were about twenty yards offshore, they rested on their oars and sat watching him carefully. Cent was in the boat, too, and on espying Barnard his tail began to wag and he tried to jump into the water to rejoin his master, but Ansel hung onto him.

'Why don't you come ashore'? Barnard called out.

James Louder acted as spokesman. 'We wish to land', he shouted, 'but we are fearful that we have so offended you that you do not want us to rejoin you. We have put a hog ashore for you at the point, with some old newspapers that I picked up at the wreck, as I often heard you wish that you had some books or papers to read'.

Inwardly, Barnard was very pleased to see them, but he was not prepared to give in too easily. 'Let my dog come ashore', he replied, 'and you may go where you please with the boat. But, if you do not land him with my gun, you may depend upon it that if a ship ever arrives you will be made to repent of your late infamous conduct'.

'We wish to land and live with you again, and we hope that you will forgive us', Louder called back.

When Barnard saw that Albrook and Green were nodding their agreement, he relented, 'Come ashore then, and I will not reflect on you to account for your recent actions'.

At this, Louder, Albrook and Green broke into smiles and started to row for the shore, but were quickly stopped by Ansell, who had remained silent so far. He looked apprehensive, as well he might, because he knew that Barnard must consider him the instigator of the desertion.

'I hope you will forgive me, captain, as well as the others'? he queried, courteously, but with a touch of anxiety.

Barnard was quick to catch the use of the word 'captain', a significant acknowledgement of authority from such a man, but was still not ready to concede too quickly. 'You are four,' he told them, 'and if it is not your choice to land, let my dog come, and you may go to any other place, as I can get my living alone as well as with company. I instructed you last winter how to get yours and prevented you all from perishing. If you desire to remain here I am agreed, but I do not wish to control you, neither shall I refer to what is past, unless you commence the subject'.

At this Ansell broke into a smile and they pulled the last few strokes to the shore, Cent leaping from the bows to rush up to his master, barking loudly and wagging his tail energetically. The dog was followed by the four sailors, who, having pulled the boat safely onto the beach, rushed up to Barnard and took turns to shake him by the hand. Barnard at last felt able to show his pleasure and relief at seeing them again, telling them that he was glad at their safe return as he had been afraid that they were lost.

'We've been down to the wreck of the *Isabella*', Louder told him, 'but everything that might have been of any use to us has gone or was destroyed before they left. We have brought a few scraps of canvas and some bits-and-pieces, but that's all'.

'Did you find my baggage'? Barnard asked them, anxiously. 'There were two chests and a trunk in my cabin, with all my clothes and books, and they must have taken them ashore and left them in one of the huts for me'?

Their faces told him all he needed to know. It seemed to him to be a pointless act to deprive him of even those few things, but it was of a piece with everything else that had happened. At this point they produced a bottle containing a letter, which they had found at the wreck, but, as none of them could read, they had no idea what it said. Barnard pulled the paper from the bottle and read aloud the terse message, which was addressed to him. It told him that the crew of the *Nancy* had made every possible search for the missing five men, but, having failed to find them, had concluded that they were lost. It was signed 'W^m D'Aranda, Lieut & Comd^r' but only served to infuriate the American captain, who threw it on the ground in disgust.

Chatting amiably, they walked up to the hut, where the captain showed them the peat fire, his stock of penguin and albatross eggs, and the shoots from the potatoes, which were just poking above the ground. The sailors were very impressed and Green, Louder and Albrook at least, were clearly glad to be back with him, and to welcome someone who would exercise some sort of direction over their lives.

Thinking ahead to winter Barnard decided that they should make some sealskin blankets and was able to implement a plan which, alone and without a boat, had been impossible. It was the time of year when the fur-seals had their young and the latters' skins were ideal for his purpose. So, they rowed across to North Island, some three miles off the northern tip of New Island, where they dropped off Louder and Ansell to carry out the kill, but during the return the weather began to deteriorate so Barnard went back to take them off again, as it would have been impossible to recover them in a storm. Even in such a short time, however, they had managed to kill five young seals, so the expedition was not entirely wasted.

Days 194–196 (December 21–23)

A few days later Ansell, Albrook and Green went off on a seal-hunt, leaving Louder on cooking duties, while Barnard spent a quiet day working on skins for clothing. Barnard took the opportunity to ask the sailor, casually, about the cruise down to the wreck, but Louder looked quite alarmed and told Barnard that as recently as the previous day Ansell had warned the others that if they told 'the captain' about what had happened on the cruise he would kill them. Louder then added anxiously that Barnard should be on his guard against Sam, who, he said, was truly evil. Barnard gently persisted, however, and finally Louder hesitantly started to tell the story.

He explained that the plan to abscond with the boat and carry off Barnard's few things was proposed by Sam Ansell, who was constantly urging the others to join him, and assuring them that he was confident the brig had immediately left the Falklands, without running down to the wreck of the *Isabella* to take off those who had been left there. Ansell also told the three credulous sailors that they would be well supplied with good things from plentiful stocks that remained on Eagle Island and that when they chose to return to New Island they would load the boat with clothes, provisions and other necessaries, and then, accompanied by his girl, Bet Davis, they would all rejoin Barnard. After that, according to Ansell, they could all live quite comfortably until the arrival of a ship.

Louder paused and looked apologetically at the captain and then went on to explain that without really thinking about it, everything that Ansell proposed sounded so practicable and so very easy that the others almost considered it accomplished. On the day that they deserted him, Louder continued, they went over to Beaver Island, where they all joined hands and swore to be true to each other, and, to render the agreement the more solemn and binding, they had gone through the ancient ritual of cutting their hands and letting their blood mix together.

Having remained on Beaver Island for three or four days to catch a sufficient number of hogs, they decided that Green, the black American, was the only one that knew the Falklands waters, where the wreck lay, and how to manage a whale boat, so he should have the entire charge of the expedition. Thus prepared, they reembarked and proceeded on the passage to the wreck. It took them some three weeks, but when they arrived at the long wished for objective, all they found was a succession of disappointments; neither clothes, nor Bet Davis, nor a single one of those many good things on which their fancies had so long been feasting. Some shells, copper sheathing and iron ballast had been left behind, but that was of no use to them. Such a total failure of their hopes and expectations had made them all very melancholy, but Ansell more so than all the rest. He fretted and cried like a vexed child, Louder said, as if that could encourage his deluded comrades, but his disappointment soon found another vent in becoming very cross and brutal to his comrades – and particularly towards Louder.

The sailor paused at some memory and then continued, 'When the weather permitted we left Eagle Island for our return, being heartily tired of our expedition, as well as afraid of and disgusted with Sam, his want of judgement and his tyrannical behaviour. We desired nothing so much, apart from the arrival of a ship for our relief, as to be with you again, captain, on this island, and to submit ourselves to your guidance and control'.

'On our way back, being abreast of Port Stephens, and our provisions being expended, we landed on Bird Island, a small island, six or seven miles off the English Maloon. Green told us that he had been there before when sealing with you, captain, and that there was a rookery of penguins, where we could get eggs'.

'We found plenty of eggs, as Green said, and had loaded the boat, when Sam, without any provocation, got into one of his mad freaks and started to curse and abuse us. Then, out of sheer spite, he began to kill the penguins with his club, which really upset us and I told Albrook that Sam was a cruel man to kill these poor little innocent birds from whom we had just got a supply of eggs to support our existence. Unfortunately, Sam overheard me and ran up to me in the greatest rage, struck me on the head with his club and knocked me to the ground, raining blows on my body, foaming with rage and swearing he would kill me. Albrook was so scared that he dared not speak a word for fear that Sam would turn on him, but Green came running up and checked Sam's attempts at murdering me by reminding him of our sworn oath to be kind and forgiving to each other'.

Louder shuddered.

'We then launched the boat and proceeded towards Beaver Island. The return passage lasted more than five weeks and when we arrived at Beaver Island we immediately set fire to the tussocks on one of the small keys, which made the smoke you saw. We made several attempts to cross over to New Island to rejoin you, but we were prevented by Sam. On one occasion we even got part of the way over, when Sam took charge of the boat and turned back, saying that he hoped that you were dead, since if you were alive he supposed that you would take your greatcoat back off him'!

As Barnard digested this long story, Louder suddenly looked very anxious, and added a plea that, whatever Barnard did, he must not let out what he had just been told. If that was to happen, Louder said, Ansell would surely kill him.

Barnard reassured the anxious sailor, but added that, if the quarrel reopened, or if Ansell started to act 'out of hand' again, then he would have to take some action. He then enquired about the reaction of Green and Albrook to all this, but Louder told him that they were all three too frightened of Sam to discuss him with each other. Ansell got them together every evening when Barnard's back was turned and demanded to know what any of them might have told him, Louder adding that Ansell never gave him the title of 'captain' out of his hearing.

Barnard reflected that this whole business with Ansell was poisoning their lives and he needed to bring it somehow to a head. So he hatched a plan with Louder, telling him that when a job arose which required all hands, then all must join in and do their part. But, if Sam tried to order the others to do a job just for him, as he was very inclined to do, then they must tell him to do it himself, since the others were not his servants.

167

Day 197 (December 24)

The following morning Ansell, true to form, once again sought to bully Louder, pointing to the seal skins brought back the previous day and which had been placed in a stream overnight. 'You, Jim', he snapped, 'why don't you go and wash them skins! You're a lazy devil, you never do anything unless I tell you'.

Louder gulped and then stood up to face the bully. 'Sam, I don't expect or want any of your skins, so I won't wash them, peg them out to dry or have anything to do with them. When I want skins I shall go and get them myself'.

There was a momentary pause as everyone digested this unprecedented resistance and then Ansell, infuriated that the worm had at last turned, grabbed his club and rushed round the boat to attack Louder and bring him back under his control. Barnard was, however, ready for such a move and as Ansell raised his club to hit Louder, the captain swung his own club and knocked Ansell's out of his hands.

'What are you trying to do'? he demanded of the raging sailor.

'Kill that damned rascal who is skulking behind you', shouted Ansell, trying to get past the captain so that he could attack Louder with his fists.

'In that case, you will have to try to kill me first', Barnard told him. 'It's time we came to an understanding with you and all the hands, and to discover whether they are so weak or cowardly that they will continue to submit themselves to all your abuse'.

Ansell seemed temporarily nonplussed that anyone should stand up to him and turning to Green, told him that the villainous rascal Louder had betrayed them. Green, however, was not prepared to be considered a party to Ansell's behaviour and replied that at least Louder had never threatened to murder anyone, nor had he spoken disrespectfully of the captain. Barnard, seeing the opportunity to seize the initiative, told Green and Albrook that if they wished to join Ansell they should go and stand with him, otherwise they should come and join him, upon which they moved with remarkable alacrity and stood beside Louder and Captain Barnard, facing Ansell.

Now that the issue was fully out in the open and they had committed themselves to the captain, the three sailors told Barnard that they wanted to place themselves fully under his orders and that Ansell should be banished from their group. At this Ansell suddenly collapsed, broke into tears and came up to them asking for forgiveness. Barnard took the opportunity to warn him to behave himself in the future and relieved that the situation had not got any worse, they all hoped that the matter had been laid to rest.

Day 198 (December 25)

The next day Ansell appeared to be a reformed character, and even demonstrated that he was capable of behaving with some courage, if the occasion arose. They all wanted some more fur-seal skins and knew that there was a colony at the foot of the cliff to the north of Rookery Hill. Having climbed down to sea-level they found that they were separated from the colony of seals by a stretch of rough water but Louder, a good swimmer, took the end of a rope and swam across, followed by Green. Ansell could not swim, but was determined to take part, so Barnard and Albrook fastened him to the middle of the rope, and then controlled the rope as Louder and Green hauled him across, where he arrived without even having got his feet wet. Barnard then swam across, while Albrook stayed on the landward side.

The seals were incredibly tame, never having seen men in this inaccessible haven before, and the four men killed no less than one hundred and twenty, mostly pups, between them. They were still at work, killing and skinning, at dusk and so had to spend the night huddled on the wave-swept rocks.

Day 199 (December 26)

They finished their bloody work next morning and then passed the skins along the rope to Albrook. Finally, two of them swam across the gap, following which Ansell was pulled across on the rope and then the last man swam to join them. They were very tired, having worked hard and had little sleep, so they carried the skins only as far as the foot of the ravine where they left them while they returned to their camp, had a meal, and then fell asleep.

Day 200 (December 27)

The next day there was more heavy labour, first bringing the skins to the top of the ravine and then carrying them across the hill to their hut. Finally, however, they stood around the great pile of skins and, following the sealers' custom, took it in turn to select one skin at a time until all had been taken.*

Day 201 (December 28)

One of the three sailors took an opportunity to have a quick conversation with Captain Barnard, telling him that, despite appearances to the contrary,

* This originated from when two or more crews from different ships found themselves working on the same beach, where they would combine to kill and skin the seals, and then place the pelts in a pile and draw them in turn.

Ansell was once again plotting evil deeds. He was in a very sulky mood and the other three were positive that he was planning to injure, perhaps even murder someone, although they were not certain whom. Barnard had not himself seen any evidence of this, but he was convinced by what he was told that Albrook, Louder and Green were living in constant anxiety, so he decided that drastic action was needed and he hatched a plan to solve the problem once and for all, which he quietly passed on to the others.

Days 202–203: 29–30 December

Next morning the plan was initiated when one of the sailors proposed that they should send a party to Swan Island to fetch hogs, a task which would require, he said, four men. Barnard, playing his part, casually remarked that he would remain on New Island to watch for any passing vessel and so the four sailors set out, leaving at eight in the morning. Barnard spent a few hours up on Rookery Hill surveying the ever-empty ocean and then returned to do some domestic chores before turning in at dusk.

The next day followed the same pattern and he was fast asleep at about eight o'clock in the evening when he felt bundles of straw being pulled from under him and he heard a voice saying, 'Come away, Jim, you will alarm the captain'. But he struggled awake and went outside where he found Albrook, Green and Louder looking very pleased with themselves.

The men told him that on arrival at Quaker Harbour on Swan Island they had sent Sam Ansell off to fetch some firewood and had then put his things ashore. Looking back he had seen what they were doing and raced back, but not in time to catch up with them, so that he was left on the beach where he drew his knife and made a dramatic threat to kill himself. The three sailors rested on their oars and asked him, possibly without too much sincerity, not to take his own life, but promised that when a ship did eventually come to New Island they would then assuredly come to Swan Island to pick him up before they left for home. Ansell was distraught at this and cried that the island was haunted and that he could not survive there for more than three days. The others retorted that, although they felt sorry for him, the way he had behaved towards them left them no choice but to leave him on his own, expelled from their company. With that they rowed away to Beaver Island, where they hunted and killed some hogs, assisted as always by Cent, and then returned to New Island to report to the captain.

At the end of the story Barnard congratulated them on the success of the scheme. Then, with all of them feeling greatly relieved at being released from Sam Ansell's malevolent presence, they went to bed.

CHAPTER 20

Days 205–235: January, 1814

There now followed a period of relative tranquillity and Barnard introduced the observance of each seventh day as Sunday, based on the calendar he had instituted while he was alone. In addition, he found in one of the newspapers they had brought him from the wreck a prayer which he so much liked, as it seemed so very apposite to their situation, that he taught it to the others and which they repeated at times of stress:

'O God, who commandest us when we are in trouble to open our hearts and let our sorrows unto Thee in prayer, and dost promise to listen with compassion to our humble supplications, give us grace to approach Thee, that we offend Thee not in word or deed. Take away from us every impatient feeling, silence every unworthy expression, and let not our prayer assume the language of complaint, nor our sorrows the character of despair'.

Their spirits were cheered in a more temporal manner by the discovery that the boar and two sows which had been released from *Nanina* when she arrived back in September 1812 had now bred two litters. They caught one of the hogs with Cent's aid and found its meat delicious, but they were sufficiently far-sighted to resolve to leave the New Island animals alone, except in cases of emergency, so that they could breed.

There was a new air of confidence about the camp and the three sailors suggested to Barnard that they should return yet again to the wreck of the *Isabella* and scour the area one more time for anything which might be of use to them, such as planks, boards, nails, or pieces of rope. Barnard agreed at once and added to their list the pieces of sail which he had seen in use as roofing for the huts at Newtown Providence and also any carpenters' tools which might have been left lying around the camp. The plan agreed, they sailed away, and Barnard once more became a Robinson Crusoe, but as this was through choice, and of even greater importance, because he now had the faithful Cent as a companion, he felt quite cheerful.

This mood was quickly dashed, however, by a near disaster to both himself and the dog. Barnard had insisted that the men take most of the pork with them and when the little that remained was finished he apparently forgot their recent agreement to leave the New Island animals alone and set off with Cent to kill another hog. They soon espied a sow grazing with eight piglets and Barnard unleashed Cent, who shot off into the tussock grass after the sow. Barnard meanwhile had caught one of the piglets and was in the process of killing it when a large and very angry boar erupted from the tussock and charged at him. Taken by surprise Barnard just managed to evade the attack, catching the boar a glancing blow on its snout as it shot past, which only served to aggravate the beast yet further.

The boar turned and charged again, but Barnard grabbed hold of its ear and then called to Cent for help as he belaboured the beast on its head with his club. The dog rushed out of the grass and immediately seized the boar's other ear, but they then reached an impasse, since the infuriated boar was determined to attack, while neither Barnard nor the dog could afford to let him go. Barnard thus had no recourse but to continue to beat the boar about the head with his club and in the mêlée one of his blows hit Cent on the head. The unfortunate dog immediately released his grip and staggered off a short distance where it then stood, obviously concussed and confused by the heavy blow it had received.

This enabled the boar to devote its undivided attention to Barnard and the American, usually so determined in battle, decided that on this occasion discretion was the better part of valour. So, choosing his moment carefully, he suddenly released the boar's ear and leapt onto a high tussock, from which he was able to wield his club with both hands. These hard blows persuaded the boar that he was not going to win and he eventually desisted from his attack and, after a worrying pause, slowly retreated from the field of battle, turning periodically to glower at Barnard, who very sensibly remained on his tussock until well after the boar had disappeared from view. When he at last considered the coast to be clear Barnard descended and hastened to the dog, cuddling and making much of him in an effort to persuade the animal that the dreadful blow had been an accident. Fortunately it seemed that Cent's skull was not broken and so, pausing only to pick up the dead piglet, the two weary hunters made their way slowly back to the hut.

For the brave little dog this was only the latest in a long series of wounds and mishaps. The boars had vicious tusks sticking some four inches from their mouths and were very fierce fighters, as Barnard had just been reminded. Consequently Cent had numerous scars all over his body, had lost one eye and in one encounter had, in Barnard's words, 'received a blow which almost converted him into the neuter gender'. The normal pattern for an engagement was that Cent would search for a boar and, when he had found one, would bark loudly to attract the attention of the hunting party. When they arrived they would usually find the boar and the dog head to head a short distance apart, each trying to stare the other down. Then, as the hunters closed in, their clubs raised, the boar would suddenly turn and charge the nearest human, whereupon Cent would spring, fastening his teeth into whatever portion of the boar happened to be nearest. The humans would belabour the boar with their clubs, trying, if possible, to hit it in the small of the back, as they had found this to have the most effect. Sometimes, however, Cent would be thrown off and occasionally he was wounded, but up to now he had always been game for the next fight.

Day 236: 1 February

The summer weather continued to be relatively pleasant and Barnard led a quieter existence, helping Cent to recover from the blow to his head. He had anticipated that the sailors' voyage to the wreck would take some seven weeks, or maybe more, but at midday he looked out into the bay to see, to his very considerable surprise, the boat standing into the harbour. His mind made suspicious by previous tricks, he imagined that they had, for some reason, not been to Eagle Island, but his doubts were quickly dispelled and there was a joyful reunion as the sailors assured him that they had made a remarkably rapid passage and showed him an assortment of useful odds-and-ends which they had scoured from the *Isabella's* campsite to prove it.

Day 249: 14 February

They now decided that they would all go to Sea Dog Island, which lay some thirty miles away, just off Cape Orford, to obtain yet more sealskins. Prudently, they left a message in a horn by the entrance to the hut in case a ship called in while they were away and then, having loaded some skins for Ansell, they sailed to Quaker Harbour.

As they stood into the bay they spotted their exiled comrade and steered for a point some half-a-mile away and landed the presents for him. They then pulled away from the shore and waited until Ansell ran towards them but then they were astonished to see him fall to his knees, literally beseeching them to allow him to rejoin them. They were close enough to see that he was reduced almost to a skeleton and there was a quiet discussion in the boat, with Barnard feeling rather compassionate towards him, although Albrook was adamant that if Ansell were to be allowed to rejoin them, he would leave the boat immediately. Ansell could not hear this, but sensing that there were still some opposed to him, he changed his tack and asked them to help him move his campsite to the other side of the bay, as that would at least enable him to see New Island, which was not possible from the present site.

Those in the boat relented slightly and agreed to this. Then they relented even further and not only transported his stores, as he requested, but also took Ansell as well, although they still refused to take him back. So, once his stores had been off-loaded they insisted that he disembark too, and then they sailed to another island to spend the night.

Day 250: 15 February

Next day they sailed on to Beaver Island where they hunted for hogs, Cent eventually helping them to catch five good ones and they then prepared to make an early start the following morning. As they were about to turn in, however, Barnard suggested that they might take Ansell with them to Sea Dog Island. Then, if he misbehaved, they could always drop him back on Swan Island on the way back, otherwise they could hope that he was cured and allow him to return to New Island with them. The others eventually agreed to this proposal, albeit with some obvious misgivings.

Day 251: 16 February

Accordingly, they set off early the next morning and picked up the astonished and very relieved Ansell, who became almost delirious with joy when he understood that they were going to release him, even if only for a few days. So, reunited once more, they headed in a south-westerly direction, sailing through the islands, until they reached Tea Island just before nightfall.

Day 252: 17 February

Their cheery mood continued and the weather was fine, so they sailed along the southern coast of Swan Island in a positively jaunty mood and then on across the entrance to Smylie Channel. Just before sunset they rounded the dreaded Cape Orford, which Barnard had been so loath to attempt the previous winter when they tried to reach Eagle Island, and found a small beach on the leeward side of the headland where they made camp for the night.

Days 253–256: 18–21 February

The following morning they rowed across to Sea Dog Island where they landed Green and Ansell, together with their knives, a water-keg and half a hog. The other three then returned to the previous night's campsite, hauled the boat well out of the water and settled down to wait. After three days they saw a column of smoke rising from the island, signalling that the Green and Ansell were ready to be picked up and, on reaching them, found that the two men had collected some eighty skins of various sizes, a useful addition to their stock.

Days 257–318: 22 February – 24 April

Their intention had been to return, as they had come, along the southern coast of Swan Island, spending the night at Tea Island, but a stiff westerly was blowing and so Barnard had no choice but to go the long way around Swan Island in an anti-clockwise direction. They spent several days camping in the lee of Loup's Head, waiting for suitable weather to round the cape and while they were there they found a hair seal rookery and killed thirty, as well as some hogs.

One night they had a strange experience, when they were awakened by the barking of a strange dog, which they tried very hard to catch, so that they could tame it and train it to assist the redoubtable Cent. But, unlike so many of the animals in the Falklands, this one outwitted them and they never saw it again.

When they reached Quaker's Harbour they went ashore at Ansell's campsite, where they admired the two shelters that their untrustworthy companion had built. He also showed them two graves that he had found, although, the wind having obliterated the shallow carving, they were unable to tell whose remains lay there or what vessels they were from. Fortunately Ansell had conducted himself so well on the expedition that they now felt able to accept him back into their community, and so their little boat was very heavily laden as it took them back across the final stretch to New Island.

By this time Barnard had worked out that it was highly unlikely that any vessel would arrive before the Antarctic winter and he decided that it was time to take a longer-term view and to set the hut to rights. The walls were quickly completed, being some three to four feet thick and five feet high, while the rafters were made from the ribs of a whale which had been washed up on the shore and the roof from thatched tussock grass. While four of them went to Beaver Island hunting for yet more hogs Ansell stayed behind and in three days built an earthen bank around the hut, five foot high and with a six foot base, which he covered with grass sods, and the man, now eager to please, completed it well within schedule.

With relative tranquillity now reigning in the camp and with the confidence that stems from experience, their tastes now became slightly more sophisticated. Thus, since they already had an adequate stock of clothing, their thoughts turned to the cold winter nights and it was decided that they should all have sealskin sleeping bags for the coming winter, which would be filled with down from the geese on the island. Barnard knew of only one place where they could find fur-seal pups in the required numbers, which was at the foot of some cliffs at the southern end of New Island, which Barnard estimated to be some two-hundred feet high. There were, however, several problems, the most important of which were that they required a long rope and they also needed a lance for killing the seals and the only lance they knew of was the one they had abandoned at Hook Camp, during their first, disastrous and ultimately abortive trip to Eagle Island. The men were reluctant to repeat the voyage in which they had all so nearly perished and were also loath to have to drag the boat over the two-mile neck of land, but Barnard persuaded them that it would be worth all that labour and it was decided that all five of them would go.

Day 319: 25 April

Having placed the usual letter in the horn in case a passing vessel should call at New Island, they set off and a fine Westerly carried them past Loup's Head before nightfall and they rowed along the leeward shore until they found a good campsite.

Day 320: 26 April

The next morning they set sail early and soon found the place where they had pulled the boat across the neck of land, which arduous performance they repeated. This time, however, they experienced much less difficulty, as they were much fitter, better fed and the weather was much more pleasant.

Day 321: 27 April

After an early breakfast on 27th they set off again, with Barnard eager to discover where they had gone wrong in the earlier voyage. They could soon see Hook Camp in the distance, but to their great surprise they began to recognize familiar landmarks and Barnard suddenly realized that in the previous June when they thought that they were heading for McCockling's Lagoon they had, in fact, being going around in a semicircle and instead of heading south they had, in reality, been heading north.

The captain could now see that their error had been caused by a mixture of hopelessness, the seductive ability of land to give the appearance a desperate man wants it to have, bad weather, and the lack of either compass or map. He was even chagrined to see that at least one of their camps during

176

that disastrous voyage must have been on Swan Island, which he had thought that he knew so well! The mystery of that awful voyage resolved, they made for Doan's Head, which they now realized was the site of Hook Camp, where they recovered the lance with little difficulty and then headed south again, stopping for the night at Tussock Point.

Days 322–335: 28 April–11 May

Their spirits raised by the recovery of the lance, Barnard remembered that the previous year they had planted some wheat and left a pair of breeding hogs at Barnard's Harbour, so they decided to call in to see if any progress had been achieved. When they got there they discovered that the wheat had rotted in the ground and, although they saw traces of the hogs, which had obviously bred well, they could not find them. So, empty-handed apart from a few old, rusting iron hoops which they had found on the beach, they spent the night where *Nanina* had been moored in happier times and the next day sailed back to New Island, arriving in the evening, very tired, but reasonably content. The lance was quickly put to good use and several sealions were killed over the next few days, following which their skins were cut into circular thongs and after three days drying were knotted together to give them a good rope.

Days 336–338: 12–14 May

The time had now come to launch their project and so, the weather being fine and the sea reasonably calm, they set out in the boat and after rounding the southern end of New Island worked their way along the shore until they were abreast the seal rookery. Ansel and Louder had volunteered to be put ashore and they crouched in the bows waiting for a break in the waves, which were crashing against the rocks with great violence. Eventually Barnard decided that the moment had come, and at his command Green and Albrook pulled on the oars until they were close enough to a rock for the two men to jump. They had just managed to throw the two men a piece of pork when Barnard saw a huge wave coming and they pulled desperately to avoid it, but it hit them with great violence and flung the boat violently against the rocks, the sea coming within an ace of dashing the boat to pieces and seriously injuring the crew. Finally, however, the exertions of the oarsmen, plus, according to Barnard, a touch of divine intervention, got them off and as they returned to the other side of the island Barnard reflected that if the boat had been destroyed they would all have perished, since the rocks were so high and precipitous that there would have been no way of escape.

Once back at the camp the men assembled all the lengths of rope they could find, including the painter from the boat and, having tied them all together they found that they had a rope some fifty-five fathoms (330 feet) long. They lugged all this to the head of the cliffs above the seal rookery, where they drove a strong stake into the ground and made the rope fast to it. Green and Albrook then sat holding the rope while Barnard went to the lip and looked down. He could see two tiny figures far below, killing the seals as they had been told to do, but the noise of the wind, the roar of the breaking waves and the bellowing of the seals was such that they could not hear his shouts. He eventually attracted their attention by throwing stones and then dropped the rope, which, despite his careful calculations, still failed to reach the foot of the cliffs, leaving a thirty foot gap.

Louder, however, was able to climb up to the end of the rope and he then used it to haul himself up hand-over-hand, walking up the cliff-face with his feet. He eventually reached the top and reported that they were having considerable success in catching seals and was willing to go down again if someone would go with him. This Green and Albrook resolutely refused to do, which left the captain, who, with as good a grace as possible, descended to join in the work below. The three of them spent all day killing and skinning seals, followed by an uncomfortable and very wet night on the rocks, and then carried on through the next day and night.

On the third day they reckoned that they had had enough and started to remove the skins from the foot of the cliffs. This involved positioning one of the men half-way up, who hauled each load up to his perch, whereupon the two men on the top raised it the rest of the way. This was very slow and laborious work, but it was eventually finished and the last man was recovered by nightfall. The five men returned to their hut in the twilight, exhausted but content, with Barnard feeling distinctly relieved that a plan which had turned out to be considerably more hazardous than he had expected had, nevertheless, ended in complete success.

Mid-May – early June

They had now been marooned for a year and as their ceaseless search for food continued unabated, they once again came to the very edge of disaster. Ansell, Albrook and Green went to Beaver Island looking for hogs and as soon as they landed Cent caught the scent of a hog and shot off in hot pursuit into the tussocks. A short while later they saw the hog again, but Cent failed to reappear and so they hurried into the tussock seeking their faithful companion. They called him, but to no avail and eventually they returned to the beach where they hauled the boat up and, as usual, turned it over to use as a shelter for the night. Just before dark, however, Green suddenly announced that he could not bear to just sit and wait for the morning and set off back into the tussock to cast about for any sign of the missing dog.

He was standing on a high tussock, alternatively calling and listening, when he thought he heard a whimper from directly below where he was standing. Climbing down he pulled the straw at the foot of the tussock aside and found the entrance to a deep pit, at the bottom of which, and well out of his reach, was Cent, half immersed in water and mud. Green was so far away from his comrades that they would be able to neither see nor hear him, but, on the other hand, he was not prepared to leave the spot, as he was concerned that he would never find it again. He also thought that the dog would be extremely upset if he should now abandon him, however good the reason for doing so.

So the sailor settled down to pass the night in the tussock, but fortunately for them both their comrades became worried by his absence and, despite the darkness, set out to search for him. They soon found him and having seen the problem, one of them ran back to the boat and fetched a rope, with which they lowered Albrook, who was able to scoop up the dog and bring him back to the surface. Thus reunited, they returned to the beach, very relieved and making much of their ever-faithful companion, whom they had once again come close to losing.

Cent had, however, finally reached his limit and when they set out next morning on yet another hunt for hogs he got as far as the edge of the tussock and then just lay down. Nothing they could do would persuade him to move, and despite repeated attempts over seven days and increasing pangs of hunger, he simply refused to re-enter the tussock. The dog had clearly decided that 'enough is enough' and they were eventually forced to return to New Island empty handed and very hungry. Fortunately they discovered that Barnard and Ansell had developed a snare for geese, which had proved highly effective in catching the birds, which were returning to the island in large numbers.

August – November

With the worst of the winter past, Green, Albrook, and Louder proposed yet another trip to the wreck of the *Isabella*, leaving Ansell with Barnard, which was agreed upon and the three men set off confidently, despite the poor weather. The two left behind spent most of their time in the hut doing minor chores, with Barnard helping to pass the time by teaching Ansell to read. This was so successful that the sailor was soon able to read the scraps of newspapers that had been brought back from a previous trip to the wreck and he became so proud of this achievement that Barnard sometimes overheard him having mock conversations with his mother.

'Mother, do you have a newspaper'?

'No, what do you want with a newspaper'?

'I want to read it'.

'Poo, you can't read'!

'Can't I? Send to the Bell and borrow one; I would read it'.

One day Barnard came in at the end of one of these conversations and asked Sam what his mother had answered to this and the sailor replied with a laugh that she had asked him who had 'learned him to read'? and he had replied, 'The American captain I was so long with'. This friendly conversation between Ansell and Barnard, and especially the unconscious reference to the 'American captain', showed how far their relationship had developed and how well Sam Ansell was now responding to firm but kindly treatment.

It snowed quite heavily on 10 August continuing into the following day, when the two men were sitting in the hut only to imagine that they could hear men's voices. Running out, and thinking perhaps that rescue was at last at hand, they found instead that it was their three comrades, home very much earlier than expected. It transpired that they had only got as far as Cape Orford, where they had been driven on to a beach and the boat had been seriously damaged. They decided to return to New Island, but on the way back the wind became so strong that it carried away the mast and they had only managed to struggle back by rigging a jury sail. Once again it was the skill and ability of Green, who as usual was in command, that had enabled them to survive.

The storm continued and it was not until the 15th that they were able to get a good look at the boat, where they found that the garboard strake had started and was split in several places. It took them two days to repair her, using a red-hot wire to make holes for the last of their nails, but they then took her to Swan Island to prove the repairs.

Thus encouraged, the three men set off again, leaving Ansell and Barnard to continue their local work. When the weather was good they were always out hunting for food, but when it was bad they remained indoors, their latest project being to produce wooden plates and spoons, together with knives and forks which they fabricated from old pieces of iron, while cups were made from old pieces of tin, rivetted with copper nails and fitted with wooden bottoms. All this gave a feeling of domesticity and if all they could drink out of the cups was hot water, who was to blame them if they sometimes pretended that it was tea or coffee?

They unearthed the potatoes, which had been stored carefully, and planted them in a specially-dug plot. They also found their stock of peat running low and their original source on the hillside was now exhausted. The nearest alternative was on Burnt Island* in the harbour and fortunately they were able to cross to it at low tide, although the digging and the carrying back was very hard work.

Barnard began to worry about the boat, but she reappeared on 6 October, very heavily loaded with yet more scraps from the wreck site, including some small potatoes (which were immediately planted) and a pair of spectacles, which they had found in the ruins of General Holt's hut. The men thought that their captain would like to wear them, but the ever-practical Barnard was much more interested in their potential use in starting fires. The men told him that the journey down to the wreck had been very rough, but that their stay at the deserted Newtown Providence and the return journey had been less of a trial.

On 20 October they took advantage of the good spring weather to start work on an extension to the hut and found that they could lay the walls much better by setting the stones in a sticky blue clay, which they had discovered near the campsite. They were by no means comfortable and the requirement to hunt for food never went away, but they were now in a much better state to survive than they had been a year previously.

Having completed as much work on the hut as was possible with the materials to hand Barnard decided that he should make another routine trip to Swan Island, accompanied by Albrook and Louder. They set off for Loup's Head in a stiff breeze, but once out into open water they found that the wind was much stronger than expected and the high sea was soon threatening to swamp the boat. They were forced to alter course and make for the nearest shelter, but even so a heavy wave half-filled the boat and they had to bail desperately to avoid sinking.

They eventually reached Ansell's old campsite, where they spent a couple of days resting and sheltering from the gale. The hunting being poor and the winds too strong to attempt to reach Loup's Head, they worked their way down to States Bay, going ashore periodically to hunt, but with little success.

Day 533: 25 November

The wind was still high and so they remained where they were. They found a couple of elephant-seal pups, which they killed since Barnard knew that their skins would make excellent parchment for his journal. That night there was very heavy rain and a high wind, and they were very surprised to be woken by loud thunderclaps, the first they could remember hearing since their arrival in the Falkland Islands.

* Presumably modern Beef Island.

Day 534: 26 November

They spent the remainder of the night chatting quietly under the upturned boat and were up at first light. The wind was too strong and the seas too high for a return to New Island, so Barnard decided to go up a nearby hill to examine some bushes which he had once noticed secreting a resinous gum that acted as an effective cure for cuts and stings. The three men toiled up the hill and then parted, Barnard and Albrook continuing to climb, while Louder went off round the hill to see what he could find.

Suddenly, there was a sharp cry from Louder, as if he had suffered a serious injury, frightening Barnard and Albrook, who immediately imagined that some disaster had befallen him. They dropped the boxes they were carrying as they rushed to their comrade's aid, while Cent, also hearing Louder's screams and sensing the excitement, shot past like an arrow. When they arrived Barnard and Albrook found Louder rolling on the ground, crying and shouting, with the dog jumping over him and barking loudly. Suddenly Albrook, who was younger and faster than his captain and had recovered more quickly, went pale, staggered, turned round and grasped Barnard's hand, whereupon he burst into tears, gabbling incoherently.

Barnard was quite taken aback by this extraordinary performance and thought for a moment that their diet had tipped both men over the edge into insanity. But he eventually managed to make out that Albrook was gabbling, 'Two ships! Two ships'! Then Louder contained himself sufficiently to get to his feet and with the sailors holding Barnard's hands, the three men stood looking across the sea to where, in the distance, two undoubted ships were standing in towards New Island. The sailors cried uncontrollably, hanging on to their captain, Cent jumped up and down, barking wildly and sharing in the excitement which he could feel but not fully understand, while Captain Barnard at long last felt a single tear trickle down his cheek. 'Come, come, boys', the ever-cautious captain counselled them, 'don't let this glad sight overjoy you, for fear that they may pass without stopping at New Island'.

But, in their hearts they had no doubt that salvation was at last, and totally unexpectedly, to hand and they sat on the hillside, their search for balsam completely forgotten. As they watched, the two vessels bore down towards Swan Island for several hours, before tacking to head for New Island.

Finally, the three could contain themselves no longer and rushed down to the shore, where Barnard had to restrain the others from launching the boat immediately, because the surf was high, a heavy sea was running and the wind was dead against them. They curbed their impatience with difficulty and waited until mid-afternoon for low tide, when they rowed up towards

Quaker Harbour in order to be well to windward, in preparation for a run down to New Island the following morning. Their impatience lent them wings, however, and they made such good progress that they were able to put the helm down and head for New Island that same afternoon.

As they sailed across towards New Island Barnard donned his last shirt, or what was left of it after he had cut the sleeves and tail for use as tinder, and they discussed what they would say when they boarded the strange ships. The two British sailors told Barnard that they were determined to claim to be Americans, which would, they hoped, prevent them from being 'pressed' if they came across a British man-of-war and had even been learning New York street names from Green to reinforce their subterfuge.

Just before six o'clock they reached the two vessels, which had anchored in Ship Harbour, just where, in fact, *Nanina* had once been. They discovered that the arrivals were both British whalers: one the *Indispensible*, William Buckle, master; the other *Asp*, John Kenny, master. The three excited men came alongside *Indispensible* and climbed a ladder to the deck where they were greeted by William Dunkin, the mate, who directed Captain Barnard to go below to join the two British masters, who were waiting to greet him. Barnard, however, declined this invitation because, for the first time in many months, he was acutely embarrassed by his wild and unkempt appearance, and so Buckle and Kenny had to come on deck instead.

Barnard's face was almost completely covered in a beard some eight inches in length, which was much denser than those of his younger comrades. He was clothed entirely in home-made seal skins, which included not only a jacket and trousers, but also moccasins and a hat, the whole giving an impression very closely resembling that of the fictional Robinson Crusoe. As he stood on the deck of the *Indispensible*, feeling once again that almost-forgotten motion of a ship riding at anchor, Barnard felt rather overcome by the sudden and unexpected change in their fortunes.

Kenny told him that his ship, *Asp*, had been the first to reach New Island and they had been very surprised when they espied two strangely clad figures, standing on a rock and shouting. He had sent an officer in a boat to find out who the men were, but with orders not to bring them off. Their entreaties were, however, so painful to see that the officer had relented and brought them aboard where Green had immediately shown his value by piloting the vessel into a safe anchorage, Captain Kenny being a stranger to the island.

Kenny had then taken the two men aboard *Indispensible*, where Buckle had asked what ship they were from and they had both, including Ansell, immediately said that they were Americans off the brig *Nanina* of New York. At this, Buckle immediately knew who they were and asked them where Captain Barnard was and, on being told that he was on another island with the other two sailors, he had become suspicious, threatening to put the two men ashore again until their captain reappeared. Green accepted this phlegmatically, but Ansell fell at once to his knees and begged, in God's name, that they be allowed to remain, although, fortunately for him, at that moment Barnard's boat was seen approaching from Swan Island.

The two Englishmen then asked Barnard whether the sailors had treated him respectfully and obediently, this always being a matter of concern to masters, Captain Buckle reminding him that sometimes, in situations such as he had been in, the men either treated their captains badly or proved disobedient. Perhaps Barnard paused for just a moment as he recalled Ansell's misdeeds, but, if he did, his two questioners did not notice and he answered that they had all exerted themselves to make the situation as comfortable as the severity of their sufferings allowed.

Buckle then explained that all British ships had been warned to keep an eye out for Barnard and his men, through a letter distributed by Admiral Dixon at Rio de Janeiro. They then chatted about the war, the Englishmen telling him that the conflict was still going on and describing how the *Essex* had been captured, and about the engagement between the *Shannon* and *Chesapeake*, all of them British victories, and it was not until much later that Barnard was to discover that his two rescuers had completely overlooked the many American triumphs.

November 27–28, 1814

The next two days were devoted to foraging ashore, where the five survivors showed-off their hunting and trapping skills to the British sailors. The two ships replenished their water tanks and stocked up with peat and then, late on the 28th, when the wind abated slightly, they weighed anchor and sailed away, Green and Ansel in *Asp*, and the other three aboard *Indispensible*.

It was over and they had survived.

CHAPTER 21

Precisely five hundred and thirty-four days elapsed between the abandon-ment of the five men by the mutineers aboard the *Nanina* and their rescue by the two English vessels. During that time they had endured two Falklands winters, overcome numerous crises and undergone almost constant hardships and privation. Astonishingly, not one of them suffered any serious illness, nor did they even appear to suffer from scurvy. There was certainly no fruit and the only vegetables Barnard mentions are the potatoes, but James Choyce, the second mate aboard *Asp* went ashore on New Island and recorded in his memoirs that, 'they had also made a garden, in which they were growing sixty potatoes, the produce of one root they had planted the year before, besides kidney beans, turnips, celery &c'.[91]

Their primary preoccupation throughout this ordeal was always the hunt for food, which engaged them every day in one way or another. Fortunately there were quite a number of animals and plenty of birds for them to eat, provided only that they could be caught. Some, like the geese and the younger hogs, were not at all difficult, while others, and especially the boars, were always a challenge. Barnard occasionally talks of finding very small fish in streams and they also caught some mullet on one occasion, but they do not seem to have gone in for any serious fishing.

Not only did they not get ill, but they also never suffered a serious injury, despite repeatedly being placed in positions of the greatest danger. They were regularly sore or bruised, but for the humans, at least, there was not even one broken limb. The same could not be said, however, for the ever-faithful Cent, who had an eye gouged out by one of the ferocious boars and was repeatedly wounded, his body being covered by scars. Despite all this, only once did he show any sign of reluctance, which was after he had fallen down the pit on Swan Island, and he seems to have recovered from that fairly quickly.

Of the men, the only one to cause any trouble was the Englishman, Ansell. He proved to be a born trouble-maker, first aboard *Isabella* during the voyage across the Pacific and later in the camp at Newtown Providence, following the shipwreck. He had, by his own admission, been involved in the conspiracy to take over *Nanina* and it is curious that he volunteered to go with Barnard on that fateful day, even though he well knew that the others were only waiting for Barnard to be out of the way to take over his ship. Perhaps he was given some promise that he would be picked up later if he cooperated in getting Barnard out of the way, or perhaps it was just a case of there being no honour among thieves.

Whatever the reason, there is no doubt that during the first part of the period on New Island Ansell's behaviour was appalling, in part towards Barnard, but even more so with his fellow sailors. His bullying tactics enabled him to terrify the others into obeying him and he fully deserved his period of exile. However, he eventually came round, partly through pressure from his fellow sailors, but mainly because Captain Barnard, through a mixture of toughness, kindness (for example, in teaching him to read) and Christian charity, finally mastered him.

The other two British sailors, Albrook and Louder, were pleasant enough and capable young men, but it was Green, the black American who was the outstanding member of the group. His one weakness was to allow himself to be persuaded into joining the conspiracy to desert Barnard, and he must have found Ansell's violent temper and repeated threats of injury quite frightening. Nevertheless, the respect in which he was held by Albrook and Louder clearly eventually rubbed off on to Ansell as well, and apart from the first few days when they abandoned Barnard, Green was always the accepted leader in Barnard's absence.

Green eventually led four expeditions down to the wreck of the *Isabella*, a long and hazardous voyage in those dangerous waters and in such a small boat. Three of these trips came to within an ace of disaster, but they survived and Green always brought them safely back to New Island.

The whole group was, in fact, regularly on the verge of total disaster. During the first, abortive attempt to reach the *Isabella*, when Barnard became so confused, there were many occasions when they could have been thrown onto a rocky shore and perished from either drowning, starvation or exposure. Similarly, when they went round to the windward side of New Island to catch the fur-seal pups in May 1814, all five men were committed and if their boat had been damaged on the rocks they could well have found themselves trapped at the foot of the cliffs where they would have been slowly killed by starvation and exposure.

Above all, however, in this epic of human survival there shines the character of Charles Barnard. Plunged into this predicament by one of the shabbiest tricks in maritime history, he found himself with one boat, one dog and four sailors, only one of whom was actually under his command. There must have been occasions in the dark of the night when he felt like giving up, when he might have joined the four sailors in bewailing their fate and, with them, crawled under the upturned boat to wait for death. But Barnard knew that if he gave up, even for a moment, their chances of survival would just disappear.

In addition to everything else, during the period of his abandonment Barnard spent several months totally on his own. Although he kept himself busy it is clear that his mental state was gradually beginning to deteriorate and the frights he was given by the skuas, the owl and the clicking spoons all show a man approaching his mental limits. Fortunately, the other four men returned before too long and, with them to look after once again, Barnard quickly returned to normal.

Like so many commanders in different fields, he alone had nobody else to turn to. The four sailors could moan to each other, shout, scream, weep or pour their troubles out to Barnard, but for the captain himself there was no shoulder to cry on. Well, no physical shoulder, perhaps, but there can be no doubt that his faith was a rock, and his belief that the Almighty would see them through kept him going through many a dark moment.

Perhaps the only sign of emotion he ever showed was when he sighted the two ships approaching New Island. He was a man steeped in the austere Anglo-Saxon and New England traditions that the strong keep their weaknesses to themselves. But, on this occasion, and after all that he had been through, not even the sternest and most puritanical critic could blame him for a solitary tear.

PART 6

The Aftermath

CHAPTER 22

To tie-up the loose ends of the story it is now necessary to return to *Nanina* which had arrived in England under command of Prizemaster Marsh in April 1814. While Marsh was being court-martialled the well-established routine for the reception of prizes was set in motion and to the staff of the Navy Yard the American brig was simply the most recent in a large number of 'Yankee' ships to have been taken during the war. The brig's details were recorded, the cargo itemized and the paperwork prepared so that the responsible legal body in London, the ancient High Court of Admiralty, could hold a preliminary hearing, which took place on 2 June, 1814.[92] The cause for the hurry was that some of the cargo was beginning to rot, as was clear from the decision of Samuel Parson, Esquire, Doctor of Laws, who held a meeting in his Chambers at Doctors' Commons and noted that 'it appears by the said Attestation that the Cargo had received Damage from being so long on board and prayed – and the Surrogate at his Petition decreed – the usual Monition and Commission of Unlivery'.

Once the monition had been issued it was possible for the cargo to be offloaded and a legal notice of intended action was then officially posted, although no objections were lodged, which was hardly surprising as the only people who might do so were still either en route from Rio de Janeiro to the United States, or in the case of Charles Barnard, fighting for his life in the Falkland Islands. So, when the issue was brought before the Prize Court on 29 November, 1814, the case of '*the American Prize, Nanina*, Valentine Barnard, Master,' appeared quite straightforward and the High Court of Admiralty duly pronounced: 'the said Ship, her Tackle, Apparel and Furniture, and the Goods, Wares and Marchandizes therein taken, to have belonged at the time of the Capture and Seizure thereof to Enemies of the Crown of Great Britain, and as such, or otherwise, subject and liable to Confiscation. And condemned the same as good and lawful Prize taken by His Majesty's Ship *Nancy*, William D'Aranda Esquire Commander'.

At this point D'Aranda must have been feeling financially secure, since as captain he would receive the lion's share of the prize money. The only thing to lie between him and this goal was the seemingly minor legal formality of a one year delay, during which an appeal could be lodged. Unknown to D'Aranda, however, events were starting to move in the United States. Barzillai Pease was the first to bring *Nanina*'s story to public attention in the United States when he took a copy of the statement the four captains had made before Mr Rutter in Rio de Janeiro to the editor of the *Hudson Bee* in New York State. This was one of the leading New England newspapers and the editor was delighted to publish the protest in full, prefacing it with an unequivocal statement:

'We request the attention of the reader to the following account of the almost unparalleled ingratitude and treachery of the crew of a British ship to the crew of an American vessel – the latter having saved the lives of the former, whose vessel had been wrecked, and they in return for this humane act, seized and made prize of the vessel and property of their preservers! Were it not that such a nation as Britain existed, this act of treachery might be correctly styled unparalleled; but British history is full of incidents of such black ingratitude. Such conduct, even in our enemy, cannot fail to call forth the indignant feelings of every American who has a drop of patriotic blood flowing in his veins'.[93]

Valentine Barnard, who had been abandoned at Rio de Janeiro on *Nanina's* departure for England, did not reach the United States until 23 November, 1814, and he immediately reported to the joint-owners, Messrs John B. Murray & Sons, in New York to give them the full story of the loss of their vessel. Shortly afterwards the War of 1812 was ended by the Treaty of Ghent, which was signed in that Dutch city on 24 December, 1814, although as always in that period, the news took some time to reach those most affected, the announcement not being made in New York until 11 February, 1815.

When they heard this welcome news the Murray brothers decided that more than mere rhetoric was required and, believing in the rightness of their case, as well as exhibiting a touching faith in British justice (and, of course, wanting their money back!) Mr John Murray went to London to see what he could do. He arrived in June, 1815, armed with all the documents he had been able to assemble, including an affidavit signed in New York by Valentine Barnard and Barzillai Pease as recently as 19 May.

Once in London Mr Murray engaged an agent and they both visited the Admiralty where they discovered that they were still well within the year's grace for an appeal. They were received with considerable courtesy, since their appearance, although unexpected, had coincided with the arrival of a letter from Admiral Dixon, in which he expressed some unease about the validity of the capture of the prize.[94] Pulling these two strands together, the Secretary of the Admiralty, John Croker, decided that a proper legal opinion was needed.

The wheels of the British judicial system now began to turn, the lead being taken by a legal office known as 'Doctors' Commons'. Mr Gostling of that office decided that he needed more information from D'Aranda and the latter, no doubt very surprised to be contacted by such an august person, hastened round to lay out his case in greater detail. On 30 July all the papers were sent to the Advocate-General for his opinion and this was duly given on 15 September, 1815.[95]

The 'opinion' came as a bombshell and boded ill for D'Aranda, since the Advocate-General, while agreeing that more evidence needed to be garnered, nevertheless wrote that:

'Mr Murray should appeal instantly from the Condemnation, for the purpose of enabling the Crown to interpose its Authority, to direct restitution if that be deemed advisable. . . . There is Reason to think, from the Acts done by Admiral Dixon and the propositions for Restitution and other Circumstances, that perhaps the Capture ought not to have been made'.

Meanwhile, in the United States the Department of State made low-level representations about the case in 1816, followed in 1817 by a formal letter from the Acting Secretary of State addressed to the British Ambassador, which stated that the capture of the *Nanina* had not been justified. His language was flowery, but the message clear:

'It would appear that the Crew of the *Nanina* had the strongest titles to the treatment due to generous friends, instead of being handed over to hostile captivity. On behalf of the owners, the peculiar and affecting circumstances attending this loss of their property makes a powerful appeal to the fairest principles of comity between nations. Without doing more than barely to advert to those principles, I venture, with entire confidence, to ask the favor of your good offices, in laying their case before your Government in such a way as you may deem fit, that a door to enquiry may be opened, and such indemnity afforded, as a spirit of kind and liberal justice may be found to dictate'.[96]

A surprising feature of this letter is that it concentrates solely upon *Nanina*'s capture and does not once refer to the abandoning of Charles Barnard and Jacob Green (the United States government was hardly likely to protest on behalf of the three British sailors). This may have been because Barnard had returned to the United States on 23 October, 1816, and this letter was written six months later, but the fact that the men had survived did not excuse the initial act of their being castaway on New Island.

In London, the case dragged on for many months, with opinions divided as legal arguments centred upon two issues. The first, and most obvious, was the sequence of events in the Falkland Islands, but the other was the actions of Admiral Dixon and Captain Valentine Barnard in Rio de Janeiro. Concerning the latter, one school took the view that Admiral Dixon had tacitly admitted the validity of the American case by his repeated offers to return the ship to Valentine Barnard, while the other school considered that the American had prejudiced his case by declining the offers. All agreed, however, that it was a complicated legal issue and that it was best left to the highly-trained legal minds of the appeal court to unravel.

It was not until 5 February, 1818, that the case was finally heard by the Prize Appeal Court of the High Court of Admiralty, but their finding was brief and unequivocal:

> '*Nanina*. The Lords . . . Pronounced for the Appeal, reversed the Sentence appealed from, retained the principal Cause and therein admitted the Claim given in this Court for the Ship and Cargo, pronounced the same to belong as Claimed and decreed the said Ship and Cargo to be Restored, or the value thereof to be paid to the Claimant for the use of the Owners and Proprietors thereof on payment of the Captors' Expenses – Nicholl then acknowledged the Receipt of said Expenses and Jenner acknowledged that his Party had received the Nett Proceeds after deducting said Expenses'.[97]

The only minor sting in the tail was that the owners had to pay the captor's expenses, but the Murrays seem to have accepted that without a quibble and there the case ended. The capture of the *Nanina* was finally judged to have been unjustified and Lieutenant D'Aranda and his crew never received the prize money they had so eagerly anticipated. Also, old Valentine Barnard's obstinate stance in Rio de Janeiro had paid off and the owners received full compensation for the whole loss, rather than just the bare and ransacked hull that he had been offered.

CHAPTER 23

The principal characters in this drama all had many years of their lives left and we shall now see what happened to them after they left the Falkland Islands and what effect this great adventure had on the rest of their lives.

Charles Barnard's return home from New Island was by no means either easy or quick. He departed from New Island on 28 November, 1814, aboard the *Indispensible*, accompanied by Louder and Albrook, both of whom were still posing as Americans, and, of course, Cent. *Indispensible* doubled Cape Horn and when they were off the Peruvian coast Barnard and his companions decided to land and so they were dropped some 40 miles offshore in their boat, which they had brought with them aboard the British whaling ship. The voyage to the shore turned out to be more hazardous than expected, even for such hardened and experienced sailors, and then, to cap it all, when they eventually made it to the shore they were identified as Englishmen, arrested and imprisoned for a time in a Spanish fortress.

After various adventures with the Spaniards Barnard reached Lima in Peru, from whence he sailed in the *Eliza*, a British whaler, on 16 May, 1815. After three months aboard this ship, Barnard asked to be put ashore on the island of Mas á Fuero, where he intended to catch seals in an effort to recoup his financial losses. He was given plenty of provisions and with an American sailor to keep him company he was duly dropped off, *Eliza's* captain promising to pick them up in three months' time.

Unfortunately, Barnard did not find as many seals as he had expected and he was very relieved when an American vessel, the *Millwood*, called in for water. He was even more pleased when the master, who knew the Barnard family, offered the two men a passage, which both he and his companion were happy to accept. They left in mid-October and by December were in the Sandwich Islands, where the ship took on a cargo of sandalwood and then sailed for Canton in China, arriving on 4 April, 1816. There the *Millwood* took on a new cargo destined for the Netherlands, so Barnard transferred to the *Trumbull*, another American vessel, in which he reached Martha's Vineyard on 23 October, 1816.

It was four years and four months since he had left the United States, and a month short of two years since he had left New Island. As he made his way home he promised himself, as sailors so often do, that he would never again venture abroad. But, and again as sailors so frequently do, his domestic intentions proved to be short-lived and he undertook many further voyages. Indeed, in 1821 he was back at New Island, albeit this time not as a castaway, where he met the British Captain James Weddell, who recorded their conversations in his memoirs.[98] Barnard published his book '*A Narrative of the Sufferings and Adventures of Captain Charles H. Barnard*', in 1829 and was certainly alive in 1831 when he was elected a member of the Marine Society of the City of New York, but no record of his death can be found.[99]

Valentine Barnard remained in Rio de Janeiro to try to obtain the release of the *Nanina*, which ended in failure in December 1813, as described in Chapter 15. He then had some difficulty in finding a ship to take him home and he did not reach the United States until 22 November, 1814, where he stirred Messrs Murray and Sons into action before retiring to his home in Hudson. He welcomed his son home in 1816 and was able to explain to Charles all that had happened aboard the *Nanina* following his departure on that fateful overnight trip to Beaver Island. Not surprisingly, Valentine never went to sea again and he died in 1823.

Barzillai Pease left Rio de Janeiro in early October 1813 and reached his home in December of that year, where he was greeted with the news that his son had recently been drowned. He quickly apprised the United States authorities of the events in the Falkland Islands and had in his possession a copy of the report sworn before Commercial Consul Rutter, which he gave to a local newspaper, the *Hudson (NY) Bee*, and which was duly published.

Pease then became commander of United States government transport vessels on Lake Ontario from 1815 to 1824, following which he spent several years in various vessels operating along the New England coast. He stumbled on evidence of buried treasure and set off to find it, but, in common with many of his undertakings, the expedition was dogged by ill-luck. First, the ship taking him to the site caught fire and sank, which was the fourth time he had been in such a marine disaster, and then the treasure proved to be an illusion.

William D'Aranda returned to England in 1814 a sick man and took up residence in London, which was fortunate, because he soon found that he was required to make frequent visits to the Admiralty and to the lawyers at Doctors' Commons to give further evidence on the events in the Falklands. Once his health had improved he was able to obtain a new seagoing appointment in 1816, which was no mean achievement in a post-war period of retrenchment, when thousands of other naval officers were being placed on half-pay. He served briefly as first lieutenant in two ships on the West

Indies station (HMS *Pique* (28 April–15 June, 1816) and HMS *Junon* (16 June–16 August, 1816), following which he spent rather longer aboard HMS *Niger* (4 September, 1816 – 22 September, 1817) on the North American station, where he must have found himself uncomfortably close to some of his former captives at times! The inevitable could not, however, be delayed for too long and when his ship returned to England in September 1817 he was placed on half-pay.

The decision of the Prize Appeal Court in February 1818 came as a real blow, since he had confidently expected a large sum of money as his share of the proceeds of the sale of the *Nanina* and her cargo, and it caused him a bitterness he was to harbour for the rest of his life. Quite regardless of the *Nanina* issue, however, it would appear that he could reasonably have expected some compensation from the owners for the rescue of the passengers and crew of the *Isabella*, plus the sale of that part of her cargo which was brought back to England. It is, however, quite clear that he did not, as he stated in the somewhat sarcastic reply he made to the editor of O'Byrne's '*Naval Biography*' in 1845, where, in outlining his career, he stated that he had 'saved 46 persons from shipwreck – and had the honour of sacrificing his Health and Fortune in the Service'.[100]

In 1819, despite being placed on half-pay, D'Aranda, then aged 31, married Elizabeth Dixon, a thirty-five year old widow whom he had known since they were both children in Billericay. She had inherited a considerable sum of money from her first husband, an Essex brewer, which must have alleviated the loss of the prize money for D'Aranda. Just over a year later, she gave birth to a son, who was also christened William, and these new responsibilities led D'Aranda to seek a return to full-time service. He therefore wrote to three of his former superiors (Admiral Dixon, Captain Greene and Captain Heywood) asking them to write testimonials on his behalf to the Admiralty, which they duly did. Unfortunately for D'Aranda many other officers were doing the same and the letters had no effect.[101]

D'Aranda was a dogged man, however, with a keen sense of grievance and in 1827 he again returned to the attack, submitting a 'Memorial' to the Lords Commissioners of the Admiralty. When this achieved nothing he then took the final course open to him and petitioned the King, but by this time he was clearly regarded as something of a nuisance and he still got nowhere. His reply to O'Byrne has already been quoted and he was still pursuing the same bitter line when he responded to an official Admiralty questionnaire in 1848, where he stated that he had 'rescued 46 British subjects from wreck and starvation in which service I lost the use of my limbs. I *never* received reward or compensation'.[102]

Like so many former naval officers, D'Aranda turned to the merchant service and by 1848 he was able to state that he had become familiar with the new-fangled steam propulsion through service aboard steamers, one such being the curiously-named SS *Pestonjee Bouranji*. He was master of this vessel from August 1842 to February 1843, which operated in the Caribbean and the St Lawrence under his command, although it normally transported emigrants and convicts to Australia. D'Aranda relinquished command at once, however, when he was offered re-employment by the Royal Navy, who gave him a job on 'emigration service' in African waters aboard SS *Senator* until 1845. At this point he and his wife moved from London to Southampton, where they took up residence at 24, Bugle Street, a delightful and old-fashioned thoroughfare, which opened on to the waterfront and which, more probably by accident than design, was no more than fifty yards from the church where his great-great-great-grandfather, Maitre Elie D'Arande, was buried.

Then, in a development which is surprising by today's practice, he returned to full-pay from 1845 to 1854, during which period he served as 'Admiralty agent for mail' in the Mediterranean. He had been a lieutenant since 1808, but in 1854 he was given the newly-instituted rank of 'Commander (Retired)', which enabled him to leave the navy with dignity and a small pension.

The D'Arandas' only child, their son William, married in 1842 and moved with his wife Charlotte to Southampton in 1848, where they and their three children lived close to his parents. When Elizabeth died in 1858 she was buried in the nearby St Michael's church, within feet of the grave of her husband's distant ancestor, but it would seem that by that time William junior and his family had left the area, since William D'Aranda senior remained in the city, moving in as a lodger with a widowed dressmaker. He died there on 10 October, 1872, at the ripe old age of 84 and no trace of his Will can be found, although he seems to have left his possessions to another Southampton family to which he was distantly related.[103] So, his final years were spent within sight and smell of the sea, which he had loved so much and which had cost him so dearly.

The Durie family reached Buenos Ayres aboard HMS *Nancy* where they bade farewell to D'Aranda and were back in Scotland in late 1813, taking up residence in Edinburgh. Their daughter Eliza Providence was baptized at Lamlash on the Isle of Arran in the Firth of Clyde on 27 February, 1814, exactly one year and one week after her birth on another, but much more remote, island in the south Atlantic. A son, Charles, was born in 1815, followed by two more daughters: Susan in 1817, and Agnes in 1818. The Duries' first daughter, who had been born in New South Wales and lived through all the adventures in the Falklands, had also been called Agnes, and the use of the name for a second daughter suggests that the first Agnes had died some time after the family's return to Scotland.

For some reason Durie waited until November, 1814, a full ten months after his return, before sending a letter to the Admiralty commending Lieutenant D'Aranda's conduct in rescuing them, which ended with fulsome praise for 'this meritorious officer to whose determined perseverance in surmounting every obstacle towards effecting our relief we are so much indebted'. Mr Croker, the Secretary to the Admiralty, had, however, already seen a lot of correspondence on the subject and merely made a tart note on the corner of the letter that 'their Lordships have already been informed of Lieutenant D'Aranda's conduct' and consigned Durie's tardy letter to the file.[104] Robert Durie was still not entirely free of the *Isabella*, since he became involved in the legal proceedings over the prize appeal and was required on several occasions to send statements to London concerning various aspects of their adventures in the Falklands.

Durie inherited the family estate in 1819, becoming 'Robert Durie of Craigluscar,' but he began to ail and trustees had to be appointed in January 1825. Joanna-Ann took him to Edinburgh, presumably for medical treatment, where he died on 24 April, 1825, at the early age of 48 and still a captain. Joanna-Ann had him buried in the family vault in Dunfermline Abbey, where his remains lie in the family tomb just one hundred feet from the grave of Robert the Bruce, and then this determined woman once again set about ensuring the survival of her family. She had already written to the Commander-in-Chief of the Army about her son Malcolm by her first marriage, as a result of which the young man was commissioned into the 23rd Regiment of Foot on 10 April, 1825. Meanwhile, she still had four children by Robert Durie to look after, who were then aged twelve, ten, nine and seven, respectively, so she wrote a lengthy 'Memorial' to the Commander-in-Chief asking for a pension to help her to bring them up.

'Your Memorialist', she told him, 'on this voyage home had so extraordinary an escape that I am induced to state the particulars to your Royal Highness. On 10 February, 1813, our ship was wrecked on one of the uninhabited Falkland Islands in the Pacific and on 20th (I) was delivered of my eldest daughter which circumstances connected with our forlorn situation rendered my case the more extraordinary to compassion. Your Memorialist after enduring the privations incident to such a calamity and without any expectation of relief were after a lapse of five months rescued from our dreary abode by the appearance of a ship in a disabled state nearing our island and which was His Majesty's Gun Brig *Nancy* and who learnt of our shipwreck by the most providential arrival of a boat our sailors constructed and manned to gain the coast of South America, a distance of some 1500 miles and which they so fortunately covered in six weeks to Buenos Ayres and was the cause of our escape. . . . . Your Memorialist concludes in the hope that your Royal Highness will take her memorial into consideration and grant her with her four children such pension as your Royal Highness may think proper.'[105]

Joanna-Ann's geography was at fault in placing the Falkland Islands in the Pacific rather than the Atlantic, and her memory was selective in omitting any mention of the Americans and the *Nanina*, but her 'Memorial' was probably as unusual as any received by the Commander-in-Chief. The outcome of her petition is not known, although it is to be hoped that it was successful, but her family certainly prospered. Charles became a doctor and inherited the estate on achieving his majority in 1837, although he died at the early age of 29, while his three sisters all married well and went on to have children of their own. So, this remarkable and determined lady should have felt some satisfaction that after all her adventures, and despite the loss of two husbands, she achieved success through her children.

Richard Lundin left *Nanina* at Rio de Janeiro where Admiral Dixon made him write a short description of his adventures, which the Admiral then forwarded to the Secretary of the Admiralty with a strong recommendation that the young officer's gallant conduct be commended to the Commander-in-Chief of the Army.[106] Having apparently abandoned Mary-Ann Spencer at Rio de Janeiro Lundin then returned to England in a packet ship, arriving at Falmouth on 2 December and he then travelled overland to London, where he was at last able to deliver Governor Macquarie's despatches.

He was promoted in January 1814 'without purchase,' a sure mark of official approbation, although, unfortunately for the young Scotsman, there was no vacancy in his own regiment, as a result of which he was made a captain in the York Chasseurs, an English regiment raised solely for service during the Napoleonic Wars. Then, as with so many other officers following Napoleon's defeat at Waterloo, Lundin became a victim of the peace and was placed on half-pay in 1815. He seems to have spent most of the remainder of his life quietly at Auchtermairnie, inheriting the title and the estate on the death of his father Christopher in 1823.

There are only two further traces of him, the first being a War Office form he completed in 1828, where he stated that he had returned some five years previously to his family home at Auchtermairnie. He also confirmed that he was still unmarried, which suggests that the romance with Mary-Ann Spencer, which had been of such importance as to spur him to return to the Falklands in the *Nancy*, did not endure in the harsh realities of life ashore. He died in November 1832, still unmarried, although some relative must have discovered his manuscript as the last trace of this courageous officer is the article published in the Edinburgh Review of 1846. He is buried in the family grave in Kelloway, Fifeshire, in Scotland.

Sir Harry Hayes returned to Ireland in late 1813, where he was described by an eyewitness as 'a portly person, wearing striped trousers, and a blue coat with brass buttons, having a rubicund face, charged with effrontery, and shaded by the broad leaf of a straw sombrero'.[107] The rest of his life seems to have passed quietly, although he tried to regain his previous social position, but without any great success, and although he had numerous male friends, women, not surprisingly, kept well clear of him. He died in Cork in May 1832, aged 70, and was buried in the family vault in the crypt of Christ Church, Cork. His daughter became the wife of Mr Burnett, later the Colonial Secretary in Van Diemen's Land, while a nephew became the editor of *The Australian*. An obituary in an Irish newspaper stated that 'the suavity and gentlemanly manner he possessed made him endeared to every person who had the honour of his acquaintance' – a view with which Miss Pike and many in authority in New South Wales would certainly not have agreed![108] Both his houses still stand, with Vaucluse House in Sydney now a State monument where the story about the snakes still arouses interest; indeed, a recent investigation confirmed that there are still traces of Irish peat in the grounds surrounding the house. His house in Cork, a fine Regency building, is now the headquarters of the Munster Motorcycle and Car Club, a body of which the fast-living and adventurous Sir Harry would doubtless have approved.

'General' Holt also returned to his native Ireland on 5 April, 1814, where he settled in Dublin with his wife, the ever-faithful Hester, and younger son. He used his money to purchase a public house, but, sadly, this venture proved to be an expensive failure and he sold up, moving to Dunleary where he built some houses and spent the rest of his life quietly, living on the rents. He died on 16 May 1826, bitterly regretting ever having left New South Wales and after his death his younger son wasted little time in returning to the colony, where he rejoined his elder brother.

Of the four sailors who endured so much on New Island, Jacob Green and Samuel Ansell left aboard the *Asp*. There is no further trace of Ansell, but Green transferred to another British whaler, the *Cyrus*, and was aboard her when she called at Callao, Peru at the time that Barnard was in that port. The captain of this British whaler was very impressed by the American's skill and behaviour, and asked Barnard to persuade him to sign on aboard his ship, which was duly done and Barnard also presented the ship's captain with his dog, Cent. After some more whaling in the southern oceans the *Cyrus* returned to England from whence it is presumed Green found another ship to take him back home to the United States. Louder and Albrook stayed with Barnard until they reached Callao, where they shipped aboard the British vessel *Wildman* and then they, too, disappear from this story.

Captain Brookes made his way to England from Buenos Ayres after his epic voyage in the open boat, where he bought a new vessel, the *Spring* and sailed her out to New South Wales, arriving on 5 March, 1814, accompanied by his wife and children. He eventually purchased a large estate, became a Justice of the Peace (a far cry from his days aboard the notorious *Atlas!*), and died in 1834 after being gored by a bull on his farm.

His court martial appears to have been the last straw in his naval career for Midshipman Marsh. Even though he had been found 'not guilty', he decided to leave the navy, giving as his reasons the outbreak of peace and the lack of any friends in influential positions to advance his career.[109]

Like many others in this affair, the owners of the *Isabella*, Messrs Keir, Buxton & Co, sought to make good their losses and wrote a letter to the First Lord of the Admiralty, which is a model of the disingenuous commercial communication and stretches the truth to its very limits – and, in some places, beyond. They averred that the *Isabella* had put in to the Falkland Islands for water, which was not strictly correct, since although that had been Higton's original intention, he had, in fact, changed his mind well before they approached the shore. The owners then went on, however, to try to place the blame for the disaster elsewhere, their letter stating that, 'As there is strong reason to believe that the detention of this vessel at the then approaching stormy season and the necessity created by the addition to the number of persons on board of putting into the said island was the cause of the serious loss'.[110]

In other words, they were trying to put at least part of the blame on Governor Macquarie in far-off New South Wales, because he had held the vessel back for eleven days and had placed sixteen additional passengers aboard (fourteen Royal Marines, plus two wives)! This preposterous charge overlooked two basic facts. First, that the stormy season in the Falklands is from May to September and the wreck occurred in February. Secondly, according to both Holt and Lundin, who were not only present on the night concerned but also sober, the weather on the night of the wreck was mild and visibility good.

The purpose of the company's letter was to seek early payment from the Admiralty for the demurrage and the cost of transporting the fourteen marines. There was not one word of thanks in this impertinent communication either to the Admiralty or to the captain and crew of the *Nancy*, nor was there any mention of reimbursement for the rescue of the people, whose plight was due to the incompetence and drunkenness of the master they had appointed. It is to be hoped that they did not receive payment.

CHAPTER 24

It is now time to make a reckoning and to decide who, if anyone, was to blame; who behaved well and who badly? First, there can be no doubt that Higton was a thoroughly poor ship's master. From the moment that the *Isabella* left Port Jackson he was regularly seen to be drunk, which was serious enough. Worse than that, however, not only did he hazard his ship off Campbell Island, but he also failed to retain command. Captain Brookes may well have been the more experienced mariner, but he was a passenger, and any reasonably competent and self-respecting master in Higton's position would have thrown him off the quarterdeck when he tried to interfere in the running of the ship. That Higton did not do so is evidence of his lack of assurance and competence, which is reinforced by his drunken confession to Holt on the evening before the *Isabella* ran aground.

It would appear that Higton was trying to obtain water free of charge and without having to pay harbour dues, both of which would have cost him money had he called in at a South American port. Further, as some of his crew were suffering from scurvy, it could be that he was also intending to find supplies of fruit and vegetables. But, whatever the reason, his decision to put into the Falklands was totally misguided, since he had no adequate charts.

The shores of the Falkland Islands are littered with shipwrecks, but that of the *Isabella* must be one of the least excusable. Higton had seen the islands clearly on the day before they hit Eagle Island, and that night the weather was clear and the wind moderate, while a glance at a chart shows that, having decided to go round the Falklands to the south, he failed to lay-off sufficiently.

Even after that, however, the first contact with the rocks, despite the loss of the rudder, was not fatal and, again, a competent master could have taken advantage of the calm inside the reef to resolve matters and refloat the vessel. Higton had, however, lost control of the sailors, who became involved in an almighty and, as they thought, terminal carouse. Indeed, according to both Holt (who was an eye-witness) and Barnard (reporting the views of other passengers after the event), Higton was himself so drunk that he was unable either to save his ship or to supervise the safe evacuation of the passengers.

Despite all this, once they were all ashore, Higton retained both legal and moral responsibility for both crew and passengers, but again failed to exercise it. Initially, the hull of the ship was still sound and, even though the mainmast was broken, the ship might have been refloated and a jury-rig used to sail to South America. Higton, however, once again failed to control the situation and when some of the crew hacked holes in the hull in an endeavour to reach the pipes of madeira the hull became beyond repair.

The one initiative that Higton did take was the construction of the boat intended to take the remaining survivors to Buenos Ayres. However, both Holt and, in particular, Barnard, criticized the location chosen for the construction as being extremely ill-advised, since it would have been virtually impossible to launch the vessel had it ever been completed. Finally, in this litany of incompetence, Higton took no discernible action to condemn the abandoning of three members of his ship's crew - Albrook, Ansell and Louder – nor did he make any attempt to speed their rescue. It is thus clear that Higton totally failed in his duties as the master of the *Isabella*.

Mattinson was undoubtedly the mastermind behind the taking of the *Nanina*, as stated by Ansell, who was one of his henchmen, to Charles Barnard, and confirmed later by Valentine Barnard. Mattinson claimed to be a former Royal Navy sailor and had talked about the value of the *Nanina* as a prize as soon as he had recovered from his brush with death in Falklands Sound. He first caused trouble several days later while in Barnard's Harbour and then caused yet more while the brig was lying at New Island, before Barnard left on his ill-fated trip to Beaver Island. Finally, he led the takeover itself.

Quite apart from the illegality of his actions, the most disgraceful aspect of Mattinson's actions is that he had himself been rescued from almost certain death by Barnard, when he and his comrades had been plucked from the jolly-boat in the middle of Falklands Sound. Coupled with this singular piece of ingratitude, Mattinson was also totally unconcerned that his fellow conspirator, Ansell, was one of those abandoned with Barnard. It is, thus, difficult to avoid the conclusion that Mattinson was a truly evil and callous man, for whom no excuse can be found.[111]

While Charles Barnard had absolutely no responsibility for the loss of the *Nanina* he did, nevertheless, exercise poor judgement in several respects. First, it is difficult to understand why, when he left Eagle Island to collect the *Nanina*, he took no less than twenty people with him in the shallop, of whom such a large proportion were British, including six sailors and seven Royal Marines, the latter even taking their firearms with them. He could not, of course, have forecast that he would, quite by chance, come across the jollyboat, and thus have to take four additional British people on board, but, even so, the proportions were unwise, since he left the Americans in a minority both in the shallop and on Eagle Island.

Secondly, it seems an odd choice that he should have personally led the foraging trip from New Island to Beaver Island. There had already been several instances of trouble aboard the *Nanina* and in his absence the only Americans remaining aboard were his elderly father, the somewhat erratic Pease, and Havens Tennant, a foremast hand who was unlikely to influence the issue. It would thus appear that, if the trip to Beaver Island really was essential, he should at least have tried to persuade someone else to lead it, because he was the one man still preventing an enforced takeover of the vessel.

Barnard, however, had been brought up as a Quaker and was essentially a man of peace, and at the very worst he can only be accused of a considerable degree of naïveté. There are suggestions in Barzillai Pease's diary that Charles Barnard was difficult to get on with, but there is no evidence from any other source to support this and, in any case, Pease himself was an odd and unpopular character.

Set against this, however, are Barnard's magnanimity in undertaking to abandon his sealing enterprise in order to rescue the distressed survivors of the *Isabella* and his splendid achievement in ensuring the survival of the four marooned sailors. The details of his account cannot, of course, be corroborated since the sailors who were with him left no records, but there is no reason to doubt his word. Indeed, the simple fact that, 534 days after being abandoned, they were on New Island, all alive, and not only uninjured but in robust health, is sufficient testimonial to his skill, determination and leadership.

Valentine Barnard tried to hold out against the mutineers at New Island, even though the Americans were heavily outnumbered, but when he appealed to Durie for support, the British officer declined to come to his assistance, which left the American with no chance of preventing the takeover. His actions in Rio de Janeiro where he took the lead in the negotiations with Admiral Dixon are more difficult to account for. The British Admiral tried very hard to persuade him to take over the *Nanina* and ensured that the vessel had been put to rights in preparation for the voyage to the Falklands. Dixon was also fully prepared to give the Americans a certificate of safe conduct, which would have been honoured by any British man-of-war that had chanced upon them during their voyage from Rio to the Falklands and then onwards to New York.

Despite all this, Valentine Barnard still held out, insisting that there must be an undertaking that by accepting the return of the *Nanina* he would not nullify any future claim for full compensation. This seems strange when the first priority should have been to embark as soon as possible for the Falklands to rescue his son and his four comrades. D'Aranda's appearance on the scene in Rio did nothing to resolve the issue; indeed, his offer to return the vessel provided the Americans undertook to pay all the harbour fees seems to have been cynical, to say the least, although an appeal by Barnard to the American commercial agent or the consul for funds could well have been successful.

Barzillai Pease is something of an enigma. His diary is of considerable value and he is one of the few to have kept such a journal who made the majority of entries on a daily basis. He seems to have quarrelled with most people at some time during this voyage and he was certainly on bad terms with Charles Barnard on *Nanina's* voyage south, although it is probable that there were many personal disputes in the confined quarters of any nineteenth century vessel during such a long voyage.

Far more serious, is Pease's claim that he twice took charge of the brig. On the first occasion (20 April, 1813) he states that following the dispute at Barnard's Harbour 'at length the charge of the Brig was excepted by me and on 20th sat Mr Mattinson free',[112] a claim that is not supported by Barnard's account. Then, following the British takeover at New Island, Pease took charge of sailing the *Nanina* to Eagle Island, which he does not mention at all in his journal, although that he did so is made clear in the deposition made by the Americans in Rio de Janeiro:

'The marines and the crew immediately commenced getting her in readiness for the sea and on the following day got under way. B. Pease represented the situation of the vessel to capt. Dure and the risk she would run sailing among the islands when there was no person acquainted, and that in case they would stop at Beaver Island he would act as pilot on the occasion'.[113]

Valentine Barnard confirmed this to his son, when they met following Charles' return to the United States.[114] This does not mean that Pease conspired with the mutineers, but it does suggest an ambivalence in his behaviour, in which case his dislike of Charles Barnard may have played a part.

Captain Brookes, despite his cruel and disastrous voyage in 1801/2, proved to be a tower of strength during the voyage of the *Isabella*. He saved the brig from shipwreck on Campbell Island and there can be no doubt that his prompt actions after the vessel hit the first rocks on Eagle Island saved many lives. Like all master mariners he would have been very sensitive to the dignity and responsibilities of the *Isabella's* master, and so, despite Higton's undoubted incompetence he held aloof, except when the lives of those aboard would be at hazard unless he intervened.

Brookes' third achievement during this voyage was however, his greatest. The difficulties and dangers involved in sailing a seventeen-foot boat, loaded down with men and provisions, across one thousand miles of the stormiest waters in the world cannot be overstated. Brookes, however, seems to have been most matter-of-fact about the whole business and quietly disappeared from the scene once he was certain that a Royal Navy brig was being despatched and he never, as far as is known, published an account of his remarkable experience.

It has to be admitted that Durie laboured under three disadvantages. First, his attention was undoubtedly diverted from wider matters by the presence of his wife and children, for whom he naturally felt a very direct responsibility. Secondly, and related to this, he appears to have been under the influence of his strong-willed wife, whose sole priority was, quite simply and very understandably, the survival of her family. Thirdly, as an army officer, he was essentially a land animal and consequently must have found the ship-board activities uncongenial, although he did have some experience of nautical matters, both through his naval grandfather* and through his long voyage to New South Wales several years previously.

Until the arrival of Lieutenant D'Aranda, Durie was the senior King's officer on the islands and he had been given direct command of the only military force, the fourteen-strong Royal Marine contingent, by the Governor. He had also been a Justice of the Peace in New South Wales and thus should have had more than the usual knowledge of legal matters. There should, therefore, have been little doubt that had he given direct orders to the Marines they would have been obeyed, except, possibly, during the drunken orgy at the time of the shipwreck.

Durie was not only a signatory to the agreement made with the Americans on Eagle Island, but he had also been directly involved in drafting it, so he could not claim that he did not understand precisely what had been agreed. Further, Durie's position was always respected by Charles Barnard, who claims to have consulted him at every stage while on Eagle Island, in the shallop and on board the *Nanina*. Finally, according to Barnard (and there is no reason to disbelieve him), it was the pleas of Captain Durie and the tears of his wife that persuaded the American to agree to take the party in the shallop and which led to all the subsequent troubles.

Charles Barnard is quite explicit that, when the *Nanina* arrived at New Island in April, 1813, he discussed the whole question of what to do next with his father, Pease *and* Durie. Barnard is also clear that Durie fully endorsed the decision to remain at New Island for the time being. At the time of the British takeover there were nineteen people aboard the *Nanina*,

* See Appendix C

207

of which three were Americans, and five were women and children, which means that the takeover was conducted by ten people: Mattinson, four of *Isabella's* sailors and five Marines. Durie's behaviour may, of course, have been influenced by the tales of other mutinies (of which there had been a number during the Napoleonic Wars), and he would also undoubtedly have been anxious because his wife and two very young children were on board. He may also have remembered the scenes of drunkenness when the *Isabella* hit the rocks, where discipline had totally broken down.

At the time of the takeover off New Island, however, the *Nanina* was in no immediate danger and there was no panic. It would, therefore, have been astonishing if a strong word of command from him could not have stopped what was going on, at least with the Royal Marines, and they were the only group with any weapons. Nevertheless, it seems from the American evidence that he did not even remonstrate with the men and the deposition made by the Americans to Mr Rutter at Rio de Janeiro includes a telling phrase:

'Captain (Valentine) Barnard requested of captain Drure that he would use his influence with the marines and prevent them from their proceedings and assured him that as soon as the boat returned the vessel should proceed; but captain Drure refused to act on the occasion..'.[115]

Durie later claimed that when they were on New Island he gained the impression that Charles Barnard intended to remain there until Spring, ie, for a period of some five months. This does not seem tenable, however, and both Charles Barnard's journal and the other Americans in their statement in Rio de Janeiro (the 'Rutter document') are adamant that a delay of, at most, several weeks was intended, since the weather was so bad. In addition, Durie and the other British people seem to have overlooked the fact that the major proportion of the American crew had remained on Eagle Island and thus Barnard was bound to return there.

There was one possible justification for taking over the *Nanina*, which Durie might have been expected to advance: namely, that the two nations were at war and had he not done so, he could have been accused of dereliction of duty. In none of his subsequent explanations, however, did he ever make such a claim, relying instead on the statement that it was because the Americans had gone back on the undertakings set out in the written agreement.

Finally, Durie could have acted with greater determination when the *Nanina* sailed past Beaver Island by insisting that a more thorough search be made for Barnard and the four sailors. He later told the Admiralty Proctor that he thought that Charles Barnard had gone direct to Eagle Island and that they would thus overtake him, but this seems an implausible explanation.[116]

All these actions (or lack of them) makes Durie at the very least an accomplice in what went on, but, by virtue of his rank, he cannot avoid the main responsibility. Charles Barnard, however, (who, it must be said, was not a totally disinterested commentator) was scathing where Durie was concerned, writing that:

'This contemptible Sir Jerry had surrendered all his manliness to his lady wife, for safekeeping, for the sake of being occasionally warm at a dinner party or review. He had emasculated himself in feeling, and was a mere puppet that moved as she pulled the strings, so it was she that actually held the balance; for like the boy who governed his mother, and she the father, and he the people; Madam Durie governed the automaton Durie, he the marines, and they the sailors and passengers'.[117]

This is reinforced by Lundin, who says that:

'without sufficient determination of character to quell these and similar acts of misconduct, Captain Durie eagerly availed himself of the opportunity which was now presented of extricating himself'[118]

Holt mentions Durie frequently in his *Memoirs*, but nowhere does he criticize him directly. However, in alluding to the events on New Island, he makes one of the strongest of any condemnations in his book stating (with considerable justice) that abandoning the five men was:

'a disgrace to the British flag, and much worse in every respect than the seizure of the *Nanina*'.

The legal proceedings in England were extremely slow, but in the end provided an excellent example of justice at work, although the refusal of Valentine Barnard to accept the return of the *Nanina* in Rio de Janeiro caused the court some hesitation. The lawyers tended to concentrate upon the issue of the taking of *Nanina* as a prize by Lieutenant D'Aranda, but Sir Christopher Robinson at the Doctors' Commons also addressed the question of the earlier taking of the American vessel at New Island:

'If the persons who had been rescued had risen as captors on their benefactors, it might have been said that there was that debt of natural gratitude between them that ought to have surpassed the Rights of War accruing to such captors'.[119]

That seems to come as close as a careful legal mind could come to condemning the action at New Island. Indeed, it would appear that, had the courts decided to pursue this matter, then Durie, rather than D'Aranda, might well have been the man in the dock.

Mrs Joanna-Ann Durie occupied no official position, but undoubtedly had a considerable impact on events, as Charles Barnard indicates. She appears to have been a woman of some charm and she swept Robert Durie off his feet during his brief sojourn on the Isle of Wight. Barnard seems initially to have liked her and refers with apparent pleasure to his first evening on Eagle Island, when she described the others on the island, 'with great spirit and humour, but, unfortunately, if correct, they were too deeply shaded to rely on the honour of those described'.[120]

Joanna-Ann's personal problems should not be underrated. She had an eighteen-month daughter to look after and during the shipwreck she was subjected to stresses which no woman in her ninth month of pregnancy should have to undergo. Then a few weeks later she gave birth to Eliza Providence while lying on the earthen floor of a ramshackle hut, assisted by two women with little experience of midwifery and in a situation where, had anything gone awry, there was absolutely nobody to offer any form of help. Charles Barnard regarded her as a most formidable person and attributed many of his problems to her activities and, in particular, to her influence over her weak husband. One thing is certain, however: Joanna-Ann was determined that her family would survive and in that she succeeded.

From the moment he arrived in the Falkland Islands, Lieutenant D'Aranda was the most powerful man there, with an armed man-of-war and a formed body of sailors and Royal Marines under his command. What he thought and did were, therefore, of crucial importance.

He was certainly aware from very soon after his arrival of the written agreement between the shipwrecked people of the *Isabella* and the Americans. His own official report on his activities in the Falklands states that:

'. . . upon landing I was informed that a Shallop belonging to the American brig *Nanina* of New York had in April anchored in a bay on the opposite side (of the island) and that in consequence of an agreement entered into with the people on board of her..'.[121]

None of the remaining records state who kept this document in the period following its signature on 4 April, 1813; it could have been retained by either Durie, Higton or one of the Barnards, or there may even have been more than one copy. If it was in the possession of one of those left on Eagle Island it would certainly have been shown to D'Aranda and even if it had been taken by Charles Barnard in the shallop to be placed with *Nanina's* other papers there can be no doubt that one of those remaining on Eagle Island (Higton, Holt, Fanning or Hunter) told him what was in it.

It is, however, quite certain that the document passed into D'Aranda's hands at some stage, because it was one of a number of documents he handed to the Admiralty Proctor in London on 22 August, 1815.[122] Despite this he did nothing to release the Americans he had seized on his arrival and when the shallop and, subsequently the *Nanina* herself arrived he made the remaining Americans prisoners, too.

As with any officer in command of a man-of-war, D'Aranda's major preoccupation was, quite properly, with the state of his own vessel. There can be no doubt at all that by the time she reached Eagle Island *Nancy* was in an exceptionally poor condition, having been dismasted in the storm on the coast of Uruguay, condemned as unfit for further service and then sent south after hurried repairs. D'Aranda was also concerned that he would be unable to accommodate all the remaining survivors aboard *Nancy* for the voyage back to Buenos Ayres. In his report he says that if *Nancy* had been the only vessel available, he would have been forced to take the people to a nearby island with better shelter and a more plentiful supply of animals, and then go back, with just a few of the survivors, to the River Plate for another vessel. Thus, he argued, *Nanina* was essential to his plans:

'We had suffered so much in our passage to the Islands, Crew sickly and the Vessel a complete Wreck, no person being able to sleep dry on board, stem parted, – Bows apiece – and sundry other defects, for which I beg to refer you to the two reports of Survey, one made previous to quitting this Anchorage, the other since our return, that but for the American Vessel I could not have brought more of the Wrecked People from the Island in the *Nancy* than I at present have on board, but could merely have removed them to one of the Islands upon which were Cattle or Pigs'.[123]

D'Aranda was thus counting upon the use of the *Nanina*, but there seems to be no reason why he could not have come to some arrangement with the Barnards to achieve this, without actually having to take *Nanina* from them by force.

But, from the moment he met the first American on the beach at Eagle Island, he appears to have decided to treat them as prisoners and to seize the *Nanina* as a prize, and his log records repeated warnings to *Nancy's* crew to keep a good lookout for 'the American.' Their vigilance was heightened after the arrival of the shallop and D'Aranda, from discussions with those on Eagle Island, knew precisely who should be aboard the American brig when she arrived. That he then chose to carry out a boarding operation seems both overdramatic and unnecessary, but perhaps he harped back to the days in the Baltic when he led cutting-out expeditions while serving on board HMS *Woodlark*. What D'Aranda could not have predicted, of course, was that when *Nanina* arrived she would already be in British rather than American hands, nor was he responsible for Charles Barnard, together with one American and three British sailors, being abandoned.

Whether unintentionally or not, D'Aranda occasionally stretched the truth and made rash allegations. His misrepresentations in *Nancy's* log have already been mentioned, but there were also later examples. One such occurred in a rather ill-tempered letter he wrote to the Secretary of the Admiralty in 1817, in which he stated that:

'The infamous proceedings of the Americans and the inhuman treatment the Wrecked People received from them prior to my arrival rendered *Nanina's* detention indispensible, and had not the American consul effected her crew's liberation and despatched them previous to my arrival, they most assuredly would have been brought to a just sense of their villainous conduct.

I am satisfied that it was never the intention of the Americans to remove the Wrecked People from Eagle Island. *Nanina* filled with plunder from the Wreck could not have carried them, the greatest precautions were taken to prevent a sufficient number of marines from getting aboard to take possession. The treatment several individuals received when first on board the *Nanina* was unpardonable'.[124]

The first paragraph is not correct, since the crew of the *Nanina* had been released in Rio de Janeiro by Admiral Dixon and not by the American consul. Further, most of them were still there when D'Aranda arrived on 6 December, as he well knew, since he had met Valentine Barnard at the British Consul's office.

As to the second paragraph, if *Nancy* had not arrived and *Nanina* had thus been left to carry all the remainder, the total to be transported would have been sixty-two. This would, indeed, have been something of a crowd for the *Nanina*, but there were three possibilities. First, *Isabella's* survivors would have been prepared to undergo almost any hardship to get away from the Falklands and would, thus, have been prepared to accept overcrowding. Secondly, if that was not feasible, then Barnard could have left some of his crew behind with the shallop to continue sealing, which was his original plan, anyway. Thirdly, he could have left some or all of the *Isabella's* cargo behind, to be collected later. Nor does D'Aranda's third allegation stand up to scrutiny, since Charles Barnard took no less than eight marines with him on the shallop, which was quite enough to take over the *Nanina*, even without the additional two who were picked up from Mattinson's boat in Falkland Sound.

There are certain points that must be made in D'Aranda's defence. First, Great Britain was at war and the Royal Navy maintained its supremacy by aggressive action. Indeed, there were several cases where commanders had been judged not to have been sufficiently aggressive and were court-martialled as a result. Enemy merchant ships were legitimate targets and there can be no doubt that if the *Isabella* had not been wrecked and she had then come within range of the frigate USS *Essex*, which was cruising in the South Atlantic at the time, then the American vessel would have taken her as a prize, and quite properly so. Prize money was a very great inducement to the whole of the Royal Navy and captains, not unnaturally, gained the lion's share, which, in *Nanina*'s case, might have amounted to several thousand pounds, no mean sum in those days. This must therefore, have appeared to be a very great opportunity to young D'Aranda and one which may have clouded his judgement.

D'Aranda was, without a doubt, under immense pressure. His ship was in an appalling state, officially declared unfit even to operate along the South American coast, let alone venture a thousand miles across some of the worst waters in the world. To put it bluntly, she was falling to pieces and even the shortest periods in harbour had always to be devoted to continuous repairs to the vessel and her sails, and it is significant that on her return from the Falkland Islands the *Nancy* was sold out of the service without further ado.

In addition, his crew was in a generally poor state of health, which became worse the longer they stayed in the Falklands and by the time they returned to Buenos Ayres half of them had to be admitted to hospital. The lot of the British sailor was a hard one, but for those on board *Nancy* it was especially miserable. The weather was bitter and getting worse with every day they remained in the Falklands, both the hull and the decks leaked, they were involved in ceaseless maintenance, and the interior was so overrun by rats that they were forced to smoke them out.

These problems were made no easier for D'Aranda by the absence of his sub-lieutenant, which left him with just the newly-promoted Second Master Shepherd, and the young and inexperienced Midshipman Marsh. The other warrant officer, Assistant-Surgeon Brison confined himself either to his medical duties or to drinking prodigious amounts of liquor.

One possible explanation of D'Aranda's action is that he may have felt that the prospect of prize money would act as an inducement to his crew.

There is no documentary evidence that he saw the capture of the American vessel in this light, but the fact is that while there were numerous floggings prior to the capture of the *Nanina* there was only one after it, suggesting that such a success could well have had an effect on the men and their morale.

There seems to be no doubt that by 1813 D'Aranda, like many other officers of the Royal Navy, and probably many of the senior ratings, too, was immensely tired. The navy had been at war since 1792, with just a 14-month break between March, 1802 and May, 1803, and officers like D'Aranda had known nothing but war since they joined. Killwick's lunacy and the constant quarrels among other officers suggest such exhaustion and the voyage of the *Hermes* typifies the whole situation, with opposition of the lieutenants to their captain, the very public row between D'Aranda and the captain, and the courts martial on their arrival in Plymouth all indicating that the people involved were not at their best.

Even the naval commander in the Brazils, Admiral Dixon, and the British Ambassador at Rio de Janeiro, Lord Strangford, quarrelled so seriously that they found it impossible to be civil to each other and, despite the state of war, indulged in a vitriolic correspondence, every letter of which was copied to either the Admiralty or the Foreign Office. The affair culminated in Dixon lodging a formal complaint with the Admiralty, although the latter body avoided taking sides on the grounds that by the time Dixon's letter arrived Strangford was no longer in post.[125] Thus, during his time in the Falklands D'Aranda not only had a very tired ship, but was also suffering from this general tiredness. Together, they had had a very unpleasant voyage down and were faced with the prospect of an equally bad, if not worse, voyage back to Buenos Ayres.

Finally, it must be remembered that, despite his naval experience, D'Aranda was a young man – just twenty-four years old at the time of the events in the Falkland Islands. He had a great weight of responsibility on his shoulders and, for the first time in his career he was totally on his own, with no superior close at hand to help or advise him; thus, he, and he alone, had to make the decisions.

Nevertheless, D'Aranda cannot avoid three responsibilities, the first of which is that he should not have captured the *Nanina* and treated the Americans as prisoners. There is no doubt that the Americans were involved in a mission of mercy and that he knew this to be so. Secondly, his efforts to find the missing men were, at best, very half-hearted, and even after the failure of the shallop to find them, he should have ensured that *Nancy* called in at New Island on her way past, a task he could hardly have delegated to *Nanina*, since Marsh was very inexperienced and had no navigation equipment. Thirdly, his entry in the log for June 15, 1813, was misleading to say the least. His statement that he 'took possession of her in consequence of maltreatment experienced by every one on board of her and the infamous conduct of her master' suggests that he learnt of the misconduct and then took possession, whereas he had, in reality, acted first and asked questions afterwards.

There was, however, never any question of D'Aranda being officially censured. Many captains had their prizes disallowed for one reason or another and there was little disgrace involved in that. Indeed, the Royal Navy treated D'Aranda better than many other officers in the post-Napoleonic period, employing him as an Admiralty agent for many years. D'Aranda's greatest critic appears to have been himself and he harboured a sense of bitterness over the affair to the end of his days.

Admiral Dixon was the first to indicate that the capture of *Nanina* was less than justified and it is to his credit that he first released the Americans and then tried so hard to give the vessel back to the Valentine Barnard. He certainly had her repaired, and also ensured that replacement equipment and provisions were placed aboard, but Valentine Barnard's repeated quibbling appears to have tried his patience too far. Admiral Dixon did not send a vessel to look for Charles Barnard, but that was scarcely possible under the conditions of war against both France and the United States. However, he did issue a notice to all British mariners to the effect that if they ventured near the Falkland Islands they were to keep a watch out for any trace of Barnard and his party. Finally, although he never failed to support D'Aranda, he still had the moral courage to inform the Admiralty of his doubts about the justice of the capture.[126]

One of the saddest aspects of this whole episode is that had the Americans not chanced upon the castaways on Eagle Island, *Nancy* would still have turned up in answer to Brookes' and Lundin's arrival in Buenos Ayres, and D'Aranda would then have achieved their rescue somehow, even if he had to make two trips. On the other hand, had the draft of Royal Marines not been present aboard *Isabella*, or had Barnard not agreed to take so many British people in the shallop, then Mattinson would not have been able to assemble sufficient armed force to realize his plan to take over the *Nanina*. Thus, Charles Barnard's sojourn on New Island would have been avoided and D'Aranda's subsequent life and career might have been less unhappy.

It is less certain what might have happened if the *Nancy* had not arrived, since the *Nanina* would still have been captured at New Island. It does seem possible, however, that without the presence of D'Aranda and HMS *Nancy*, the Americans and British might somehow have worked out an agreement with each other to enable them to make a more serious search for the missing men. All that is, however, a matter of supposition.

The people involved in this drama were very ordinary men and women

215

who suddenly found themselves thrust into a series of very hazardous situations, where most of them, for most of the time, felt that they were fighting for their very lives. They were as typical a cross-section of humanity as could be imagined: there were a few very good people, while a few were very bad; some were undoubted heroes and some were cowardly; some were very religious and found their faith a rock upon which they could depend for survival, while others had no religious beliefs at all. And, in all these cases, the majority lay somewhere in between. Even the best of them made mistakes: Charles Barnard, for example, was quarrelsome on occasion and made some errors of judgement, while Jacob Green, whose conduct was otherwise exemplary, allowed himself to be persuaded into taking part in the desertion of Barnard.

Mattinson was undoubtedly wicked, Higton an incompetent drunkard and Hayes simply a scurrilous and unprincipled rogue, despite his title. Ansell, on the other hand, was an ill-educated and mean bully until Barnard and his companions decided to treat him with equal toughness. Having taught him his lesson they then accepted him back into their company and, at least in Barnard's case, treated him with kindness, so that by the end of their time on New Island Ansell seems to have found some sort of redemption.

Not one of those in authority 'progressed' in a material sense after their great adventure in the Falklands. The British Service officers all remained virtually what they were in the Falklands: Durie stayed a captain, Lundin was promoted to captain and then put on half-pay, while D'Aranda had to wait many years for his promotion to commander, and even then it was, to all intents, an honourary rank. Charles Barnard, Brookes and the American masters all had further commands of similar types of vessels, Higton disappeared into well-deserved obscurity and the older men, Valentine Barnard, Holt and Hayes, all returned to their native countries, where they lived out their lives without any further excitements.

The majority of the Marines and sailors of the *Isabella*, *Nanina* and *Nancy* simply carried out their orders and did their best in very testing circumstances, as such people always do. Even the British Marines and sailors who took part in the takeover of the *Nanina* felt themselves to be in a desperate situation and responded to Mattinson's demagoguery, although it seems highly probable that firm and determined leadership from Durie could have set things quickly to rights.

There is no evidence that either Durie or D'Aranda were dishonourable men and both came from honest families with strong Christian backgrounds. But, as has been shown, they made mistakes, although they almost certainly, but for different reasons, considered that they were taking the correct action for the best of motives.

Durie's weaknesses would probably never have been shown up in a more conventional setting, where he would have had more experienced superiors readily available to direct and support him. D'Aranda, on the other hand, was not weak, but he was under a variety of very strong pressures, which led him into errors of judgement. Setting aside the issue of the taking of the *Nanina* as a prize, however, D'Aranda deserves considerable credit. His brig was in a shocking state and he was faced with a situation unlike anything in his experience. Despite this he took his vessel to the Falklands, found the people he had been sent to save and got them all back to South America, just as he had been ordered, which was no mean achievement.

One of the most inexplicable episodes in this curious story is the refusal of the Americans, while in Rio de Janeiro, to accept the return of the *Nanina* in order to go back to the Falkland Islands to search for the missing men. Admiral Dixon said that he had ensured that the brig had been 'put to rights' and since he knew that the intention was to go back south and as he seems to have been an honourable man, it may be assumed that she was, therefore, ready for such a voyage. He was also fully prepared to give Valentine Barnard a certificate of safe conduct, which would have covered the brig not only in the South Atlantic, but also all the way to the United States. Valentine Barnard may well have had a deep resentment about the way he and his comrades had been treated and all the American captains obviously wanted to obtain some financial return for what was, from their point of view, a commercial disaster. Nevertheless, it seems very odd that they should have put such considerations before the rescue of the missing men, unless, of course, they had successfully convinced themselves that those men must already have perished.

Jacob Green, on the other hand, played a most distinguished role throughout the voyage and especially during the survival of the group that was so cruelly abandoned. He kept his head at all times, was repeatedly at the point of maximum danger and skippered the small boat on all three voyages to the wreck. In an era supposedly full of prejudice, his colour seems never to have been an issue; both Barnard and Lundin mention it just once, and then only casually. Indeed, all that mattered was that he was a fine and experienced seaman, for which he was greatly admired and respected by Charles Barnard, but perhaps the most important tribute to his capabilities is that, in the absence of Barnard, he was the man the British sailors turned to as their leader.

There can be no doubt that Charles Barnard acted to save the lives of the survivors of the *Isabella* by agreeing to take them to South America, an act whose humanity was not diminished by the subsequent appearance of the *Nancy*. In addition, he saved the lives of Mattinson and Ansell, both of whom repaid him in a most disgraceful fashion, Mattinson by taking his ship and Ansell at New Island by making his group abandon the one man who was offering them all a chance of survival. Above all, however, there towers Barnard's achievement in keeping five men alive over a period of two years in an extremely hostile environment. They faced a constant threat of starvation and were repeatedly on the verge of disaster, if not death, but they all survived and this must rank as a major feat of leadership in a great epic of survival.

All of these men and women, however, were in a desperate situation, quite beyond anything their previous experience had prepared them for, and in a setting well outside the bounds of what they considered to be the civilized world. Throughout their time in the Falklands their very survival was at stake and they acted accordingly. For the survivors of the *Isabella* there was a long period when rescue seemed impossible and the possibility of a long, lingering and very unpleasant death must have seemed very real. What might have transpired as the weaker among them started to die and people such as Mattinson, Ansell, Hayes and Higton began to gain the upper hand can only be a matter for conjecture. Then, once Charles Barnard arrived in the shallop, that dreadful prospect receded only to be replaced by a quite different one, where they were all faced with a curious contradiction, where the Americans possessed the means of escape, the *Nanina*, but no weapons, while the British had no vessel, but did have the only formed body of armed Royal Marines, while over both groups lay the knowledge of the distant war. It was, therefore, almost inevitable that mistakes would be made and misunderstandings occur.

What is incontrovertible is that this entire episode resulted in only one death, that of the seaman with scurvy, and even that occurred not in the Falklands, but at the very end of it all at the entrance to Buenos Ayres harbour. The dangers during their experiences in the Falklands had, after all, been very real and it would have been all too easy to have incurred casualties when the *Isabella* ran on to the shore or in some of their subsequent adventures on Eagle and New Islands. Then, too, Brookes' remarkable voyage in a small, open boat across a thousand miles of turbulent ocean, which inflicted such a severe battering on the very much larger *Nancy*, was hazardous in the extreme, but all six men survived totally unscathed, apart from Lundin's scalded foot.

Indeed, one more person left the Falkland Islands than had arrived there: the infant Eliza Providence Durie, who was born under conditions as adverse as can be imagined. And the renewal of birth is probably the best way to leave them; these very ordinary people who struggled, as best they could, through an extraordinary experience.

ENDNOTES

1. *The Times*, Saturday 29 January, 1814, p. 4.

2. In fact, the capture of *La Perla* was an impudent affair. *La Perla* (Rais Hadji Mustafa, master) was lying in the harbour of Bona in Algeria immediately ahead of the British privateer St Josef and sailed at 2am on Saturday 14 June, 1806. The master of the *St Josef*, Vincenzo Williams, immediately followed her, captured her one hour later when she was some three miles offshore, sent her under a prize crew to Malta and then returned to Bona to complete his loading. The Algerian authorities were, not surprisingly, furious, but the High Court of Admiralty still found in favour of the *St Josef*. PRO/HCA 42/951.

3. Her cargo included: window glass – 11 cases; paint – 102 kegs; turpentine – 50 jugs; nails – 14 casks; tinplate – 15 boxes; iron, steel and iron hoops – $14\frac{1}{4}$ tons; rivets – 1 keg; sheet lead – 4 rolls; soap, butter, cheese and candles – 140 cases, firkins and boxes; glassware – 5 casks; stationery – 9 cases; haberdashery – 37 trunks and cases; fine hats – 3 cases; cloth – 12 bales; ash oars – 83; sugar – 3 cases; tallow – 20 bales; and tobacco – 17 rolls. There were also 346 casks of wine (23,252 gallons); one cask (124 gallons) of brandy and 28 casks (3,160 gallons) of rum. PRO/CO 201/61 page 203.

4. Holt, *Memoirs*, Volume II, pp. 320–321.

5. The second battalion of the 42nd Royal Highlanders (today's Black Watch) was formed in 1780. This battalion became a separate regiment in its own right in 1786 as 'His Majesty's 73rd Regiment of Foot, a Highland regiment' and was then despatched for a long spell of duty in India. The 73rd returned from India in 1806, where it took up station in Scotland, with its headquarters at Stirling, but with numerous small detachments spread around the country.

6. The marriage certificate is with other Durie documents in PRO/WO 42/14/376.

7. *Historical Records of New South Wales:* Volume VII, No pp. 99–100.

8. New South Wales Government Order, Sydney, 16 June, 1810.

9. *Return of Christenings at St George's River, Paramatta, 25 June to 30 September, 1811.* Governor Macquarie's despatch 1/1811 in PRO/CO 201/59.

10. Barnard, *Marooned*, p. 180.

11. Holt, *Memoirs*, Volume II, pp. 32–33.

12. Holt, *Memoirs*, Volume II, pp. 321–323.

13. *Historical Records of New South Wales: Volume III*, p. 283.

14. Colonial Office letter dated 17 August, 1811. PRO/CO201/57.

15. *List of free pardons granted by Governor Macquarie, 14 October 1811 – 30 September 1812.* Despatch 8/1812 #103 in PRO/CO201/62.

16. The story of the *Atlas'* voyage is based on the account in Bateson, *The Convict Ships,* pp. 164–167.

17. The detachment comprised: one Lieutenant, one 2nd Lieutenant, three Sergeants, three Corporals, two Drummers and 39 Privates. (Field, *Britain's Sea Soldiers,* Volume I).

18. Governor Macquarie: Despatch #6/1812. PRO/CO 201/60.

19. No trace of women of these names has been found in the annals of the colony, although it is probable that they had been convicts and changed their names on being pardoned.

20. This description of Mattinson's background is taken from *Marooned* in which Charles Barnard dwells at some length on this man, the source of his information being Mrs Durie. Holt does not mention Mattinson at all in his *Memoirs.* Investigation in the PRO has failed to reveal any background on Mattinson or to validate his claims to have been a 'sailing-master' in the Royal Navy. However, like others in this story he could well have changed his name following his Court Martial.

21. Lieutenant Lundin's report to Admiral Dixon. PRO/ADM 50/98.

22. This disgraceful episode is described by two separate eyewitnesses: Holt, *Memoirs* Volume II, p. 329 and Lundin, *Edinburgh Magazine.*

23. Holt, *Memoirs* Volume II, pp. 332–333.

24. The shooting competition is described in Holt, *'Memoirs,'* Volume II, pp. 334–335.

25. Holt (*Memoirs,* Volume II, p. 341) is very specific about the name Ann. The infant was eventually baptized at Lamlash on the Isle of Arran in Scotland on 27 February, 1814, and the record shows that she was christened Eliza, although the second name – Providence – was retained (PRO/WO 42/14/376).

26. Holt comments on the plentiful supply of celery (*Memoirs* Volume II, p. 353), as does James Choyce (*Log of a Jack Tar,* p. 203).

27. Goode, *Fisheries and Fishing Industries of the United States,* p. 441.

28. The 'measurement' of an XIXth Century vessel was not a weight as such, but gave an indication of the carrying capacity. In overall terms it was calculated by multiplying the length by the breadth, and then multiplying this product by half the breadth. This product was then divided by 95, the result being expressed as a whole number of tons. Thus, *Nanina's* burthen was 132 and 35/95 tons. For the precise means of measurement see *Rees's Naval Architecture* p. 27.

29. These diaries are now held in manuscript form in the George Arents Research Library of Syracuse University.

30. Fanning, *Voyage and Discoveries in the South Sea.*

31. Barnard, *Marooned.* The details of the flora and fauna of the Falkland Islands

are taken from the appendix (pp. 267–270) to the original version of the book, published in 1832, which was not reproduced in Dodge's 1986 version.

32. There is a clear contradiction between two records here. Holt is quite specific (*Memoirs*, Volume II, p. 359) that he was offered a free passage by Captains Hunter and Fanning on 4 April, an offer which was then extended to include the Duries. Holt does not mention the departure by the Americans on the morning of the 5th and the despatch of Durie (accompanied by himself) to fetch them back, whereupon Barnard offered the Duries a passage, as described here. Barnard's version appears to be the more likely.

33. Both Holt (*Memoirs*, Volume II, p. 362) and Barnard (*Marooned*, p. 60) refer to this document. This written agreement definitely reached England, but, despite a protracted search, has not been found in British archives.

34. The map in Bertha Dodge's book (*Marooned*, frontispiece) shows this march as having started at Port Edgar. I believe this to be an error, as Barnard says that he anchored in Arch Island Harbour on the night of 13 April and that the next day, after attempting to weather Cape Meredith, *'I returned to the anchorage'* ie, Arch Island Harbour (*ibid*, pp. 63–64).

35. Rutter document.

36. All details of events in Part 3 relating to *HMS Nancy* and her activities are taken from the daily entries in Captain's Log (PRO/ADM 51/2601) and Master's Log (PRO/ADM 52/4547), unless otherwise stated.

37. Captain Greene's letter dated 31 March, 1820 is in PRO/ADM 1/2749.

38. PRO/ADM 50/98.

39. PRO/ADM 1/21. Page 5.

40. Journal of CinC Brazil; letters of 3 and 6 September. PRO/ADM 50/98.

41. Lewis, *A Social History of the Royal Navy: 1793–1815*, pp. 396–398.

42. PRO/ADM 9/9 (1817 Record of Officers' Service) Serial 2886. In that document Killwick explained his problem thus: 'Then superseded in consequence of derangement from poison administered by the Spaniards when at Montevideo on service.'

43. CinC Brazil Journal. Letter dated 20 August, 1812. PRO/ADM 50/98.

44. CinC Brazil Journal. Letter dated 8 October, 1808. PRO/ADM 1/19.

45. Killwick had been appointed a midshipman in 1801 and was captured by the French that same year. He spent two years in a French prison before escaping and returning to England. He was a midshipman aboard HMS *Victory* from 20 February – 24 September, 1804, at the time she was Nelson's flagship. He went to the Brazils in *Foudroyant* in early 1808.

46. *Reports of Sailing Qualities, HM Brig Nancy*, 5 November, 1813. PRO/ADM 95/48 #32.

47. Letter by Lieutenant Killwick to Admiral Smith dated 26 November, 1808. PRO/ADM 1/19.

48. Letter from Captain Pym to the Admiralty, dated Cawsand Bay, 27 October, 1806. PRO/ADM 1/2331 #188.

49. Admiral Dixon letter dated Sunday, 20 September, 1812. PRO/ADM 50/98.

50. This incident is described in *Nancy's* log (PRO/ADM 51/2601). In addition, D'Aranda made a statement on arrival at Buenos Ayres which was sent to Admiral Dixon and forwarded by him to the British Minister, Viscount Strangford (letters in PRO/ADM 1/21).

51. HMS *Nancy* Muster Roll. PRO/ADM 37/3851.

52. Despatches from US Minister to Brazil 27 May, 1813, to 23 February, 1817. Letters dated 13 January, and 15 January, 1813. US National Archives. Microfilm M121 Roll 3.

53. *Racoon* Muster Roll shows the two Americans from *Nancy* taken on strength 21 January, 1813, and discharged 21 January (Paine), and 22 January (Davis), the entries annotated 'by order of the American Minister, Rio de Janeiro, being American subjects.' PRO/ADM 37/4753.

54. The details of Captain Heywood's life are taken from *Marshall's Naval Biography*, Volume 2 Part II, pp. 747–797.

55. Survey carried out by Lieutenant Vere Gabriel, RN and four warrant officers, in the Rio de la Plata, 5 February, 1813. PRO/ADM 1/21.

56. Copy of this letter is in CinC Brazil's Journal: PRO/ADM 1/21. (Admiral de Courcy had been in command in Rio de Janeiro when Durie passed through on the voyage out to New South Wales in 1809.)

57. This description of their voyage is taken from Lundin's second account, which was published in *The Edinburgh Review* of 1846.

58. The details of the longboat's voyage are recorded in Lieutenant Lundin's report to Admiral Dixon (PRO/ADM/1/21) and his 1846 article in *The Edinburgh Review*.

59. *Annual Register*, 1813. Chronicle, pp. 25–26.

60. Letter, Captain Heywood to Captain Durie. PRO/ADM 1/21.

61. Letter Captain Peter Heywood 'off Buenos Ayres,' dated 1st April 1813. PRO/ADM 1/2855.

62. Muster Roll of HMS *Nereus*. PRO/ADM 37/3851.

63. The description of the events accompanying the arrival of the *Nancy* is taken from Holt's *Memoirs*, Volume II.

64. Letter Lieutenant D'Aranda to Capt Bowles, Buenos Ayres, 22 August, 1813. PRO/F 5/128.

65. This stabbing incident is mentioned in *Nancy's* Log, in D'Aranda's report to Captain Bowles, dated Buenos Ayres, 22nd August 1813 (PRO/F 5/128), and Lundin's 1846 article in *The Edinburgh Review*. None of these reports elaborates on the cause of the fight or names the participants, but Lundin says that the 'Malay dirk' (actually, a *kris*, the wavy-edged Malay fighting knife) was his, one of a number of souvenirs he was taking home to Scotland.

222

66. The description of the 'taking' of the *Nanina* is taken from the 'Rutter document' and Barzillai Pease's diary.

67. A complete schedule of the cargo and personal goods purloined was submitted to Admiral Dixon at Rio de Janeiro: PRO/HCA 42/474, Bundle 889, Document 'D.' The ripping of the feather mattresses is also described by Holt, op cit, pp. 371–372.

68. CinC Brazils Journal; letter dated 2 April, 1813. PRO/ADM 21.

69. Pease diary, (quoted in Dodge, '*Marooned*,' p. 228).

70. *Nancy* Captain's log.

71. 'Rutter document.'

72. 'I heard that the *Nanina* brig was to sail from the Falkland Islands, direct to England. . . .' (Holt, op cit, Volume II, p. 372). 'I embarked in the *Nanina*, American Brig, and sailed from the Falkland Islands on the 27th July, when on 23rd August, we were compelled for want of sufficient Provisions, for so long a Voyage, to put into Rio de Janeiro.' (Lundin, PRO/ADM 50/98, letter #104)

73. Holt, *op cit*, pp. 372–373. The editor of the memoirs left this letter in its original form to illustrate Holt's poor spelling and grammar.

74. The return, dated 'Off Buenos Ayres, November 5, 1813' is at PRO/ADM 95/48 #32.

75. Account submitted to Admiral Dixon in Rio de Janeiro. PRO/HCA 42/474. Bundle 889. Document 'D.'

76. 'Rutter document.'

77. The disposition of people between *Nancy* and *Nanina* is taken from *Nancy's* Muster Table.

78. Pease diary.

79. The original of this 'Rutter document' is in PRO/HCA 42/474 Bundle 889, with the *Nanina*'s ship's papers. The latter came to England via the Falkland Islands, while the 'Rutter document' reached England via the US State Department.

80. Letter from Admiral Dixon to Valentine Barnard dated 16 October, 1813. PRO/HCA 42/474/Bundle 889.

81. Letter Valentine Barnard to Admiral Dixon. PRO/HCA 42/474. Bundle 889.

82. This meeting between D'Aranda and Valentine Barnard is described in PRO/ADM 7/312 Folio 6.

83. Details of the entire incident are given in the court-martial proceedings: PRO/ADM 1/5442. The story is also summarized in *Naval Chronicle*, 1814, Volume 31, p. 457.

84. He was later to claim that he had 'lost the use of all his limbs' at this period, although that seems a trifle far-fetched. PRO/ADM 9/27. Entry 947.

85. All these incidents are described in a series of letters in Commander in Chief Plymouth Letter-Book: PRO/ADM 1/834.

86. All details in Part 5 are taken from Barnard's journal (Dodge, *op cit*) unless otherwise stated.

87. Barnard refers to these birds as 'rooks,' not knowing their correct appellation.

Elsewhere in this narrative I have used Barnard's own names, but in this case that would cause confusion, so they are referred to as 'skuas' throughout.

88. The only owl to be found in the Falkland Islands is the Short-Eared Owl, *Agio flambeaus sanfordi*.

89. *Eudyptes crestatus*. The penguins still use the identical site today (Author's observation).

90. The Macaroni penguin, *Eudyptes chrysolophus*, is slightly larger than the Rock-hopper and has a more extensive golden plume growing out of a patch on its forehead. The name is derived from an eighteenth century English nickname for a dandy.

91. James Choyce, '*The Log of a Jack Tar*,' p. 203.

92. PRO/HCA 30/215. Bundle 'June 1814.'

93. Quoted in Dodge, *op cit*, p. 233. Italics are in the original.

94. Admiral Dixon's letter is registered in the Admiralty Digest Book for 1815 (PRO/ADM 12) and should be held in PRO/ADM 1/22. The latter volume contains a removal slip, stating that the letter has been removed and '. . . *sent to Sir Wm Scott for opinion.*' and there is no trace of its return.

95. PRO/ADM 7/312. Folio 6.

96. PRO/FO 5/122. Part 1. Letter from the US Department of State dated 15th April 1817.

97. PRO/HCA 44/80. Appeal Assignment Book.

98. Weddell, '*A Voyage Towards the South Pole*,' pp. 89–92.

99. Dodge, '*Marooned*,' p. 22.

100. Original manuscript return for O'Byrne's '*Naval Biographies*' (British Library Manuscript ADD 38039–38054.)

101. The original exchange of correspondence is not to be found. However, copies of the three replies to D'Aranda's request are in PRO/ADM 1/2749 – Lieutenants' Letters 'A' 1827, mistakenly filed under 'Aranda' instead of 'D'Aranda.' Mention of the 1820 request is also made in D'Aranda's reply to the Admiralty's 1848 questionnaire, together with a summary of Dixon's reply. PRO/ADM 9/27 Entry 947.

102. PRO/ADM 9/27. Entry 947.

103. His final residence was 4, Portland Place, Southampton, where his landlady was Mrs Hawksworth (1871 Census: RG10/1188 #143). He was buried in Holy Trinity church, Southampton on 15 October, 1872, (parish burial register), but the church was totally destroyed by German bombing during World War Two, as was much of the centre of the city.

104. PRO/ADM 1/4518. #522.

105. PRO/WO 42/14/376.

106. PRO/ADM 50/98 Letter #105 dated Sunday 13 September, 1813.

107. '*The Story of Vaucluse House*,' Bertie, p. 21, quoting from 'Ainsworth's Magazine, Volume 7.'

108. *'The Story of Vaucluse House,'* Bertie, p. 22, quoting from *'The Cork Constitution'* of May 1832.

109. PRO/ADM 1237 Letter A.976.

110. Letter from Messrs Kier Buxton & Co, Warnford Court to Rt Hon Earl Bathurst, dated 2 November, 1815. Copy kindly supplied by I.H. Nicholson, Esq.

111. Extensive searches have been undertaken in both England and Australia to discover more about this man, but nothing has been found.

112. Pease diary quoted in Dodge, *op cit*, p. 226.

113. 'Rutter document.'

114. Dodge, *op cit*, p. 213.

115. 'Rutter document.'

116. The original letter no longer exists, but is summarized in the Advocate General's 'opinion' dated 15th September 1815. PRO/ADM 7/312 #6.

117. Dodge, *Marooned*, p. 180.

118. *The Edinburgh Magazine*, 1846, p. 310.

119. Letter Sir Christopher Robinson, Doctor's Commons, to Viscount Castlereagh, 22 June, 1816; PRO/PRO 30/28/5.

120. Dodge, *op cit*, pp. 56–57.

121. PRO/F 5/128.

122. Letter from Mr Gostling at Doctor's Commons to Mr Croker at the Admiralty Board, dated 18 September, 1815. Unfortunately, this is one of the documents that cannot now be traced. PRO/ADM 1/3903.

123. D'Aranda to Captain Bowles at Buenos Ayres, 22 August, 1813; PRO/F 5/128.

124. Letter from Lt Wm D'Aranda, RN, to Wm Croker, Esq, dated Portsmouth, 20th September 1817. PRO/F 5/128.

125. Admiral Dixon's journal; PRO/ADM 50/98.

126. Dodge, *Marooned*, p. 151.

EARLY XIXth CENTURY BRIG

THE SAILS

1 Jib
2 Headsail
3 Fore Course
4 Fore Topsail
5 Fore Topgallant
6 Main Staysail

7 Main Topmast Staysail
8 Main Topgallant Staysail
9 Main Course (furled)
10 Main Topsail
11 Main Topgallant
12 Driver

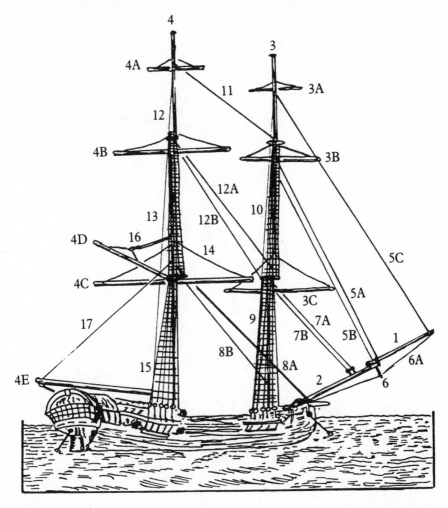

BRIG AT ANCHOR SHOWING STANDING RIGGING

(Some rigging and port shrouds omitted for clarity)

BRIG-STANDING RIGGING

1 Jib-boom	4E Boom	10 Foretopmast shrouds
2 Bowsprit	5A Foretopmast stay	11 Maintopgallant stay
3 Foremast	5B Foretopmast preventer stay	12 Maintopgallant mast
3A Foretopgallant yard	5C Foretopgallant stay	12A Maintopmast stay
3B Foretopmast yard	6 Martingale	12B Maintopmast preventer
3C Foresail yard	6A Martingale stay	stay
4 Mainmast	7A Forestay	13 Maintopmast
4A Maintopgallant yard	7B Forestay preventer	14 Mainlifts
4B Maintopsail yard	8A Mainstay	15 Mainshrouds
4C Mainyard	8B Mainstay preventer	16 Gaff peak halliards
4D Gaff	9 Fore-shrouds	17 Boom topping lift

APPENDIX A

Glossary of Nautical Terms

Aft, After. Towards the stern.

Astern. A position aft of (ie, behind) the vessel.

Aweigh. Used in reference to the anchor, when it was hanging vertically by its rope or chain and clear of the seabed; thus, *'anchor's aweigh.'*.

Batten Down. To close and secure all the openings in the weather decks. Thus, in particularly foul weather the hatches would be *'battened down'* to ensure that waves breaking over the vessel did not result in water cascading into internal spaces, such as the hold.

Bend/Bent. See 'sails.'

Bow. The forward (front) part of the vessel.

Bowsprit. The boom protruding forwards at an angle from the bow.

Brig. A *brig* had two masts, both of which were square-rigged, but with a fore-and-aft *spanker* or *driver* (qqv) on the main mast.

Burthen/burden. Eighteenth/nineteenth century measure of a merchant vessel's carrying capacity in tons.

Cable. A nautical measurement of distance. One cable equals one-tenth of a nautical mile (qv), ie, 608feet (185m). The term derives from the traditional length of a sailing vessel's anchor cable, which was 101 fathoms (606ft).

Caulk. The sides and decks of wooden vessels were constructed of planks, between which there were gaps, which were filled by a process known as *'caulking and paying.'* *Caulking* consisted of filling the gaps with cotton or oakum (qv), which was rammed into place, using a caulking iron and a caulking mallet, while *paying* involved filling and sealing on top of the filler, using an adhesive.

Chains. The metal fittings on each side of the hull to which the shrouds were attached.

Course The largest sail and almost invariably the lowest sail on a particular mast; thus, for example, *main course*, *forecourse*, etc.

Cross-tree. A single strut at right-angles to the mast, which was used to spread the shrouds.

Demurrage. The charge levied by a shipowner when a charterer caused a delay to a ship's previously agreed time or date of departure.

Dolphin-Striker. A small spar set at right-angles to and below the *bowsprit* (qv). It was used to spread the stay which strengthened the bowsprit, which was known as a *martingale*.

Driver. Another name for the *spanker* (qv).

Fathom. A nautical unit for measuring depth of water and lengths of rope. One fathom equals 6 feet (1.83m).

Fore-and-aft. See '*sails*'.

Forestay. Stay running from the head of the foremast to the stem. (Also called headstay).

Forward (for'ard). The front end of the vessel.

Jury/Jury Rig. Temporary or makeshift device, intended to replace something damaged until more permanent repairs can be made or the device replaced. Thus, a vessel which had been dismasted could make a temporary arrangement of masts, yards and sails (a '*jury*' rig) to reach the nearest port.

Hand.
    a. To furl and lower a sail (thus, a sail would be 'handed').
    b. A sailor or member of the crew (eg, 'All hands on deck').

Headsail. Triangular fore-and-aft sail, set before the foremast and *bent* (qv) to a forestay. Also known as a *jib*.

Heave-to. In very heavy weather a sailing ship would furl all its sails, and ride out the storm, known as *heaving-to*. A small sail or a *sea-anchor* (qv) was frequently used to keep the vessel's head to the wind.

Heave down. To lower topmasts, etc.

Knot. The nautical measurement of speed, where 1 knot equals 1 nautical mile (qv) per hour (1.153 statute miles per hour). The term derives from the traditional sailing vessel's method of measuring speed, when a piece of wood attached to a line was thrown over the stern. The line had equidistant knots and a sailor counted the number of knots to pass through his hands in a given time, which then gave the speed in *knots*.

Labour. A ship is said to *'labour'* when she pitches and rolls heavily in rough seas.

Larboard. Term used to describe the left-hand side of the vessel, looking forward. The term was originally *ladeboard*, which stemmed from the old practice of mooring alongside a jetty on the opposite side to that of the steering-oar, over which the cargo was then loaded (*lade* = load). Now universally called the *port* side, the change having taken place in the 1840s.

Latitude. A position on the Earth's surface, measured as an angle from the Equator and expressed in degrees and minutes north or south of the Equator; eg, 40° 45′N (forty degrees, forty-five minutes north).

League. An old measurement of distance, equal to 3 statute miles (2.6 nautical miles)(4.83km).

Lee, Lee-shore, Leeward. The *lee* is that side of a vessel opposite to that from which the wind is blowing. Thus, a *lee-shore* was highly dangerous to a sailing ship, since it meant that the wind was pushing the ship down towards the land.

Longitude. The position of a point on the Earth's surface measured as an angle east or west of the meridian (0°) at Greenwich, England and expressed in degrees and minutes; eg, 32° 21′E.

Loose-footed. The *foot* is the bottom edge of a sail. In an early nineteenth century brig, such as *Nancy*, *Nanina* and *Isabella*, the *foot* of the *spanker* (qv) was usually secured to the boom only at its forward point (*tack*) and at the after end (the *clew*) and thus *'loose-footed.'*

Masts.
   a. The *Main Mast* was the highest mast in a vessel and in a brig this was the after mast, since this carried the principal sails. Thus, the second mast on a brig, which was forward of the mainmast, was designated the *foremast*.
   b. Masts were usually made in sections, which were known (in ascending order) as the *lower mast*, *topmast*, *topgallant mast*, and (where fitted) *royal mast*, respectively.
   c. Masts were *stepped* into the vessel and when the upper masts were removed or lowered to the deck they were *struck* or *sent down*.

d. Masts were not solid pieces of timber, but were built-up from carefully constructed elements, which slotted into each other and glued to give strength.

Nautical Mile. One nautical (or sea) mile equals 1.15 statute miles (6,080feet) (1.853km).

Oakum. Teased-out fibres of unwanted hemp rope, used for *caulking* (qv) seams.

Paying. See *caulking*.

Port. The left-hand side of the vessel, looking forward. See also *larboard*.

Quadrant. A navigational instrument for measuring angles, similar to the later sextant.

Quarter. The after end of the side of a vessel.

Ratlines. Light ropes secured across *shrouds* (qv) to form ladders.

Reef. To reduce the area of a sail by rolling or folding part of it in anticipation of, or during heavy weather. A square sail had several rows of short lengths of rope across the sail and a gang of sailors had to stand over the *yard* (qv) to secure these ropes – *making a reef* – or loosing them – *shaking out a reef*. Note that the sailors did not pull the sail up, but that the yard on which they were standing was lowered to the reef, using ropes (*halyards*; literally '*haul-yards*') controlled from the deck.

Rigging. Ropes comprising the rig, which fell into two types. The *Standing Rigging* supported and steadied the masts and was tarred to extend its life. The second element, the *Running Rigging*, was used to raise, lower and control the sails and moving spars and was not tarred, since that would have prevented it from running through the blocks and tackles.

Sails.
　　a. The sails were made of heavy canvas and were either *square*, ie, approximately rectangular in shape and rigged across the hull, or *fore-and-aft*, ie, four-sided or triangular, but rigged along the line of the hull.
　　b. There was a special language for sails. Sails were *bent* to yards or booms, *spread* when *making sail*, and *handed* when *taking in sail*. In high winds the sail area could be reduced by *reefing* (qv).
　　c. Sails were described by both their mast and their position on that mast. Thus, for example, *foretopgallant (sail)*, *maintopsail*, *foreroyal (sail)*, *forecourse* etc.

Send Down. To dismount and lower a large spar; for example, a top-mast or a yard would be *sent down* for repair.

Shallop. A relatively small boat, used in American and European waters for coastal duties. The term was also used as a generic title for auxiliary vessels on long-distance voyages, which were utilized to conduct local voyages, eg, for sealing. Believed to derive from *chaloupe* (French) or *sloep* (Dutch).

Shears. Yards (qv) lashed together at one end and raised to provide a lifting tackle; eg, for raising masts.

Ship. Today the word 'ship' is a generic term for virtually any large maritime vessel, but in the sailing era the word had a more specific meaning. The *'full-rigged ship'* (or, more simply, 'ship') had three or more masts, with square sails on all masts, as well as a *spanker* (qv) on the mizzen. Thus, *Nanina* and *Isabella* were not referred to as 'ships' but as *brigs*, while *Nancy*'s correct title was HM Gun Brig *Nancy*.

Shrouds. Rope stays used to support the masts, part of the *standing rigging* (qv).

Slops. Articles of clothing and personal equipment made for the Crown and issued on repayment to Royal Navy seamen and Royal Marines.

Soundings. The process of testing to ascertain the depth of water. This could either be done from the bows of a large vessel or, particularly when close to the shore, could also be done from a small rowing-boat. A weighted line, with measurements marked, was thrown forwards, so that, as the boat passed over it the weight touched the bottom and the line was vertical, and thus the depth could be gauged accurately.

Spanker. The fore-and-aft sail rigged abaft the mainmast on a brig (also known as a *driver*). The top of the spanker was attached to a boom and the gap above this boom was filled on some vessels by a triangular-shaped sail, the *jigger topsail*.

Spreader. A pair of struts which held the shrouds away from the mast. In a single unit this would be a *cross-tree* (qv).

Square-rigged. A type of sail rig in which the principal sails are approximately rectangular in shape, suspended from yards, which, in turn, are suspended at their mid-point from a mast.

Starboard. The right-hand side of the vessel, looking forward. The term originated from the side on which the steering-oar or *'steer-board'* was originally shipped.

Stay. See '*rigging.*'

Staysails. Triangular fore-and-aft sails, rigged between the masts.

Stem. The massive timber beam which formed the forward extremity of the hull. That part of the stem below the waterline was called the *cutwater* while the top was called the *stemhead*.

Stern. The extreme after part of the hull.

Storm Sail. Special sails made of heavy canvas and of reduced area, for use in heavy weather. *Storm staysails* were set between the masts, while *storm jibs* (also sometimes known as *spitfires*) were set to the forestays.

Strake. A complete plank in the vessel's or boat's hull.

Trysail. Small, triangular, fore-and-aft sail set immediately abaft the fore-mast, usually during heavy weather.

Wale. A strake, strip or plank standing proud of the rest of the hull. For example, the *gunwale* ('*gunnel*') was the finishing strake above all others in the hull.

Warp. To move a vessel by hauling on ropes, usually from one or more rowing-boats.

Weather deck. A deck level exposed to the weather.

Weigh Anchor. To clear the anchor from the seabed and lift it clear of the bottom; see also '*aweigh*'.

Windward. That side of the boat from which the wind is coming.

Yard. A spar set across a mast, which was normally used to support a sail.

APPENDIX B

The D'Aranda Family

Lieutenant William Peter D'Aranda, Royal Navy (1788–1872), was a scion of a distinguished but unusual Huguenot family, which originated in Spain and came to England by way of the Netherlands and France in the early seventeenth century. At least one member of the family was in the Netherlands in the sixteenth century, presumably as part of the Spanish forces sent there to impose his rule by King Philip II. At some time during this period members of the family were converted to the Calvinism that was then sweeping Western Europe and were forced to flee to France during the persecutions by the Duke of Alva, the Spanish Governor, which took place during the years 1567–1573. Once in France, the name was amended to D'Arande, presumably to give it a French sound.

French Huguenots (Protestants) were, in their turn, being forced to leave France in large numbers and 40,000 of them moved to England. One Huguenot community established itself in the south coast port of Southampton, where in 1567 it leased the Chapel of St Julian (also known as the *Maison Dieu*, or God's House) from Queen's College, Oxford. In 1619 this congregation sought a new preacher and selected *Maitre Elie D'Arande*, then the pastor of the Huguenot church at Calvé in Picardy in North-East France, who moved to England to take up his new post, arriving later that year, accompanied by his wife *Elizabeth* (née Bonhomme). The family settled in Southampton, where they spent the remainder of their lives, Elie dying in post in 1633, and being buried near the church he had served so well.

Elie and Elizabeth's two sons were both born in England, of whom the younger, *Pierre* (1626–1628), died at the age of two. The elder son, *Elie Paul* (1625–1669), was brought up as an Englishman, completing his education at Oxford, where he became a Fellow of Pembroke College and was ordained into the Church of England. He survived the complications of the English Civil War (1642–1650) and was curate of several parishes in Sussex, before feeling compelled to return to his father's tradition, being appointed minister of the Walloon (Huguenot) church in Canterbury, taking up the appointment on 1 April, 1663.

Elie Paul's first wife, *Esther*, gave birth to two sons, *Paul* (1652–1712) and *George*, and two daughters, *Esther* (b. 1654) and *Elizabeth* (b. 1664), before dying in 1664. The following year Elie Paul married again, his new wife, *Francis* (née Pickering), giving birth to two more sons, *Benjamin* (1666–1739) and *Peter* (1669–1739), before he, too, died in 1669 at the relatively early age of forty-four.

Paul D'Aranda (1652–1712) turned from the church to commerce, where he achieved rapid success, being involved in the wool trade with The Netherlands. He had both a business home in London and an impressive country seat in the beautiful village of Shoreham in Kent, where he became a pillar of society, being appointed a Justice of the Peace (magistrate) in his home county of Kent. He married an heiress, *Mary Baxter* in 1682, by whom he had two sons, the younger *William Henry* (1688–1712), dying when he was just twenty-four years old.

The eldest son, *Paul* (1685–1732), inherited the property at Shoreham on his father's death in 1712, but sold it three years later and moved to Putney, which in those days was well outside London, where he bought a very large and imposing house known locally as 'Putney Palace.' Its size and importance can be gauged from its royal associations under previous owners, since Queen Elizabeth I had stayed there regularly, while King James I spent the night in the house before going to London for his Coronation. Despite this grand house, their old home in Kent continued to exert a great influence on the family and no less than five D'Arandas were taken back from Putney to be buried in the family crypt beneath the Lady Chapel in the parish church at Shoreham. The younger Paul continued his father's commercial and social success, being married in Westminster Abbey in 1722, one of only four such weddings in the capital's premier church in that year, and he and his wife *Elizabeth* (née Emilie) had four daughters and one son.

Their only son, *Benjamin* (1730–1740), continued an unfortunate family pattern, dying when he was just ten years old, while *Elizabeth* (1722–1746) died at the age of twenty-four. Two of the remaining daughters were very wealthy and did not marry at all, living to ripe old ages, *Mary* (1723–1798) to seventy-five and *Henrietta-Emilia* (1728–1810) to eighty-two. The latter seems to have become somewhat cantankerous and her Will ran to eight pages with no less than twelve codicils, since she seems to have changed her bequests according to whim.

Paul and Elizabeth's fourth daughter, *Martha* (b.1724), made up for the single state of her sisters by marrying three times, wedding her first husband, Honourable Charles Lee (third son of the second Earl of Lichfield), when she was nineteen. He died less than a year later and she was no sooner out of mourning than she married Dr Coxe, Court Physician to King George II, by whom she had three children, who were clearly favourites of their Aunt

Henrietta-Emilia, since she remembered them all in her Will. Henrietta-Emilia was, however, the last to bear the family name in this branch of the D'Arandas and with her death the D'Aranda association with Putney came to an end, although the old lady's ghost was reputed to haunt Putney Palace and the adjacent lanes nearby until it was pulled down in 1826.

The second D'Aranda line stemmed from *Reverend Elie Paul D'Aranda* (1625–1669) and his second wife, *Frances* (née Pickering), who gave birth to two sons. Both became Church of England ministers and lived long lives, the younger, the *Reverend Peter D'Aranda* (1669–1739), remaining single, while the elder, the *Reverend Benjamin D'Aranda* (1666–1739), married twice. His first wife, *Elizabeth* (née Blake), the daughter of a well-established landed family in his parish at Calne in Wiltshire, gave birth to one son, *Henry* (1701–1716), who, like so many D'Aranda males, died young; in his case at the age of fifteen. Elizabeth died in 1730 and, somewhat surprisingly, the Reverend Benjamin married for a second time at the age of sixty-eight, his new bride, *Elizabeth Oliphant* of Petersham (a village on the Thames only two miles from Putney Palace), being only twenty-seven years old. Five years later the couple were blessed with a son, although the proud father, by now seventy-three years old, died shortly afterwards.

Elizabeth herself died only three years later and the three-years-old *Peter D'Aranda* (1730–1804) was brought up by his mother's family in Petersham. Although he had not known his father, Peter became the fourth generation of the family to be ordained as a Protestant minister (1762), serving as vicar of Great Burstead in Essex for thirty-seven years, a living he subsequently combined with that of Great Wakering, a nearby parish on the coast. He married *Jane Ward* of Richmond in 1760 and they had just one child, *Benjamin* (1760–1833), who broke with family tradition by becoming a surgeon. He remained in Essex, establishing his home and practice at Billericay, within sight of his father's church.

Benjamin had four sons and two daughters. One son, *Samuel* (b. 1795), has disappeared from the records, and may well have died young, but the other three were all professional men, *Benjamin* (1789–1837) and *George* (1794–1848) becoming surgeons like their father. The eldest son, *William Peter* (1788–1872), however, took a totally new line and joined the Royal Navy at the age of twelve, where he eventually became the commander of HM Brig *Nancy*. The two daughters *Eliza-Jane* (1791–1867) and *Caroline-Lucy* (1797–1872) both moved to London and both married somewhat late in life, the former at the age of forty-eight and the latter at fifty-seven.

It is noteworthy that whereas at least some Huguenot families anglicized their names, the D'Aranda family never attempted to do so. Indeed, they reverted from the French to the Spanish spelling of the name at a time when English folk memories of the Armada were still very much alive. The name

D'Aranda appears frequently in Seventeenth Century Spanish records and there is also a D'Arande buried in St Bavor's Cathedral at Ghent in Belgium. This latter tomb shows the same Spanish coat of arms as the memorial plaque to Henry D'Aranda (1700–1716) which once hung in the parish church at Bremhill in Wiltshire, England, the arms being: *'Azure, a castle of three towers argent, with a bordure or, charged with saltiers, gules'*. (A silver castle with three towers, on a blue background, with a gold border containing red crosses.)

The English D'Aranda family is unusual because it can be traced back to one specific ancestor, who arrived in the country in 1619. In the six generations which followed the family produced six Protestant ministers, three surgeons, two very successful merchants and one naval officer. The family clearly moved with ease in the upper echelons of English society, Paul D'Aranda (1652–1712) being particularly wealthy, with a large estate and the appointment as a magistrate, while his son Paul (1685–1732) was sufficiently influential to be married in Westminster Abbey. Indeed, all D'Aranda men married well, virtually all their brides being from the landed gentry or wealthy business families, while those females who chose to marry found husbands in the upper middle class, or, in the case of the much-married Martha, from the aristocracy.

The family seems to have remained close-knit, almost clannish, with extensive remembrance of other, sometimes distant, members in many of their Wills. Henrietta-Emilia (1728–1810), for example, clearly knew her distant relative Peter (1739–1804) and left a small bequest to his son Benjamin (1760–1830).

The D'Arandas epitomized solid English middle-class values and, if any of them did behave badly, the records fail to show it. They were deeply religious, worked hard, were honest, upright and widely respected, and, like so many Huguenot families, contributed greatly to the country their ancestor had adopted in 1619.

THE D'ARANDA FAMILY TREE

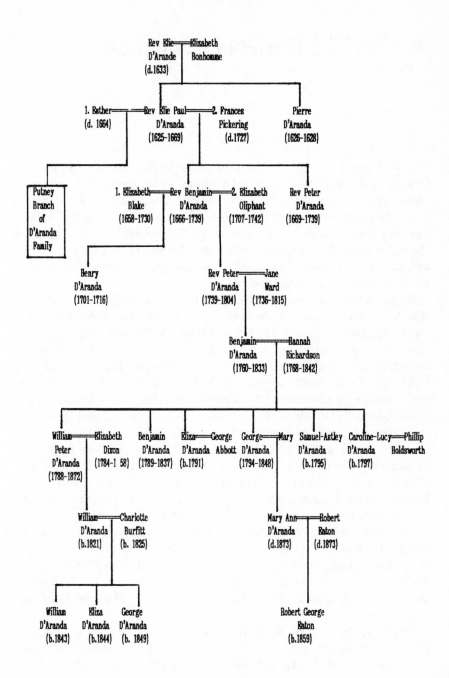

APPENDIX C

The Duries of Craigluscar

The Norman family of *de Doure* came to England with William the Conqueror in 1066 and was granted a barony by their grateful leader, but some one-and-a-half centuries later their descendants moved to Scotland under the patronage of Queen Joan, wife of King Alexander II (1214–1249). The king granted them an estate near Leven in Fifeshire, to which they gave the family name (the spelling of which had changed by this time to *Durie*) and this senior branch of the family, the 'Duries of Durie', lived on the estate for the following four hundred years.

By the start of the sixteenth century the family was prominent in Scottish affairs, becoming wealthy in the process. One of the most notable members was *George Durie*, second son of *John Durie Of That Ilk*, who was one of the most important courtiers of the period, some of his many appointments including Lord of the Council, Lord of the Sessions, and Keeper of the Privy Seal. He was a strong supporter of Mary, Queen of Scots (1542–87) and a vociferous advocate of the Scottish relationship with France, 'The Auld Alliance', for which he was given many rewards, including the appointment of Abbot of Dunfermline Abbey on 23 May, 1526.

Despite his abbacy, George Durie fathered four sons and three daughters by Catherine Sibbald and two of these sons were legitimized by Mary, Queen of Scots in 1543. He also purchased an estate just outside the town of Dunfermline at Craigluscar in the county of Fife, and from that time this branch of the family became the *'Duries of Craigluscar'*.

The abbot died in 1565 and his eldest son *Henry* inherited, the estate then passing in a direct line to *Charles Durie of Craigluscar*, the second lawful son of the fourth *George Durie of Craigluscar*, who inherited in 1768. Little is known about this Charles Durie, other than that he was described as 'having once been a soldier' and that he held the estate for no less than 54 years, dying in 1822.

Charles Durie married Agnes Greig, a member of another well-known Fifeshire family. Her father, John Greig (1734–1816), had joined the Royal Navy as an ordinary seaman and rose to the rank of senior petty officer, but, despite repeated offers, he declined to accept a commission. He eventually returned to settle in his native Scotland where, among other appointments, he became the gunnery instructor to the North Queensferry Artillery Volunteers. Another member of the family of that time, also named John Greig (1735–1788), achieved somewhat greater prominence. Having joined the Royal Navy as an officer, he volunteered to go to Russia to help improve the quality of Catherine the Great's navy and ended his life as Admiral Sir John Greig and commander of the Imperial Russian Navy.

Charles and Agnes Durie had two children: one son, *Robert* born in 1777 (the Captain Robert Durie aboard the *Isabella*) and a daughter, *Susan*. Despite the nautical connections on his mother's side, young Robert decided to join the Army and, presumably with his father's help, he purchased a commission in the 73rd Regiment of Foot, joining for duty as an Ensign (equivalent to today's Second Lieutenant) on August 15th, 1804. At this date he was 27 years old, which seems to have been rather old for someone just joining the Army, and the great majority of his fellow ensigns would have been at least eight to ten years younger.

The regiment that Durie joined had been raised as the Second Battalion, the 42nd Royal Highlanders (The Black Watch) in 1780, but was separated during a subsequent expansion of the Army in 1786 to become the 73rd Regiment of Foot. This new regiment was immediately sent to India, where it served for some twenty years, only returning to Scotland (then known as 'North Britain') in July, 1806. The regiment was then employed on garrison duties, with small detachments scattered over the country, one of them being commanded by Ensign Robert Durie.

In a further expansion of the Army during the Napoleonic Wars a second battalion of the 73rd Regiment was raised in 1808 at about the same time that the original battalion, now designated First Battalion, 73rd Regiment of Foot, was warned for a move to New South Wales. This move was necessary to restore legitimate government following the overthrow of the Governor, Captain William Bligh, Royal Navy, and the Battalion's Commanding Officer, Lieutenant-Colonel Lachlan Macquarie, was ordered to rescue Bligh and then to take his place.

Robert Durie, by now promoted to lieutenant, travelled with the First Battalion, leaving Leith on January 13, 1809. They landed at Gravesend in England a few weeks later and were then re-embarked and sent to the Isle of Wight, where they again went ashore. Whilst there, Robert Durie married Joanna-Ann Ross, who was described on the marriage certificate as a 'widow of Islington.' Nothing can be discovered of her antecedents or previous history, except that her first husband was one Lieutenant-Colonel Malcolm Nugent Ross of the 71st Regiment of Foot, who died at Inverness in 1806.

There seem to be two possibilities concerning this marriage. One is that the widowed Mrs Ross moved to the Isle of Wight following her husband's death and was living there when the 73rd Foot arrived, where she met and married Lieutenant Durie in a whirlwind courtship. The second is that Robert and Joanna-Ann had met when she was with her first husband at Inverness (where there would certainly have been a detachment of the 73rd) and that they decided to get married after Lieutenant-Colonel Ross's death.

Following their adventures in the Falkland Islands, the Duries went back to Scotland, where their daughter *Eliza Providence* was baptized at Lamlash on the Isle of Arran in February 1814. They had three more children: *Charles*, born in 1815; *Susan*, born in 1817; and, finally, *Agnes*, born in 1818. Charles was obviously named for his grandfather and Susan for her aunt, but the choice of 'Agnes' for the youngest suggests that their eldest daughter Agnes, who had been born in New South Wales and lived through all their experiences on the Falkland Islands, had died sometime between 1814 and 1818.

Robert Durie became 'Durie of Craigluscar' in 1819, three years before his father's death, but was, himself, to go to an early grave at the age of 48 and was buried in the family vault in Dunfermline Abbey. His son, Charles, qualified as a doctor, married and had two children (*Eliza*, born 1837 and *Robert*, born 1840). He inherited the estate on achieving his majority in 1836 but then died at the age of 29, as, by an unfortunate coincidence, did his son, who was also christened *Robert*.

Robert and Joanna-Ann's three surviving daughters all married, but the family name was continued through Eliza (1837–1917) their grand-daughter and sister of Robert, who had died in 1869. Eliza married Andrew Dewar in 1859 and they changed their surname to 'Dewar-Durie' to ensure the continuation of their ancient name. The family eventually left the house at Craigluscar in 1908, but the old building still stands.

THE DURIE FAMILY

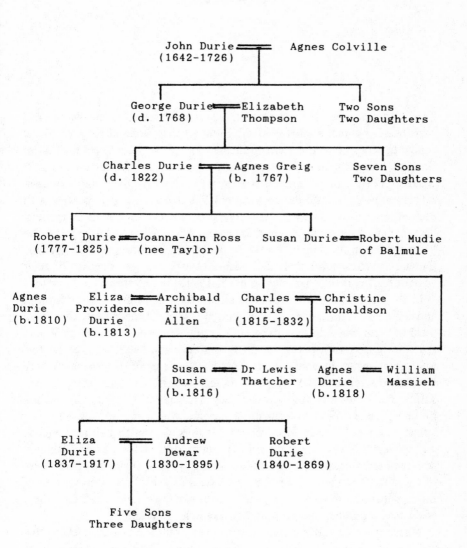

APPENDIX D

Sources

There are a number of accounts of the voyages of the *Isabella*, *Nanina* and *Nancy*, all of which are listed in the Bibliography. None of them gives the complete story, but the eight principle sources – Joseph Holt, Charles Barnard, the complaint sworn in Rio de Janeiro (the 'Rutter document'), Barzillai Pease's diary, Lundin's report to Admiral Dixon and his 1846 article in the Edinburgh Review, and *HMS Nancy's* two logs – coincide with each other to a remarkable extent. These are further supported by archival documents such as the letters and reports from Admiral Dixon, and the Press articles in the Times and the Annual Register. Unfortunately, neither Captain Brookes nor Robert and Joanna-Ann Durie left a record of their adventures, or, if they did, this author has failed to find them.

In the surviving records, there is almost total agreement on the timings and sequence of main events, even though it seems inconceivable that those making them could have collaborated in any way with each other. Where there are differences, these are relatively minor and lie either in subjective interpretation, or in omission. It would, of course, be surprising if there were no discrepancies or errors in these accounts, but two examples will suffice to show how relatively minor they are. Charles Barnard, when listing his crew, names 'William Seaman,' a surname which appears nowhere else, whilst he omits 'William Montgomery.' It thus appears that either he made a simple error or else he (or the printer) got muddled with the term 'William Montgomery, Seaman' (ie, by trade). Similarly, Holt states that there were thirty-four passengers aboard the *Isabella* and then lists twenty-three of them, which, even when the six in his own party are added, still falls short of the actual number and he omits, for example, Lundin.

Where there are differences between descriptions of the same event this author has given greater credence to the account of an eyewitness than to that of someone who was not present, unless there is good reason not to do so.

Holt's *Memoirs* are based on a journal that he claims to have started while on Eagle Island, although he later expanded the document to cover his entire life. The manuscript was left with the Keeper of Records in Ireland, and was later transcribed and prepared for publication by T. Crofton Croker, a prolific Victorian writer. Croker admits to having made amendments to Holt's description of some events, of which the most important was in suppressing the name of the man Holt blamed for unjustly reporting him to the Irish authorities in 1798. There is no reason, however, to think that Croker made any changes to that part of the *Memoirs* covering Holt's experiences in the Falklands.

Holt's description of the shipwreck is corroborated in its essentials by Lundin, while Barnard's report of the shipwreck also agrees with Holt's, although the American was, of course, basing his account on hearsay, much of it probably from Holt. Barnard, again using hearsay, states that prior to his arrival on Eagle Island, a totally informal committee consisting of Hayes, Mattinson and Ansell had actually run affairs, using a reign of terror to cow the others, particularly Holt. Holt, on the other hand, although he indicates that there were problems during this period, particularly involving drunkenness, does not mention any reign of terror, while the committee he describes did not include Mattinson.

Holt's account rarely mentions any event that he did not personally witness and very seldom includes any 'gossip' about someone else's background. Thus, for example, the only details of Sir Henry Hayes' affair with Miss Pike to be given in the *Memoirs* appear in a footnote added by Croker and are not part of Holt's own text.

Two points must be mentioned. First, Holt relates only stories in which he plays the principal part and, secondly, virtually everyone he meets immediately recognises him as a hero of the 1798 rebellion, including all the Americans, both on Eagle Island and in Rio de Janeiro. Also, everyone addresses him as 'General' and he is quite specific that when he visited *Nancy* on 18 May, 1813, he was given the honours due to a general. D'Aranda, says Holt, 'sent a boat for me, with an officer in it, and had the yards manned, when I went on board, and the same when I was coming away'. This is not mentioned in either of *Nancy's* logs and, although there seems little doubt that D'Aranda treated both Holt and his wife with great courtesy, it seems highly improbable that he would have given him the honours due to a serving general.

Although there is no doubt that Holt's name was well-known at the time of the 1798 rebellion, it seems unlikely that it would have still been so widely known fifteen years after the event, as he claims. Also, it seems more probable that when Holt visited *Nancy* the sailors simply happened to be working on the rigging, a task which they did with great regularity when in port, and that Holt, a landsman, misunderstood what they were doing.

Despite the general agreement between his journal and other records, it is, nevertheless, clear that on occasions Holt 'varnishes' the truth. To give but one example, in his *Memoirs* (Volume II, pp. 321–323) he describes how he took John Byrne up to Governor Macquarie's house sometime in August/ September 1812 to persuade the latter to grant the old man a pardon, and how he played a trick on the Governor by persuading Byrne to pretend that he was deaf. This makes an amusing story, but the truth is far more prosaic, since Governor Macquarie's Despatch #8 shows quite clearly that Byrne had been given a routine, free pardon in the normal course of events on 29 February, 1812.

Holt scarcely mentions Lundin at all, except to say that he was selected to go in the longboat and that he later returned aboard *Nancy*. More curiously, he does not mention Mattinson once, even though, according to Barnard, this man must have exercised a most malign influence over the passengers both before and after the shipwreck. Of less significance, while Holt goes into considerable detail concerning life on Eagle Island, he makes no mention of the flagpole, the bonfire and firing the cannon, although they are, of course, very obvious methods of attracting passing ships, and Barnard is quite clear that it was the combination of these that gained his attention in the first place.

Charles Barnard was certainly keeping a journal on New Island and may well have kept notes prior to that. He gives a very full account of everything to do with the *Nanina* up to the time that he was abandoned at New Island and is the only source for the description of the period that he and his four companions spent on their own. The story of the eventual rescue is, however, corroborated by James Choyce, who, although he gets some of the background wrong (for example, he gives the name of the American brig as the *Nymie*), nevertheless gives a valuable description of the men and their little camp on New Island, which ties in closely with that given by Barnard.

Unlike many other sources, Barnard makes extensive use of hearsay, most of which seems to have been garnered during conversations with the Holts and the Duries (particularly Mrs Durie) during his short stay on Eagle Island. He frequently adopts a rather ironic style and sometimes becomes very bitter, although, considering the succession of tricks played on him, this is very understandable. Occasionally, however, his descriptions are rather obtuse, and their precise significance difficult to interpret. For example, on meeting Captain Higton on Eagle Island he says that 'I accompanied him to his residence, where I saw his *cher amie*, who appeared perfectly at her ease.' It is clear that he is referring to Mrs Bindell, but quite why she should not have been at her ease is difficult to fathom, unless Barnard is simply making a veiled reference to the fact that they were not married. He takes a similarly strict view of Lundin's relationship with Mary-Ann Spencer, although, again, he refers obliquely to her as 'one of the frail sisterhood' whereas in the 'Rutter document' his fellow captains refer to her directly as 'a prostitute from Port Jackson'.

Charles Barnard is quite definite that he was the master of the *Nanina*, except that he says that his father was due to take the vessel back to New York. All other documents, such as the ship's papers and health certificates (the originals of which are now all in the Public Record Office, London) show his father, Valentine, as master, as do all the prize papers. It is therefore possible that either Charles Barnard overstated his importance, or that his father was shown as master for the sake of the return voyage, while he, Charles, was, for all practical purposes, in command during the voyage south and the subsequent sealing operations.

Barnard relates in his memoirs that he visited Messrs Murray in New York on his return to the United States in October 1816. By that time one of the partners in the firm had been over to England to lodge the appeal, but Barnard mentions nothing of this beyond 'an interesting conversation followed'. Indeed, nowhere in his book does Barnard make any mention of the appeal or of the eventual restitution made by the British Prize Appeal Court of the High Court of Admiralty.

Captains Valentine Barnard, Hunter, Pease and Fanning made a lengthy sworn statement in Rio de Janeiro on 6 September, 1813, to the Acting United States Commercial Agent, Charles Rutter (the 'Rutter document'). Since all four would have had to agree on what was written, and since they were under oath administered by Mr Rutter, it is assumed that this is an accurate version of the events described.

Pease's journal, on the other hand, while it has the advantage that, with only a few exceptions, it was written virtually daily, suffers from a distinct bias against the rest of the world. He knew the Barnards from previous voyages, but seems to have harboured a dislike for both of them, especially Charles. On several occasions his version of events differs significantly from that given by Barnard; for example, Pease states that during the final phase of the journey south there were very serious quarrels among the officers aboard the *Nanina*, whereas Charles Barnard suggests that all was reasonably tranquil. Pease's animosity towards Barnard is, however, so clear that it is difficult to give credence to his descriptions.

Lundin left two records of his adventures, the first being a fairly brief and terse official report written in Rio de Janeiro for Admiral Dixon, who forwarded it to the Admiralty. It agrees closely with Holt's version of events up to his (Lundin's) departure from Eagle Island and also with the *Nancy's* log once he had joined D'Aranda in Buones Ayres. His second record is a much longer and fuller account, which was published in the *Edinburgh Review* in 1846. Curiously, the two documents differ in some respects, most notably that while his report to Admiral Dixon makes no mention of finding the deserted Spanish settlement, which is described in great detail in the later document.

Captains' and Masters' Logs exist in the Public Record Office, Kew, for all the Royal Navy ships covered in this story, although there are some gaps in the sequences. The system was that the Master (Second Master in the case of HM Brig *Nancy*) kept a log which simply recorded weather, navigational details and matters strictly relating to the ship. The Captain's log was usually based on the Master's log, but with some added detail concerning significant events. These logs, both of which were official documents, must be assumed to be generally accurate, although it is quite clear that D'Aranda asked (or persuaded) Second Master Shepherd to add some detail to his log entry concerning the (alleged) maltreatment of the British by the Americans aboard *Nanina*.

The Muster Table of a Royal Navy vessel was also an official document, used to record the presence of every man aboard and to account for the issue of rations to him. These documents have, therefore, all been taken as accurate, although it is a curious feature of *Nancy's* Muster Table that no American from *Nanina* ever appears on it, even though all the British survivors from *Isabella* are fully accounted for. No explanation for this is given in contemporary documents, although one possibility is that D'Aranda regarded them as being accommodated aboard *Nanina* and thus eating only provisions supplied by that ship.

Captain James Weddell describes meeting Captain Charles Barnard at New Island in 1821. Naturally, the two captains talked and Barnard described his experiences, which Weddell records in his book, although, not surprisingly, this ties in closely with Barnard's own account in *Marooned*.

James Choyce was second mate in the *Asp*, one of the two ships which arrived at New Island and rescued Barnard and his companions. His description contains some inaccuracies, such as referring to the American vessel as *Nymie* rather than *Nanina*, but he does give a useful eyewitness account of the survivors' appearance and their camp on New Island.

The British service records for the Navy and Army personnel have proved helpful, but only up to a point. Neither the Admiralty nor the Horse Guards (Army headquarters at this time) appear to have maintained individual files on officers and seamen/soldiers, or, if they did, they have not survived. There are, of course, some records, but they are generally not complete, and for some reason (although probably not a sinister one) some of the people involved in this story seem to fall into these gaps.

For example, no record of Joanna-Ann Durie's first husband, Lieutenant-Colonel Ross, appear to have survived, beyond his appearance in the Army List. Similarly, although there are records of officers' wives' maiden names and dates of birth, Joanna-Ann does not appear. On the naval side, a particular effort was made by the author in England and by Ian Patterson in Australia to trace Mattinson, the cause of so many problems in this story. This has proved impossible, but may be because the man changed his name after being discharged, a by no means rare occurrence, Ansell, for example, admitting to have done so.

The British Public Record Office and the United States' National Archives proved to be fruitful sources of official documents concerning this story. Such documents have been invaluable in assembling the details of the events and people involved in them.

Unfortunately, a number of important documents have disappeared. All documents concerning the *Nanina* are known to have been forwarded to the Advocate-General in September, 1815, and are carefully listed in the covering letter (PRO/ADM 7/312 #6). Some of these documents have survived and are in PRO/HCA 42/474 Bundle 889, but these are essentially the documents of American origin, such as *Nanina's* ship's papers, Valentine Barnard's letters to Admiral Dixon and the 'Rutter document'. The papers of British origin are missing, including the agreement signed on Eagle Island, Admiral Dixon's letters and extracts from *Isabella's* log.

In all the prize cases which went to appeal a printed summary of the evidence was prepared, to which was appended a manuscript statement of the appeal court's final ruling. Bound volumes of these cases covering the years 1794 to 1819 have been found in the Public Record Office, Chancery Lane, London and the Supreme Court Library at the Royal Courts of Justice, also in London. In both cases the *Nanina* case is missing.

It is, however, beyond all doubt that the case was heard on 5 February, 1818, as there are two identical entries to this effect: one in the 'Appeal Assignment Book' (PRO/HCA 44/83), the other in 'Prize Appeal Interlocutories' (PRO/HCA 46/11). These are ledgers in which entries were made in manuscript in chronological order and it would have been a major undertaking to remove the entries concerning the *Nanina* case.

Finally, it has been discovered that D'Aranda appealed to the King in 1827 concerning the case; this is made quite clear in his letter of 12 June, 1827 (PRO/ADM 1/2749) to the Secretary of the Admiralty. The record of this appeal should be in the Privy Council file for that year, together with the others submitted by Royal Navy officers, but is not.

It is, of course, entirely possible that these papers are nestling in some forgotten and unrecorded corner of the Public Record Office or else that they may have been accidentally destroyed. It is, however, also a possibility that they were deliberately suppressed at some time in the period 1818–1830, but, should that be the case, who did it and for what reason has not been established.

Bibliography

Archive Material

Extensive use has been made of archive material, particularly from the Public Record Office, London (Kew and Chancery Lane) and the National Archives Washington, DC. All such sources are identified in the endnotes. PRO prefixes are:

– ADM	Admiralty
– CO	Colonial Office
– F	Foreign Office
– HCA	High Court of Admiralty
– PRO	Public Record Office
– WO	War Office

Books

Anon, *The Trial of Sir Henry Browne Hayes, Knt, for forcibly and feloniously taking away Miss May Pike on the twenty-second day of July 1797, before Mr Justice Day, and a most respectable jury on the thirteenth day of April 1801. Taken down by an eminent short-hand writer.* Cork: printed by James Haly, 1801.

Barnard, Charles H, see Dodge, Bertha S.

Bateson, Charles, *The Convict Ships: 1787–1868*, Brown, Son & Ferguson, Glasgow, 1959.

Bertie, Charles, H, *The Story of Vaucluse House and Sir Henry Browne Hayes*, Australian Historical Society, Sydney, 1918.

Bladen, FM (Ed), *Historical Records of New South Wales*, Volumes I to VII, Government Printer, Sydney, 1895.

Cannon, Richard, *Historical Records of the British Army: 73rd Regiment of Foot*, Adjutant-General's Office, Horse Guards, London, 1851.

Cawkell, Mary, *The Falkland Story: 1592–1982*, Anthony Nelson, Oswestry, 1983. ISBN 0–904614–08–5.

Channing, Edward, *A History of the United States*, Volume IV: 1789–1815, Macmillan, New York, 1917.

Choyce, James, *The Log of a Jack Tar; or, The Life of James Choyce, Master Mariner*, T Fisher Unwin, London, 1891. Reprinted by George Mann, Maidstone, 1973. ISBN 0–7041–0005–3.

Dodge, Bertha S, *Marooned, being a Narrative of the Suffering and Adventures of Captain Charles H Barnard, Embracing an Account of the seizure of His Vessel at the Falkland Islands &c 1812–1816*, edited and with an introduction and appendices by Bertha Dodge, Syracuse University Press, Syracuse, New York, 1986. ISBN 0–8156–0203–0.

Dodge, N.A.M, *The Wooden World*, Collins, London, 1986, ISBN 0–00–216548–1.

Fanning, Edmund, *Voyages and Discoveries in the South Seas, 1792–1832*, Collins & Hamnet, New York, 1838; reprinted by Marine Research Society, Salem, 1924. [BM AC. 8400.0].

Fanning, Edmund, *Voyages Round the World; with Sketches of Voyages to the South Seas, North and South Pacific oceans, China, etc, Performed Under the Command of the Author*, New York, 1833. [BM 1045. k.1]

Field, C, Colonel, R.M.L.I, *Britain's Sea Soldiers, A History of the Royal Marines*, Lyceum Press, Liverpool, 1924.

Gardner, John, *Warships of the Royal Navy: First Series – Sail*, Hugh Evelyn, London; 1968, ISBN 0–238–78890–3.

Goode, G.B, *The Fisheries and Fishing Industries of the United States*, US Commission on Fish and Fisheries, five sections, Government Printer, Washington DC.

Goodwin, Peter, *Construction and Fitting of Sailing Men-of-War, 1650–1850* Conway Maritime Press, London, ISBN 0–85177–326–5.

Harland, John, *Seamanship in the Age of Sail*, Conway Maritime Press, London, ISBN 0–85177–179–3.

Hawkings, David T, *Bound For Australia*, Phillimore & Co Ltd, Shipwycke Hall, Chichester, Sussex, 1987.

Holt, Joseph (Croker, T.C. ed), *Memoirs of Joseph Holt, General of the Irish Rebels*, Henry Colburn, London, 1838 (two volumes)

Lewis, Michael, *A Social History of the Navy: 1793–1815*, George Allen & Unwin, London, 1960.

Mahan, Captain AT, *Sea Power in Relation to the War of 1812*, Sampson Low, London, 1903.

Morrell, Benjamin, *A Narrative of Four Voyages to the South Sea, North and South Pacific Oceans, Chinese Sea, Ethiopic and Southern Atlantic Ocean, Indian and Antarctic Ocean from 1822 to 1831*, New York, 1832. [BM 1045. i. 16]

Nicholson, Ian, *Log of Logs*, Roebuck Society Publication No 41, Nambuer, Queensland, Australia, 1990. ISBN 0–7316–6534–1.

Pope, Dudley, *Life in Nelson's Day*, George Allen & Unwin, London, 1981, ISBN 0–04–359008-X.

Rees, Abraham, *Rees's Naval Architecture* (1819–1820) David & Charles Reprints, Newton Abbot, 1970. ISBN 0–7153–5030–7.

Salvesen, E, *The Whale Fisheries of the Falkland Islands Dependencies* in *Report of the Scientific Results of the Voyage of the SS Scotia*, Edinburgh, 4, pp. 479–486.

Smith, Thomas W, *A Narrative of the Life, Travels and Sufferings of Thomas W Smith, Comprising an Account of His Early Life, Adoption by the Gypsies his Travels during 18 Voyages to various parts of the World, during which he was Shipwrecked five Times, Thrice on a desolate island Near the South Pole.* . . . . W.C. Hill, 1844.

Steel, David, *Steel's Art of Rigging, 1818* Reprinted by Fisher Nautical Press, Brighton, 1974. ISBN 0–904340–00–7.

Weddell, James, *A Voyage Towards the South Pole Performed in the Years 1822–1824*, Longman, Rees, Orme, Browne and Green, London, 1825. Facsimile edition of the second edition (1827) by David & Charles Reprints, 1970.

Woods, Robin W, with photographs by Cindy Buxton and Annie Price, *Falkland Islands* Birds, Anthony Nelson, Oswestry, England, 1982. ISBN 0–9094614–0707.

Journals and Magazines

Lowe's Edinburgh Magazine, 1846, article, *Narrative of a Voyage from New South Wales in 1812–1813*, by Richard Lundin; pp. 281–314.

Miscellanea Genealogica et Heraldica, article *D'Aranda Family Tree*, New Series, Volume 1, page 83.

INDEX

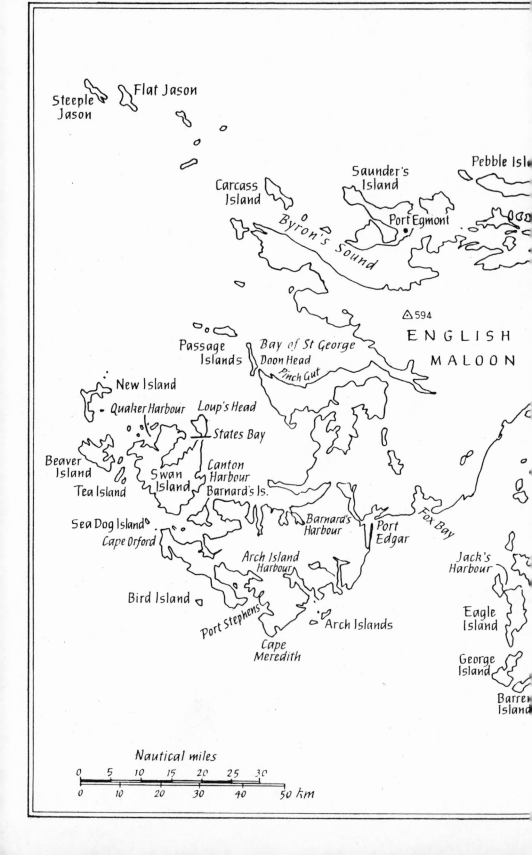

Steeple Jason

Flat Jason

Carcass Island

Saunder's Island

Pebble Isl

Byron's Sound

Port Egmont

△594

ENGLISH

Passage Islands

Bay of St George

Doon Head

Pinch Gut

MALOON

New Island

· Quaker Harbour

Loup's Head

States Bay

Beaver Island

Tea Island

Swan Island

Canton Harbour

Barnard's Is.

Sea Dog Island

Cape Orford

Barnard's Harbour

Port Edgar

Fox Bay

Jack's Harbour

Arch Island Harbour

Bird Island

Port Stephens

Arch Islands

Eagle Island

Cape Meredith

George Island

Barre Island

Nautical miles

0   5   10   15   20   25   30

0   10   20   30   40   50 km